nations in darkness:
China, Russia,
and
America

Consulting Editor: Inis L. Claude, Jr.   University of Virginia

nations in darkness:

China, Russia, and America

John G. Stoessinger

The City University of New York
at Hunter College

RANDOM HOUSE   NEW YORK

Trade Edition: ISBN: 0-394-47147-4
Text Edition: ISBN: 0-394-31236-8

Library of Congress Catalog Card Number: 79-150716

Design by Jack Ribik

Manufactured in the United States of America

First Edition
987654321

FOR CAROLINE

For now we see through
a glass, darkly; but
then face to face: now
I know in part; but
then shall I know even
as I also am known.

St. Paul
*First Epistle to
the Corinthians*

preface

This is a deeply personal book. It has grown out of my life experience: youth as a Jew under Hitler, flight across Stalin's Russia, refugee life in China, and the chance to build a new life in America.

There are two fundamental ways in which a man can deal with tragic experience: he can get stuck in the past and do battle with its ghosts, or he can come to terms with it and try to fashion it into strength. This book represents an effort to take the latter course.

During the first twenty years of my life in Europe and in China, tragedy seemed to be the most basic existential fact of life; during the second twenty years I discovered that America was still relatively innocent of tragedy—despite the Civil War, a depression, two world wars, and a growing inclination toward violence. There is a need to try to build bridges from America to Russia and China—two-way bridges between those nations that now hold the fate of the world in their hands.

Today it is no longer enough for nations to understand each other with their minds; they must now learn to *feel* each other with their souls. Intelligence and knowledge alone cannot prevent catastrophe. Also needed is the kind of empathy that flows from the knowledge in one's mind that ultimate tragedy is truly possible and from the subsequent realization in one's heart that all men—in their brief and precarious journey through life—are truly brothers. Americans, I believe, still do not know that men can build *both* cathedrals and concentration camps. They still do not know, in other words, that everything is possible.

I hope that the new perspectives I have opened may show the panorama of world politics in a deeper and richer hue. I also hope that a spirit of reconciliation may help to still the counsels of despair and soften the harshness of the political climate. But above all, I hope that this book may give new strength to the voice of reason in the affairs of states.

Many dear friends have helped me in this quest: Bernard E. Brown, Zbigniew Brzezinski, Inis L. Claude, Jr., Walter Kaufmann, Hans J. Morgenthau, Harrison Salisbury, Arthur M. Schlesinger, Jr., and Ethel Sherman. Two former students, now close friends, have been a steady source of strength: Brenda Forman and Robert G. McKelvey. I have also been blessed with three fine and understanding editors, Susan Gilbert, Elizabeth Kaye, and Barry Rossinoff, and with valuable secretarial assistance from Pamela Nicholas.

Finally, this book is not the product of teamwork or of a massive research apparatus. It is in essence a product of reflection. There is, in my view, no substitute for the writer's lonely discipline. In that sense, this is an old-fashioned book, and the ultimate responsibility for both its strengths and its weaknesses is truly mine alone.

John G. Stoessinger
New York City
February 1971

contents

nations in darkness:
China, Russia,
and
America

one
INTRODUCTION

More than two thousand years ago, Plato, in the seventh book of his *Republic,* conjured up a melancholy scene. Inside a cave, a group of men are chained in such a way that they can only look at the wall before them and are unable to turn their heads. Behind them a fire blazes and, between them and that fire, other men walk up and down, some talking and some silent. The chained men can only see the shadows of their fellow-men. To them, the shadows are in fact the men, and the voices come from the passing shadows. To these chained men, in Plato's words, "The truth would be nothing but the shadows."

The shattering symbolism of this allegory has haunted mankind for generations. And well it might because we still wear the chains of which Plato spoke. All too often we mistake the shadows for the men and dim echoes for their voices. In Plato's time such shadows did not have the power to obliterate the species. In our time they do. To draw attention to this danger is, in essence, the purpose of this book.

The last three decades of the twentieth century may well be dominated by the political constellation of the world's three great powers: the United States, China, and Russia. Two of them now wield the power to incinerate the planet and the third may soon possess it. This work attempts to shed light on *one* facet of this constellation in the past. It is my hope that the material uncovered may serve as warning for the future.

During the past century the struggles between the United States and China and those between the United States and Russia were not waged solely on the basis of objective reality. They were also fought in the realm of imagery and illusion. At times, great gaps developed between image and reality, and these gaps deeply

3

exacerbated tensions and made more difficult the task of political accommodation.

The assumption underlying this thesis is that international relations are often what people *think* they are; or, to put it in other words, that under certain conditions, men respond not to realities but to fictions that they have themselves created. To say that there are no objective problems in Sino-American or Russo-American relations would, of course, be folly. But the stage of world politics lends itself all too easily to the development of wide gaps between what reality is and the way it is perceived. Because of this fact, perception probably plays almost as important a role in international relations as does objective reality itself.

Misperceptions among nations may have disastrous effects on policy decisions. Stereotyped images on one side may elicit similar ones on the other, compounding the distortion. Even worse, if one believes a stereotype long enough, it may *become* reality by setting in motion the mechanism of self-fulfilling prophecy. Thus, if a nation believes that another is its implacable enemy and reiterates this often enough, making it the guideline of its national policy, it will eventually be right.

The task in this book is to examine ten empirical case studies in which misperceptions had concrete and specific effects on policy decisions. Five of these deal with milestones in Sino-American relations. The first vignette looks at the earliest encounters between these two nations during the last decades of the Chinese empire; the second traces the complex relationship between Chiang Kai-shek and the United States; the third deals with the Communist Chinese intervention in the Korean War; the fourth examines the United States–Chinese relationship during the French phase of the war in Indochina; and the fifth concludes with a study of Sino-American relations during the Americanization of the Vietnamese war.

The second set of studies examines the great watersheds in Russo-American relations. The first of these concerns the volatile relations between the United States and Czarist Russia in the days of Catherine, Alexander, and Nicholas; the second deals with the encounter between Woodrow Wilson and V. I. Lenin in the crucible of world war and the Bolshevik Revolution; the third examines Soviet-American relations leading to the establishment of diplomatic relations; the fourth traces the beginning of the cold war spiral and the division of Germany; and the fifth analyzes the interaction between President John F. Kennedy and Premier Nikita Khrushchev during the Cuban missile crisis of 1962.

These ten case studies, drawn from two vital areas in world politics, provide valuable empirical material for conceptual conclusions about the effects of misperceptions on policy decisions. I am fully aware that anyone who purports to undertake the task of distinguishing illusion from reality in world politics may justly be accused of hubris, for he is venturing into areas that pose formidable problems of an epistemological and even metaphysical nature. Nevertheless, an attempt must be made to determine when perceptions are accurate, when they are partially false, and when they are completely false. I have made a determined effort to maintain a balanced and objective attitude and to adhere to a pragmatic approach. While perception is the main subject treated, it is only *one* factor among many; it has never been systematically analyzed in the context of international relations. This work is not meant to be a single-factor analysis. But like any effort at theoretical innovation, it emphasizes *that* conceptual insight which is considered original and new. Unlike a photograph, the analysis does not attempt to reproduce every detail of the truth; more like a portrait, it tries to uncover a new truth.

I have attempted to analyze perception in terms of four distinct, yet interrelated, categories: first, each nation's *self-image;* second, each nation's perception of the *character* of its adversary; third, each nation's perception of its adversary's *intentions;* and finally, each nation's perception of the other's *power* and *capabilities.*

The methodology is traditional in that it avoids excessive quantification of data and complex behavioral jargon; but it is innovative in the sense that it refuses to compartmentalize the social sciences. Insights are drawn, wherever relevant, from the fields of political science, history, psychology, and philosophy.

The book is essentially a diagnosis. It tries to show how great nations struggle not only with each other, but also with their perceptions of each other. To move from diagnosis to prescription is yet more difficult. In the concluding chapter, I attempt to determine the conditions under which national leaders manage to correct their misperceptions. Finally, I have suggested some guidelines for building policies on the basis of reality.

Facts are usually quite complex. When one learns to respect them, nuances appear instead of black-and-white or good-and-evil categories. Nations, like people, must learn to think in color rather than in black and white.[1] Once again, man must escape from Plato's cave in which he perceives only shadows. Toward this end this book is dedicated.

---

[1] I am indebted for this phrase to Professor Walter Kaufmann's article, "Beyond Black and White: A Plea for Thinking in Color," *Midway* (Winter 1970), pp. 49–79.

part one
the role of perception in sino-american relations

two

CHINA AND AMERICA: THE BURDEN OF THE PAST

History, in psychological terms, is the memory of nations. It is the repository not only of objective events, but also of illusions and misunderstandings that filter down to our own time. Many Americans are profoundly anxious about the course of Chinese-American relations, but far too few are aware of the psychological roots of the present encounter. These roots go deep and are grounded in a soil of misperceptions that have marred relations between China and America since the very beginning. Perhaps an analysis of this tragic past may better equip us to deal with the even more tragic present.

THE FIRST ENCOUNTERS

This is the first century in over 2,000 years in which China has not considered itself to be at the center of the universe. For two millennia the Chinese empire conceived of itself as the hub of civilization, the great school of the world—much as Athens had once considered itself the school of the ancient Mediterranean world. Although dynasties came and went, the political structure of the empire remained essentially stable: the emperor, aided by a small intellectual elite, controlled the government; he ruled by the Mandate of Heaven; and his edicts had the authority of a philosopher-king. His vast realm, which stretched from Siberia to the Tropics, was known as "everything under heaven."

The world beyond the Great Wall of China did not hold much interest, since, in the eyes of the Chinese, it was populated by barbarians. Hence, the foreign relations of the empire for 2,000 years were in essence tributary relationships: long caravans laden with gifts for the emperor would weave their way across the land to the Imperial Court at Peking; the envoy would kowtow before the Son of Heaven and present the tribute. The act of kowtow, for example, left no doubt as to the personal superiority of the emperor. The ritual consisted of three separate kneelings, each accompanied by three separate prostrations, all performed to the command of a court usher: "kneel," "fall prostrate," "rise to your knees." All envoys went through this calisthenic exercise, and its proper performance was regarded merely as good manners by the court. The Chinese believed that it was perfectly self-evident that their empire was a superior civilization and the act of kowtow was a symbolic recognition of this axiomatic truth.

This view of themselves made the Chinese a stay-at-home people. Since the empire contained everything of value, no one wanted to go abroad and thus be removed from civilization. There was no interest in the conquest of strange lands of lesser value; an Office for Barbarian Affairs handled all foreign, that is, tributary, relations. On reading the descriptions of "Western Barbarians," one is struck with a fuzzy-minded, fairy-story quality not unlike that which dominated the descriptions of Western travelers to "Cathay." The barbarians were thought to inhabit small islands separated from civilization by "intervening wastes of sea." They were described as having skins of "dazzling white color," beaked noses, and flaming red hair. No distinction was made among the multifarious "tribes" of barbarians. In all cases, the Chinese attitude was a mixture of indifference and contempt.

The first attempt by a Westerner to pierce this curtain of ignorance took place in the sixteenth century. It was the attempt of a Jesuit Father—Matthew Ricci—to convert China to Catholicism. Marco Polo's travels to China in the twelfth century had had a significant impact on Europe but almost none on China. Ricci arrived in China in 1583, strongly influenced by the Catholic Counter Reformation, and engaged in a thirty-year effort to convert China from the top. This resourceful Jesuit mastered the Chinese language, dressed in the garb of a Confucian scholar, and adapted himself to the customs of the land. His knowledge of mathematics and astronomy earned him the respect of Chinese scholars and even got him an audience with the emperor. His first mission, as he saw it, was to show the Chinese that their view of the world was false:

Their universe was limited to their own fifteen provinces, and in the sea painted around it they had placed a few little islands to which they gave the names of different kingdoms they had heard of. All of these islands put together would not be as large as the smallest of the Chinese provinces. With such a limited knowledge, it is evident why they boasted of their kingdom as being the whole world, and why they called it Thienhia, meaning, everything under the heavens. When they learned that China was only a part of the great east, they considered such an idea, so unlike their own, to be something utterly impossible . . .[1]

Ricci's effort met with such resistance and even fury that the Jesuit had to settle for a tactful compromise. While he did include the Western empires on a map that he made, giving them Chinese names in the process, he retained China's central position:

They could not comprehend the demonstrations proving that the earth is a globe, made up of land and water, and that a globe of its very nature had neither beginning nor end. The geographer was therefore obliged to change his design and, by omitting the first meridian, he left a margin on either side of the map, making the Kingdom of China to appear right in the center. This was more in keeping with their ideas and it gave them a great deal of pleasure and satisfaction.[2]

When Matthew Ricci died in China in 1610, his famous map did not long survive him. It had made a sufficient impact, however, to fix in the minds of the ruling Confucian scholars the names of the great Western empires, although their exact location in the world was soon forgotten. During the next two centuries, right up to the time of the Opium War, total confusion dominated Chinese perceptions of the outside world. Contemporary maps showed islands named France, Spain, Portugal, England, Italy, and America, rotating like satellites around the great sun of the celestial empire. Ricci's role had been to lift the veil briefly, but soon after his death it descended again, and the barbarians were relegated once more to obscurity. Only vague memories of strange names connoting quaint and faraway places remained.[3]

When in 1793 Lord Macartney, leader of a trade mission from Great Britain, refused to perform the kowtow upon his arrival in

[1] Matthew Ricci, *China in the Sixteenth Century: The Journals of Matthew Ricci: 1583–1610,* Louis J. Gallagher, S. J. (tr.) (New York: Random House, 1953), p. 166.

[2] *Ibid.,* p. 167.

[3] John K. Fairbank, *Trade and Diplomacy on the China Coast* (Cambridge: Harvard University Press, 1953), Vol. I, p. 10.

Peking, he was denied an audience with the emperor, who sent the following rebuff to King George:

> You, O King, are so inclined toward our civilization that you have sent a special envoy across the seas to bring to our Court your memorial of congratulations on the occasion of my birthday and to present your native products as an expression of your thoughtfulness. On perusing your memorial, so simply worded and sincerely conceived, I am impressed by your respectfulness and friendliness and greatly pleased.
>
> The Celestial Court has pacified and possessed the territory within the four seas. Its sole aim is to do its utmost to achieve good government and to manage political affairs, attaching no value to strange jewels and precious objects. The various articles presented by you, O King, this time are accepted by my special order to the office in charge of such functions in consideration of the offerings having come from a long distance with sincere good wishes. As a matter of fact, the virtue and prestige of the Celestial Dynasty having spread far and wide, the kings of myriad nations come by land and sea with all sorts of precious things. Consequently there is nothing we lack, as your principal envoy and others have themselves observed. We have never set much store on strange or ingenious objects, nor do we need any more of your country's manufactures . . .[4]

The American Revolution, which occurred toward the end of Emperor Ch'ien Lung's reign, must have seemed to Ch'ien like an insignificant squabble between white barbarians somewhere in the outer darkness. Perhaps he never even heard of it. At any rate, when the first American ship, the *Empress of China*, reached Canton in 1784 "in the adventurous pursuit of commerce," her master, Captain John Green, was received as just another white barbarian, although he managed to sell for an enormous profit his cargo of furs, cotton, and ginseng weed, which, the Chinese believed, could restore their virility. By 1789, the year George Washington was inaugurated as President, fifteen American vessels were carrying on trade with China.

The first serious controversy involving Americans and Chinese clearly demonstrated the Chinese attitude. In 1821, a Chinese woman peddling fruit on board the ship *Emily*, anchored in Canton, fell overboard and drowned. The captain of the *Emily*

---

[4] Quoted in John K. Fairbank and Ssu-yu Teng (eds.), *China's Response to the West: A Documentary Survey* (Cambridge: Harvard University Press, 1954), p. 19.

claimed that the death was an accident, but the Chinese officials at Canton insisted that an American sailor, one Francis Terranova, had caused the woman's death by hurling a heavy object at her. They now demanded a life for a life and insisted that the sailor be handed over to them or all trade with the Americans would be stopped immediately. The Americans, in a quandary, refused to hand over Terranova but permitted the Chinese to try him on a murder charge aboard the *Emily*. The Chinese declared him guilty and demanded his custody for execution of the sentence of death by strangulation. The Americans reluctantly complied, and Terranova was executed by the local Cantonese authorities. Shortly after the sentence was carried out, an imperial edict reached the Americans that permitted them to continue their trading but left no doubt in their minds about the emperor's view of them. "As the dispositions of these foreigners are depraved by the education and customs of countries beyond the bounds of civilization," the edict read, "they are incapable of following right reason; their characters are formed; their perverse obstinacy is untameable; and they are dead to the influence of our renovating laws and manners."[5] The Son of Heaven was moved to compassion, however, by a people so dependent upon the products of the Celestial Dynasty that he was willing to permit them to continue their tribute-bearing activities.

These conditions prevailed until the year 1839 when the flourishing opium traffic off the China coast precipitated a major crisis between the British government and China. In the autumn of that year, the Chinese emperor was so disturbed about the ravages of the drug upon the Chinese population that he sent a stern protest to Queen Victoria:

We find that your country is sixty or seventy thousand li (three li make one mile, ordinarily) from China. Yet there are barbarian ships that strive to come here for trade for the purpose of making a profit. I have heard that the smoking of opium is very strictly forbidden by your country; that is because the harm caused by opium is clearly understood. Let us ask, where is your conscience?[6]

The emperor then stated, in conclusion, that "the barbarians could not get along for a single day without two major Chinese exports,

---

[5] Quoted in Foster Rhea Dulles, *China and America* (Princeton: Princeton University Press, 1946), p. 13.
[6] Quoted in Fairbank and Teng, *op. cit.*, p. 25.

tea and rhubarb" and threatened Queen Victoria with an embargo: "If China cuts off these benefits with no sympathy for those who are to suffer, then what can the barbarians rely upon to keep themselves alive?"

The protest went unheeded, and finally the emperor appointed one of his officials, Commissioner Lin, to blockade British merchants at Canton and to destroy their opium. The British interpreted this seizure as an interference with freedom of trade and as an act of aggression. Instead of ending the smuggling of opium, Commissioner Lin had precipitated the Opium War. The war was little more than a skirmish during which the British destroyed the Chinese forts at Canton and imposed upon the empire the Treaty of Nanking of 1842. The Opium War, which signified the first violent encounter between China and a Western nation, came as a terrible shock to the Chinese. There was no room for this phenomenon in the Chinese universe. It was as if the world had suddenly been turned upside down. Strange and inferior people, known to them only through folklore and myth, had suddenly assaulted them out of nowhere and broken their ramparts with superior firepower. As one Chinese edict to the British put it, shortly before the Treaty of Nanking was signed: "Except for your ships being solid, your gunfire fierce, and your rockets powerful, what other abilities have you?"[7]

The Treaty of Nanking compelled the Imperial government to open not only Canton but four other Chinese ports—Amoy, Ningpo, Foochow, and Shanghai—to British trade. Moreover, Britain exacted from China a heavy indemnity and the cession of the island of Hong Kong. At the time the treaty was being signed, an American sea captain, Commodore Lawrence Kearney of the *Constellation,* was anchored in Canton. The captain sized up the situation and immediately demanded from Commissioner Chi-Ying, the Chinese negotiator, that "the trade and commerce of the United States be placed upon the same footing as the nation most favored."[8] This demand was granted, and shortly thereafter the first United States emissary to the Chinese empire, Caleb Cushing, a lawyer from Newburyport, Massachusetts, arrived with a naval squadron of four vessels to formalize the agreement. The first Chinese-American treaty that granted the United States

---

[7] Quoted in *ibid.,* p. 36.
[8] Lawrence Kearney, quoted in Dulles, *op. cit.,* p. 28.

equal privileges to those exacted by Britain was signed at Wanghia in July 1844.

The Chinese negotiators were simply defenseless in the face of Western guns. But they deeply believed in their own cultural superiority and the "backwardness" of the white barbarians in everything but firepower. Chi-Ying, before sitting down with the British and Americans, made it his business to study these strange tribes. A short excerpt from his discoveries is revealing:

> As to these various countries, although they have rulers, they may be either male or female, and they may rule variously for a long or short time, all of which is far beyond the bounds of any system of laws. For example, the English barbarians are ruled by a female, the Americans and the French are ruled by males, the English and French rulers both rule for life, while the ruler of the American barbarians is established by the campaigning of his countrymen, and is changed once in four years—after he leaves the position, he is of equal rank with the common people.[9]

Chi-Ying hoped that if the barbarians would be exposed for a short period to the impact of a superior civilization, they would recognize this self-evident fact and depart from the soil of China with their profuse apologies. Hence, the correct way of dealing with the barbarians was to conciliate them and to play them off against each other. For example, Chi-Ying thought nothing of giving the Americans, in 1844, the right to try their own citizens who committed crimes on Chinese soil. An arrangement whereby the barbarians would administer justice to their own nationals and assume responsibility for their good behavior could only be of advantage to the Imperial government. Upon concluding the Treaty of Wanghia with Ambassador Caleb Cushing, Chi-Ying stated that "he could not restrain his spirit from delight and his heart from dilating with joy."[10] This was the beginning of American extraterritorial rights in China.

Early American images of China were deeply colored by the Marco Polo story. At the time the *Empress of China* sailed into Canton harbor, Cathay was described as a great, ancient, and exotic culture devoted to the arts and sciences. By and large,

---

[9] Chi-Ying, quoted in Fairbank and Teng, *op. cit.*, p. 39.
[10] Chi-Ying, quoted in Dulles, *op. cit.*, p. 29.

Americans were much too busy with the affairs of revolution and the building of a nation to be concerned with an oriental potentate at the other end of the globe. But the early American writings that exist are permeated with a feeling of profound respect and admiration. The information that the Chinese had invented such things as paper, gunpowder, and the compass and had great sages and philosophers was known to the founders of the American republic. Symbolic of this period was the American conception of Confucius as a venerable Chinese sage who had developed a profound ethical system centuries before the West had become civilized. Actually Confucius had preceded Plato by a little over a century.

Once the seafaring Yankees of the Canton trade had established actual physical contact, American images of China changed drastically. Most of the Americans who came to China in these early days were interested either in making a profit, making converts, or both. Merchants and missionaries soon began to see China as a "backward" nation. The exotic now acquired a tinge of the inferior. In almost all of these early American travelogues there are stories about pigtails, bound feet, ancestor worship, female infanticide, and a host of other sinister practices. Life in China was no longer described as superior but as upside down. The people read from right to left, wrote their surnames ahead of their given names, made soup the last course of a meal, and made a gesture for "come here" when they meant "good-by." The respected Chinese became "Chinamen"; the bearers of a superior civilization became "teeming faceless millions"; and the originators of a profound ethical system became godless heathens. The attitude of superiority of Chinese officials toward Americans was perceived as grotesque arrogance. In Harold Isaacs' telling phrase, the Age of Respect was giving way to the Age of Contempt.[11]

The American reaction to the Terranova incident was already symptomatic of this transition. The murder trial was described as a farce, and only the lack of effective protection by their own government, fear of losing their lucrative trade, and their helpless position in Canton made the Americans give up Terranova to the Cantonese officials. However, the captain of the *Emily* expressed the bitter feelings of the Americans in the following note to the Chinese government:

---

[11] Harold R. Isaacs, *Images of Asia* (New York: Capricorn Books, 1962), p. 71.

We are bound to submit to your laws while we are in your waters, be they ever so unjust. You have, following your ideas of justice, condemned the man unheard. You have the power to compel us. We believe the man innocent, when he is taken from the ship; the commander strikes his colors.[12]

Twenty years later the Americans had reversed the balance of power.

Ambassador Caleb Cushing, who arrived in Canton in 1844 to formalize the Treaty of Wanghia, was to take no presents to the emperor so that no tribute would be inferred. Instead, a varied collection of scientific objects was assembled to impress upon the Chinese the technological achievements of the United States. A list of these objects is worth mentioning: a pair of six-shooters, models of a steam excavator and a steam vessel, a daguerreotype apparatus, a telescope, a barometer, and the *Encyclopedia Americana*. Cushing carried with him a letter of introduction from President John Tyler that addressed the Son of Heaven in a tone customarily reserved for petty American Indian chiefs:

Great and Good Friend: I hope your health is good. China is a great empire, extending over a great part of the world. The Chinese are numerous. You have millions and millions of subjects. The twenty-six United States are as large as China. Our territories extend from one great ocean to the other . . . I therefore send to your Court Caleb Cushing, one of the wise and learned men of this country. On his first arrival in China, he will inquire for your health. He has then strict orders to go to your great city of Pekin, and there to deliver this letter . . .[13]

Cushing's mission, as we have seen, was a great success. The Americans received the most-favored nations' privileges they had come for, including extraterritorial rights. While these rights were granted by the Chinese in the hope of persuading the foreigners to withdraw after they realized their own inferiority, the Americans interpreted the Chinese concessions as appeasement stemming from weakness. They had come to force the Chinese to treat them as equals. In the process, American perceptions of China changed so greatly that the positions were completely reversed. It was now the Chinese who were treated as inferior. This first

---

[12] Quoted in Dulles, *op. cit.*, p. 15.
[13] John Tyler, quoted in *ibid.*, p. 26.

encounter between the nations was thus a surprise to both sides: the Chinese found themselves unable to eject the barbarians through moral suasion; and the Americans encountered almost no effective military resistance.

The most striking observation about the early images that China and America held of one another is how little they resembled reality. This is not too surprising since nothing in the history of these nations prepared them for the violent encounter to follow. Matthew Ricci's effort to teach the Chinese about the outside world remained a ripple on a sea of illusions that had been placid for thousands of years. When Caleb Cushing's naval squadron entered Canton harbor, Confucian scholars had to learn about America like children in school. The first Chinese researcher on the United States, Hsu-chi-yu, wrote a primer in 1848 with the following description of Washington:

There was a certain Wa-sheng-tun (Washington) born in 1731 (sic). When he was ten he lost his father, and his mother educated him and brought him up. He had cherished great ambitions in youth and was gifted in both literary and military matters. When the time came for the multitude of the people to revolt against the British, they urged Tun (Washington) to be their commander . . .[14]

The Americans, on their part, brimming with ideas of innovation and revolution, quickly lost respect for a civilization that placed little value on expansion and technical progress. Admiration for a superior culture quickly changed to disdain for a backward people. Americans had little patience with a static bureaucracy that could not even defend itself.

Almost everything about the two societies was different. Ancient China venerated tradition above all else. All inspiration came from the past, and history was the queen of the sciences. Early America, on the other hand, looked to the future. Age was a liability, not an asset. The earth's resources had to be harnessed, and the frontiers had to be explored.

What finally brought the two societies into contact in the nineteenth century was the coming of the new imperial age and the growing expansionary drive of America. The two nations met in a world in which one regarded itself as the bearer of tradition and

---

[14] Hsu-chi-vu. quoted in Fairbank and Teng, op. cit., p. 44.

the other became associated with the destruction of tradition. The expansion of Europe which created this new America had also destroyed the old China, and China made her stand against this modern world, stunned and bewildered.

It is reasonable to assume that had the West not forced open the Chinese door, China's perception of itself and of the West would have continued undisturbed. But given the dynamism of Western expansionism, the meeting between China and America was probably inevitable. What made it a tragedy, however, were the illusions that the main participants harbored about one another. The Chinese self-image left no room for learning from the outside world; barbarians would always remain barbarians. The Americans, on the other hand, held directly opposite views: they went to slay dragons in a land where the dragon stood for almost everything that was good. Thus, this first encounter, steeped in misperceptions on both sides, became the seedbed for the great conflicts to follow.

THE BOXER UPRISING AND THE OPEN DOOR

The story of China's dismemberment at the hands of the Western powers in the nineteenth century has often been told. Yet most Western accounts do not fully grasp the fact that this event was probably the greatest disaster that befell China in her entire history. A civilization that saw itself at the top was brought low by the gunboats of a group of assorted barbarians. After the Opium War, a scramble for concessions in China had taken place that considerably reduced China's sovereignty. By 1900, the British, the French, and the Japanese had all defeated China and exacted territories and spheres of influence. Russians and Germans had followed suit and carved out extraterritorial rights with the result that, in most of China's coastal cities as well as in the capital of Peking, foreign laws reigned supreme, and the Chinese were treated as inferiors in their own country. I still recall how, upon arrival in Shanghai in 1941, I was shocked to see a sign affixed to a foreign club in the international settlement: "Chinese and dogs not permitted." The United States fought no colonial wars in China but benefited from all the concessions exacted by the other Western powers. She, too, enjoyed extraterritorial rights and all the special privileges accorded foreigners under the unequal treaties of the nineteenth century. While the British had brought the first gunboats into the harbor of Canton, Caleb Cushing had also brought his naval squadron. And in 1858, while British and French gunboats besieged Tientsin, an American emissary waited some distance up the river and then joined with the other envoys in signing a treaty that secured for America a share of Chinese territory.

What reduced the old China to dust was, of course, the superior firepower of foreign cannon. But if we are to understand the Chinese reaction at a deeper level, we must ask the question: Why were they so slow to respond? The answer can be found in the Chinese perceptions of themselves and of the West, particularly on the matter of physical force.

Throughout the entire history of the Chinese empire, the ultimate sanction of rule was virtue by example. The right conduct of the Son of Heaven would move all others to respect and obedience, and his virtue would command their loyalty. In all their foreign relations, the Chinese kept this myth intact, even when they were weak. When 3,000 Mongol horsemen threatened Peking, they were given lavish gifts by the emperor, but he insisted that their visit be called a tribute mission. Thus, the fiction of superiority was kept intact; and since the recorded "facts" substantiated the theory, it became self-perpetuating. Physical force seemed unimportant in this context.

Hence, when five major Western powers intruded into China, the one thing that could have stopped the assault was lacking in the Chinese attitude: the resolution to meet force with force. Instead, old techniques were applied to the new situation. The barbarians were conciliated or played off against each other, usually with disastrous results. The Chinese army was decades behind its Western counterparts. It was simply a rabble provided with bags of rice and an assortment of antiquated weapons, including umbrellas, fans, gaily colored flags, and heavy swords. There was no medical staff, and the wounded either died or recovered in the nearest ditch. Pay was unpredictable and the soldiers usually survived by living off the countryside. When they were not on the march, soldiers spent their time smoking, gambling, or prowling after women. Discipline was erratic, though officers thought nothing of beheading conscripts who incurred their displeasure. Men of good family would not join the army, since it was known everywhere that Confucius had held that "good iron is not used for nails and good men are not used for soldiery."

Until the scramble for concessions threatened to swallow up China altogether, Emperor Kuang Hsu was complacent in his conviction that the time-honored techniques would work. There were a few men who perceived reality more accurately, but they remained voices in the wilderness. One of these was Kang Yu-wei, a reformer who appealed to the emperor in 1895 urging a thorough overhaul of the empire if the situation was to be saved. His memorial is a poignant document:

If Your Majesty will not decide, or will prefer to remain in the old grooves of the Conservatives, then your territories will be swallowed up, your limbs will be bound, your viscera will be cut up, and Your Majesty will scarcely manage to retain your throne or to rule over more than a fragment of Your ancient Empire.[15]

Unless China would modernize and develop firepower to expel the foreign devils, "she would sink in the earth, be buried in ruins, burst like an egg, and be torn to shreds." At the very thought of this, Kang concluded, he was so angry that his "hair stood on end, his eyes stared out of their sockets, and he was not able to endure it for a single day." Finally, in 1898, Kuang Hsu listened and attempted some reforms, but with little success. The resistance of the Confucian conservatives was too strong, and later that year the old Empress Dowager Tzu Hsi deposed him in a coup d'état and assumed control of the government. The short-lived reforms came to an abrupt end. The old empress nurtured a fierce hatred for the "foreign devils." In an edict of November 1899, she complained that "the various powers cast upon China looks of tiger-like voracity, hustling each other in their endeavors to be the first to seize upon her innermost territories."[16] Yet she refused to meet the challenge realistically, and when the old China finally did respond with violence, the result was a failure.

At about the time of the empress' edict, a popular movement began to flare up in northern China describing itself as the Fists of Righteous Harmony, to be known later and more popularly as the Boxers. These bands were held together by fierce hatred of the Westerners and their ceaseless pressure and interference with indigenous customs. Many of the Boxers believed, for example, that the foreign devils had built railroads and telegraph lines for

---

[15] Kang Yu-wei, quoted in William L. Langer, *The Diplomacy of Imperialism* (New York: Knopf, 1935), Vol. II, p. 677.
[16] Tzu Hsi, quoted in *ibid.*, p. 693.

the express purpose of murdering the good spirits of the harvest, for when it rained, the wires would rust and reddish drops would fall to the ground, obviously the blood of good spirits impaled on the wires. The barbarians had also built buildings steeper than any in China, obviously constructed so that benevolent spirits, flying low over the countryside, would crash to death. Worse, the foreigners had disturbed the ancestral burial grounds, desecrated holy places, and made a tourist attraction of the Temple of Heaven in Peking. By early 1900, armed bands roamed the countryside, burning foreign property and taking the lives of "secondary devils," Chinese converts to Christianity. By the spring, Peking was encircled by fanatical bands who robbed, pillaged, burned, and killed as they advanced. They no longer concealed their objective of driving all the barbarians into the sea. The empress, herself fiercely antiforeign, gave the movement her tacit and, at times, open support.

The story of the Boxers' siege of Peking is well known and will not be recounted here. What is less well known is the image the Boxers held of themselves that led directly to their disastrous defeat. They believed, in effect, that they were invulnerable, that Western bullets could not harm them, since right and justice were on their side. In April 1900, for example, placards appeared all over Peking proclaiming that God Himself had come down to earth to support the Boxers in their struggle:

In a certain street in Peking some worshippers at midnight suddenly saw a spirit descend in their midst. The spirit was silent for a long time. Then a terrible voice was heard saying: I am none other than the Great Yu Ti (God of the unseen world) come down in person. Disturbances are to be dreaded from the foreign devils; everywhere they are erecting telegraphs and building railways. Their sins are numberless as the hair on the head. Therefore am I wroth and my thunders have pealed forth. I have given forth my decree that I shall descend to earth at the head of all the saints and spirits and wherever the I-ho Chuan (Boxers) are gathered together, there shall the Gods be in the midst of them. Therefore I expressly command you to make this known in every place . . .[17]

Encouraged by their self-proclaimed invulnerability and "800,000 spirit soldiers," the Boxers burst into Peking in June 1900, assas-

---

[17] Quoted in G. N. Steiger, *China and the Occident* (New Haven: Yale University Press, 1927), pp. 144–145.

sinated the German and the Japanese ministers, and laid siege to the foreign legations. During the fifty-five days of the siege, the empress vacillated. One day she would send supplies to the beleaguered legations and on the next urge the Boxer leaders to destroy them. At any time, she could have lifted the siege or crushed the foreigners. But she did neither. One cannot be quite sure about the old lady's state of mind during those crucial days. But it is likely that her inaction stemmed from the conflict of her Confucian convictions against violence, and her desire to get rid of the barbarians. At any rate, when the international relief expedition entered Peking in August and the siege was lifted, the empress had left the capital in headlong flight, leaving the responsibility of dealing with the victorious foreigners to a veteran Chinese diplomat, Li Hung-chang.

After the Boxer fiasco, China could not but agree to the harsh terms imposed upon her by the Western powers. The Boxer Protocol of 1901 included several items that were bitterly resented by the Imperial Court, but there was no alternative but to accept them. The leaders of the uprising were to be executed, and monuments to foreigners who had lost their lives were to be erected in each of the foreign settlements. The importation of arms and ammunition was to be prohibited for five years, and an indemnity of 450 million taels was imposed on the Chinese treasury. In the words of one thoughtful student of the period, the function of the Manchu government now became little more than a debt-collecting agency for the foreign penetration.[18]

At the time the Boxer rising was beginning to smolder in the Chinese countryside, the United States was deeply preoccupied with the Spanish-American War. But after Admiral George Dewey's victory and President William McKinley's famous decision "after having walked the floor of the White House all night," to annex the Philippines, the attention of the United States government shifted to the Far East. The quest for concessions by the European powers worried American business interests who feared that they might be excluded from China altogether. Pressures for a more spirited United States Far Eastern policy mounted during 1899 and finally led to the famous American circular letter to the European powers known as the Open Door notes.

---

[18] Chester Tan, *The Boxer Catastrophe* (New York: Columbia University Press, 1955), pp. 215–236.

A great deal has been written about these notes and, hence, a brief summary will suffice here. What is interesting for our purposes is the astounding difference between what most American leaders at the time believed the Open Door to be and what it really was. Many of these misperceptions have lived down to the present day.

The Open Door notes of September 1899 are usually associated with the American Secretary of State John Hay. Actually, they were deeply influenced by two other men, one an American, the other a Britisher. When John Hay assumed the office of secretary of state in late 1898, he had no adviser on Far Eastern affairs. He had never been to China and had only a most cursory knowledge of the Far East. Thus, he brought with him to Washington an old friend, William W. Rockhill, who had served in the diplomatic corps in China. Rockhill, however, had not been to China in seven years and was somewhat out of touch with the rapidly changing events in that country. In June 1898, a friend of Rockhill's, the Englishman A. E. Hippisley of the Chinese Imperial Customs Service, then under the command of Sir Robert Hart, passed through Washington on his way to England. Hippisley was concerned about the threat of other European powers to British commercial interests in China. Britain controlled about 80 percent of Western trade with China and wanted to maintain the status quo.[19] Hence, Hippisley urged Rockhill to persuade Hay to approach the European powers and to get from them an assurance that there would be no interference with foreign trade in each other's spheres of influence. Spheres of influence, he said, were here to stay and had to be treated as existing facts.[20] Rockhill sensed a congruence of British and American interests in China. He realized that an American initiative to the European powers would serve a double purpose: it would restate the most-favored nation principle, which the United States had enunciated at the Treaty of Wanghia in 1844, but it would also put the United States on record as being against the further dismemberment of the Chinese empire. Hay was impressed and, after some initial reluctance to play into the hands of Great Britain, decided to go along with Rockhill's recommendation. The result was a circular memoran-

---

[19] George F. Kennan, *American Diplomacy 1900–1950* (New York: Mentor Books, 1952), p. 27.
[20] *Ibid.*, p. 34.

dum dispatched on September 6, 1899, to London, St. Petersburg, and Berlin and a month later to Paris, Rome, and Tokyo, in which the United States asked the six powers concerned not to interfere in each others' treaty ports and spheres of influence and to observe trade equality for everyone. These were the original Open Door notes.

Upon close scrutiny, the notes did not amount to very much. First, they were inspired by a British subject and were in essence a restatement of British policy. William Langer asserts, in fact, that "the American position was exactly that of Britain."[21] Second, they represented no novel departure for the United States, but merely reasserted privileges claimed by, and granted to, the United States half a century earlier. Third, the replies of the six powers were evasive and noncommittal. The American ambassador at St. Petersburg, for example, warned Hay that the Russian government "did not wish to answer the propositions at all and finally did so with great reluctance."[22] Nevertheless, Hay announced on March 20, 1900, that he had received "satisfactory assurances from all the powers addressed" and that he regarded each as "final and definitive."[23] Finally, the notes had little if any impact on the fate of China. They were dispatched only a few months before the Boxer fiasco and its bitter consequences for the Chinese empire.

The interpretation put upon the Open Door notes by the American public at the time was very different. Almost without exception, the American press hailed the notes as a triumph of American diplomacy. The Chicago *Herald* declared that "there had never been a more brilliant and important achievement in diplomacy," and the New York evening *Post* described the notes as a "noble work of peace." The two major political parties voiced their approval. The prevailing opinion was well summed up by one contemporary publicist:

The "open-door" policy in China was an American idea. It was set up in contrast to the "spheres-of-influence" policy practised by other nations . . .

The "open-door" is one of the most creditable episodes in Ameri-

---

[21] Langer, *op. cit.*, p. 687.
[22] Tyler Dennett, *John Hay* (New York: Macmillan, 1933), p. 294.
[23] John Hay, quoted in A. Whitney Griswold, *The Far Eastern Policy of the United States* (New York: Harcourt, Brace, 1938), p. 78.

can diplomacy, an example of benevolent impulse accompanied by energy and shrewd skill in negotiation. Not one of the statesmen and nations that agreed to Hay's policy wanted to. It was like asking every man who believes in truth to stand up—the liars are obliged to be the first to rise. Hay saw through them perfectly; his insight into human nature was one of his strongest qualities.[24]

The gap between reality and the American perception of the Open Door is not difficult to explain. The Hay notes committed the United States to absolutely nothing. There was no sacrifice of any kind. Yet, the formula had a lofty and idealistic ring and sounded good at home. It made the United States appear as the arbiter among the self-seeking European powers and the protector of the weak. The very term "Open Door" conjured up rights of equal opportunity without fear or favor. And the United States was to be their guarantor.

Actually, the Open Door notes were quickly overtaken by events. Three months after Hay noted his satisfaction with the responses of the European powers, the Boxers laid siege to Peking. On July 3, 1900, in the midst of the siege, Hay sent a follow-up circular note in which he reiterated the points made earlier and added that it was "the policy of the Government of the United States to seek to preserve Chinese territorial and administrative entity." Once again, the reaction of the American public was favorable, and the image of the United States as the protector of China permeated the contemporary American press. However, as George F. Kennan points out, this second set of notes had no practical effect outside the United States.[25] In fact, by August 1900, the international relief expedition was on its way to Peking. Of the 19,000 allied forces, 2,500 were American troops. Furthermore, the United States was one of the signatories of the Boxer Protocol of 1901.

While the United States government was hesitant at first to take an active part in the suppression of the Boxer rising, the siege of its legation in Peking tipped the scales. The American minister in Peking, K. H. Conger, encouraged legation guards to open fire on Chinese troops and called these actions "exhibitions of skill

---

[24] Mark Sullivan, *Our Times: The Turn of the Century* (New York: Macmillan, 1926), p. 509.
[25] Kennan, *op. cit.*, p. 38.

and courage that would serve as good object lessons."[26] Americans generally regarded the Boxers as ruffians who deserved the same treatment as ordinary criminals. Most contemporary American diplomats tended to regard the Protocol of 1901 as a lenient settlement for China.[27]

The final irony occurred in November 1900 when John Hay, the author of the policy of the Open Door, instructed his minister in Peking to seek to obtain for the United States a naval base and territorial concession at Samsah Bay in the province of Fukien, thus abandoning the basic premise of his entire policy. This American attempt to join in the scramble for concessions was thwarted by the Japanese government, which politely pointed out that Fukien was within its sphere of influence and noted its surprise that the United States, of all powers, should attempt to interfere. Hay abandoned the venture in disillusionment, and Rockhill, in a letter to Hippisley, expressed the hope that it would be "a long time before the United States would get into another muddle of this description."[28] Thus ended the American policy of the Open Door in China.

The misperceptions that plagued the relations between China and America during the latter half of the nineteenth century added enormously to the tragedy of the encounter. Half a century separated Caleb Cushing's arrival in Canton from the Boxer rising. During that period, the leadership of the Chinese empire did not yield up its self-image of moral and cultural superiority or its conviction that the barbarians would recognize these qualities and behave like the tribute-bearing missions of old. Nor did it recognize the Western cannon as a totally new factor to be reckoned with, but rather it preferred to meet physical force with the time-honored tactics of conciliation. Even extraterritorial concessions were not resented at first, but were seen by the Chinese as convenient devices whereby the barbarians would apply their own laws to their fellow-barbarians without involving China. There was little if any feeling of Chinese nationalism in those early days.

As the European powers began to carve up China in earnest and the competition for concessions gathered speed, the Imperial

---

[26] K. H. Conger, quoted in Steiger, op. cit., pp. 221–222.
[27] Edward Thomas Williams, China Yesterday and Today (New York: Thomas Y. Crowell, 1923), p. 424.
[28] William W. Rockhill, quoted in Griswold, op. cit., p. 83.

government was forced to acquiesce almost without resistance. Only in 1900, when the capital itself was divided up and the hated barbarians had reached the Temple of Heaven, did the Boxer uprising take place. And even then, there was almost no awareness of reality. The Boxer myths of invulnerability in the face of Western guns and of countless armies of "spirit soldiers" led straight to their defeat. The self-image of the old China was only shattered on the rock of the Boxer Protocol.

The attitude of the United States toward the Chinese empire was also one of moral superiority. The Americans had not waged war against China, but they had received the same privileges as the European powers. Nevertheless, they wished to draw a clear distinction between themselves and the "imperialists." This the American government attempted to do through the Open Door notes. As we have seen, these circular memoranda of 1899 were little more than a free trade "me too" claim, although those of 1900 made an unsuccessful effort to uphold the integrity of China. Yet the myth was established that "in this episode of the Open Door notes, a tremendous blow had been struck for the triumph of American principles in international society—an American blow for an American idea."[29] Neither their ineffectiveness nor American unwillingness to enforce the notes, nor in fact Hay's departure from the goals set forth in them—"none of these things succeeded in shaking in any way the established opinion of the American public."[30] The Americans saw the Chinese as their wards and themselves as superior to the petty power politics of the Europeans. To America, the Open Door was a democratic policy guaranteeing equal opportunity to all and at the same time protecting the integrity of China. To China, the Americans had arrived late at the Western holdup, but just in time to share in the spoils. The door of China had never opened voluntarily; it had been crashed in.

The Boxer rising was never perceived in the United States as a legitimate nationalist movement. Rather, the Boxers were seen as criminals and fanatics. One contemporary American diplomat describes the edicts of the empress dowager as "the cruel decrees of a selfish ruler" and the uprising itself as "the barbarity of a frenzied mob."[31] Hence, when the empire finally responded with

---

[29] Kennan, *op. cit.*, p. 41.
[30] *Ibid.*
[31] Quoted in Williams, *op. cit.*, p. 423.

force, the United States felt virtually betrayed by its protégé. So pervasive had the American self-image of the benevolent protector become that the Chinese attempt at self-assertion was met with fury. This explains why an American minister was able to order his troops to open fire on the Boxers "as an object lesson" and why another described the Boxer Protocol as "lenient." It also explains the United States participation in the suppression of the Boxer rising through force of arms.

Communist historians in China today describe the early relations between China and America in terms of a capitalist plot intended to victimize China, creating an image of victimization at the hands of a great evil force invading China. In the words of a leading scholar, "this makes for self-pity, resentment, and the need for an explanation of history in terms of evil and injustice."[32] The Opium War and its aftermath left a more lasting impression on the present Communist leaders than on the apolitical peasants of the preceding century. The American response, on the other side of the gap, generally is a startled "Who, me?" when confronted with the historical data. The self-image of moral superiority coupled with one of benevolence toward China persists even today.

Reflection shows that neither the American nor the Chinese images tally with the facts. No one-dimensional, Communist-devil theory showing how American capitalism attacked, betrayed, and exploited the Chinese people, diverting their otherwise "normal development toward Communism," will do. Nor is the typical American textbook history of the period any more satisfactory. It is true that in general the Western impact was a disaster for China and that the United States was a part of that impact. But this disaster was not the result of a plot; rather, it was the predictable result of Western civilization expanding and coming into contact with the last remaining separate, distinct, and isolated empire in the world, one that conceived of itself as superior to all others. Under this impact, the old China crumbled. As John K. Fairbank puts it: "circumstances made China the worst accident case in history."[33] The reciprocal images that accompanied these historical circumstances deepened the tragedy even further and made it echo down into the next century.

---

[32] John K. Fairbank, "Why Peking Casts Us as the Villain," *The New York Times,* May 22, 1966.

[33] Testimony of John K. Fairbank in U.S. Senate Committee on Foreign Relations, *U.S. Policy with Respect to Mainland China,* 89th Cong., 2nd sess. (1966), p. 102.

three

CHIANG KAI-SHEK AND THE UNITED STATES

The twentieth century brought many profound upheavals in Chinese society. The shock of the Boxer defeat forced many Chinese intellectuals to reevaluate their positions in relation to the West. The year 1901 had demonstrated in the most explicit terms that whatever the barbarians' cultural inferiority might be, their fire power was overwhelmingly superior. Consequently, a whole new generation of students began studying the West in an entirely different light. They largely ignored its culture, its art, and its literature. Instead, they carefully studied its science and technology for the express purpose of using this knowledge to expel the foreigners from China.

Accompanying this development was a widespread movement for political reform under the leadership of Sun Yat-sen. The Manchu dynasty was doomed, for although it had managed to survive the upheavals of the nineteenth century, it had lost an irretrievable amount of face with the Boxer defeat. In 1911, it succumbed to the revolutionary movement and the Republic of China was formally declared.

The republic, however, was beset by internal weakness. It had been born as a parliamentary democracy—with a representative legislature, an elected chief of state, and a judiciary—but with little of the requisite life force. There was no tradition of self-government on the national level, and the revolutionary party was a loosely organized group of intellectuals with little, if any, popular support. It fell prey almost immediately to factional strife within its own ranks. Yüan Shih-k'ai, who had become the first president of China, attempted to declare himself emperor, and only his death in 1916 ensured his failure. The next seven years were a confused time of local revolt and internecine struggle within the revolutionary movement.

The revolution entered a new phase in 1923 when Sun Yat-sen embarked upon a complete reorganization of his party, the Kuomintang. His requests for aid from the West having been ignored, he turned to the Soviet Union for counsel. The USSR responded with material aid and expert advisers in the technique of revolution and helped to establish in 1924 a military academy at Whampoa to train officers for the Chinese army.

The next step was seen as the subjugation of various northern warlords entrenched in their respective satrapies. Sun Yat-sen died in 1925, however, and the northern expedition was carried out under the leadership of a young general who had risen rapidly in Kuomintang politics to become Sun's successor. This young man was Chiang Kai-shek, later generalissimo of China. His northern expedition was a success, but internal strains were soon evident within the Kuomintang. In 1927, Chiang Kai-shek purged all Communists from his party and spent the following years consolidating his power against recalcitrant dissidents and warlords. From 1931, moreover, he was under increasing pressure from the Japanese, who had begun their encroachments into Chinese territory.

During this time, Americans were largely unaware of events in China. American missionaries continued their efforts to convert China to Christianity and sent back periodic reports on their work to the faithful at home. The Western powers confined themselves to preserving their extraterritorial privileges in the face of the revolutionary turmoil in China, but there was little understanding even at the policy-making level of the nature of the revolution in which China was enmeshed. As for the public-at-large, it was dimly aware that China was the scene of considerable fighting, but the impression was one of general chaos in a remote land whose political impact on the United States was negligible.

Only the Sino-Japanese War brought China to the attention of the American public. The Japanese bombardment of Shanghai and the savage conquest of Nanking were greeted with horror in the United States, while China's continued resistance against heavy Japanese odds excited increasing admiration. As the 1930s drew to a close, the American people's image of China grew to heroic proportions—an image of a dogged, patient, indomitable people fighting with boundless determination against a brutal foreign intruder.[1]

---

[1] See Harold Isaacs, *Images of Asia* (New York: Capricorn Books, 1962), chap. 7.

This image was well described by an American who spent the war years in Chungking and several Chinese provinces:

I had come back that summer [1940] with a full set of standard ideas about the Kuomintang's war, acquired from the American press: the gallant losing battles, the brave and clever guerrillas, the millions of determined refugees fleeing west; later, the firmly held fronts beyond which there would be no retreat, and behind them a new country a-building; the factories in the caves, the busy co-ops, the new roads and schools and hospitals, and looming over the whole united land, the massive figure of the Generalissimo, his attractive wife only slightly in the background. As a prewar visitor to China, when I read about such things in America I had marveled: "How different from the place I knew!" The idea that a new China was emerging from the war was one reason why I returned.[2]

Such images are frequently personified in an individual figure, particularly in moments of high historical drama, for strong feelings of admiration or horror are not easily applied to abstract entities such as nations; they run deep and require a human recipient. Thus, the Third Reich became "Hitler's Germany"; England was embodied in the formidable figure of Churchill; and it was only natural that the image of a heroic China was personified in the figure of the Kuomintang leader Chiang Kai-shek.

America's apotheosis of China between 1936 and 1945 came to be the apotheosis of the generalissimo. The image grew to extravagant dimensions, portraying Chiang as a hero, a soldier-saint, and a savior of modern China. Above all, Chiang was shown as a defender of democracy—a tough and seasoned soldier whose fight was the same as that of America. "If the United States must face the Axis on two fronts," declared *Fortune* magazine in 1941, "it can do so for one reason: that a Free China is fighting the Battle of the Pacific. . . . The future history of China rests on him [Chiang]; and he has so far discharged his responsibility with superb skill."[3]

Time magazine designated Generalissimo and Madame Chiang "Man and Wife of the Year" in 1938 and asserted that the generalissimo "had remade China" and that "after centuries, the Chinese people had at last found a leader."[4] Much was also made

---

[2] Graham Peck, *Two Kinds of Time* (Boston: Houghton Mifflin, 1950), p. 35.
[3] "China the Ally," *Fortune*, 24 (September 1941), 44, 49.
[4] *Time*, 31 (January 3, 1938), 14–15.

of the fact that Chiang was a Christian, and the missionary press acclaimed him widely.

To the missionaries, Chiang's acceptance of Christianity raised limitless hopes. Many even believed that China would now become a Christian nation. For the first time they could look forward to official support for their endeavors. And in return for this bright promise, the missionaries and their supporters at home gave Chiang Kai-shek and his wife, from 1930 on, their passionate and uncritical support.[5]

The hero image rose to even further heights. A pamphlet published by the Institute of Pacific Relations in 1942 compared Chiang Kai-shek to George Washington and drew analogies between the Chinese and American revolutions:

> As revolutionary America produced a great leader in war and peace—George Washington—so revolutionary China has produced a great leader—Chiang Kai-shek. Revolutionary China of today is not behind the revolutionary America of more than a hundred and fifty years ago . . . Her war is a people's war and its impact has stimulated both the spirit and the practice of democracy in wartime China . . . China is at last awake to modern techniques and modern ideas. She has acquired both chiefly from America . . . Her future form of government will be an adaptation of Western democratic institutions to her own conditions and national genius.[6]

During the civil war between the Nationalists and the Communists in the late 1940s, Americans added yet another facet to the image of the generalissimo. Not only was Chiang Kai-shek a leading defender of democracy; he now became the United States' trusted friend in the common struggle against communism. Chiang Kai-shek, the Christian general, would fight side by side with America against the threat of atheistic communism. This image permeated American thinking during the 1940s and provided the basis for most decisions on China policy. A perusal of Chiang's record reveals a picture that is at great variance with the image described above. Let us first examine the extent of the Chinese leader's commitment to democratic rule.

---

[5] Felix Greene, *A Curtain of Ignorance* (Garden City, N.Y.: Doubleday, 1964), p. 12.
[6] Robert W. Barnett, "China—America's Ally," *Far Eastern Pamphlet No. 5* (New York: Institute of Pacific Relations, 1942), pp. 24–25.

Chiang Kai-shek's political model for the Kuomintang came not from the democratic West but from China's Confucian past. Once he was in complete power after the purge of the Communists in 1927, Chiang looked more and more for his inspiration to the example of Imperial China. In November 1928, he urged the officers of the Kuomintang army to delve into the Confucian classics in their leisure time. In 1931, he declared Confucius' birthday a national holiday, and Nationalist troops were ordered to give special protection to Confucian temples throughout China. In 1934, Chiang decreed the canonization of Confucius, and the Confucian temple at Kufow became a national shrine.

It is particularly significant that, after Confucius, the figure that Chiang Kai-shek admired most was Tseng Kuo-fan, the political architect of the T'ung-Chih Restoration, that short-lived decade in the 1860s described by a leading scholar as "the last stand of Chinese conservatism."[7] Tseng Kuo-fan made a last determined effort to renovate the Manchu dynasty, to restore the traditional Confucian virtues, and to prevent the massive Western incursions into China. The effort failed because the problems faced by Imperial China could not be solved by the restoration of the Confucian order. In essence, Tseng Kuo-fan was a political anachronism. Nevertheless, Chiang Kai-shek admired him as one of the greatest men in Chinese history.

It is easy to see that Chiang Kai-shek hardly fitted the American perception of the democratic leader. The Confucian leader governs by precept and example, not through elections; he stands at the top of a political pyramid whose hierarchy and structure he controls. The concept of a "loyal opposition" is unknown to him; he governs not by mandate of the people, but by the "Mandate of Heaven."

There is little wonder that a few leading Americans, upon close contact with Chiang, were shocked and surprised at what they saw. General Stilwell, for example, the United States military adviser to the Kuomintang, made the following entry in his diary on August 2, 1942:

His [Chiang's] obstinacy refused description. He has lost all habit of discussion in fact because everybody around him is a yes-man. No

---

[7] Mary C. Wright, *The Last Stand of Chinese Conservatism* (Stanford: Stanford University Press, 1957).

one dares tell him an unpleasant truth because he gets mad. . . . He is not taking a single forward step, or doing anything concrete to improve the position of China, and so, incidentally, his own.[8]

Chiang Kai-shek was no enemy of democracy. He simply came from a completely different tradition, which he tried his best to restore and with which Americans had no empathy whatsoever.

The American perception of Chiang's violent anticommunism was equally far from the mark. While it is true that, after the purge of 1927, Chiang turned against the Communists, there is strong evidence that the origins of the Kuomintang and of the Communist party in China were almost the same. Both were conceived in the anti-Western reaction that swept China in the early 1920s. Chiang's political power base, at that time, was the Whampoa Military Academy of which he was the commander. He openly collaborated with the Communists and many leading members of the Chinese Communist party occupied prominent posts in the Kuomintang. Mao Tse-tung's first significant appearance on the historical stage, for example, took place in 1924, when he was elected an alternate member of the Kuomintang Central Executive Committee. Stuart Schram, author of a leading political biography of Mao, observes that: "In this triangular relationship of Moscow, the Kuomintang, and the Chinese Communist Party, the position of Mao Tse-tung during the crucial years 1925–1927 was on the whole closer to that of the Kuomintang than to that of either Stalin or Chen Tu-Hsiu [the Head of the Chinese Communist Party]."[9] Schram also states that it is probable that "Mao was more at ease within the Kuomintang than within his own party."[10]

While these observations may seem startling to Americans, exposed for decades to the image of Chiang as an anticommunist, the following excerpt from a speech he made in Changsha in 1926, provides revealing evidence of his views:

Only after the overthrow of imperialism can China obtain freedom. In the present world revolution, there is the Third International, which can be called the general staff of the revolution. If we want our revolution to succeed, we must unite with Russia to overthrow imperialism.

---

[8] Joseph W. Stilwell, *The Stilwell Papers*, Theodore H. White (ed.) (New York: William Sloane Associates, 1947), p. 133.
[9] Stuart Schram, *Mao Tse-tung* (New York: Simon and Schuster, 1966), p. 71.
[10] *Ibid.*

If Russia aids the Chinese revolution, does that mean she wants to oblige China to apply Communism? No, she wants us to carry out the national revolution. If the Communists join the Kuomintang, does this mean that they want to apply Communism? No, they do not want to do that either; they want to apply the Three People's Principles. I am persuaded that the Communists who have joined our party do not, at the present time, want to apply Communism, but want rather to carry out the national revolution. The Chinese revolution is part of the world revolution. We want to unite the partisans of the world revolution to overthrow imperialism.[11]

There is a striking similarity between these words and an article written by Mao Tse-tung in 1926, the first item of his *Selected Works*. Mao was in fact the head of the Peasant Institute of the Kuomintang in 1926, and, Lin Piao, his favorite disciple, was a student at the Whampoa Military Academy, which was supported with funds, advisers, and weapons by the Soviet Union.

All this is not to imply that Chiang Kai-shek was a Communist. It is merely to point out that, during the early part of his career, he made common cause with the Communists against Western imperialism in China. Chiang had suffered no harm at the hands of the Communists but he had witnessed the dismemberment of China by the Western powers. And to him that was a greater evil than communism. Most Americans perceived the Nationalists and the Communists as radically antithetical movements, with Chiang Kai-shek, the Christian general, battling the Communists on behalf of the forces of freedom and righteousness. This perception was at odds with reality. Chiang's desire to restore the Confucian imperial tradition and Mao's goal of a Communist peasant revolution made them allies in the common cause of national self-assertion against the Western presence in China. The break between them in 1927 and the events that followed were essentially the manifestations of a struggle for power, not a conflict over ideological differences.

The progress of relations between China and America was further complicated by perceptual errors on the part of Chiang. These included Chiang's self-image, as well as his view of the United States.

In 1926, an American reporter named Lewis Gannett interviewed the young commander-in-chief of the Chinese Nationalist army.

---

[11] Chiang Kai-shek, quoted in *ibid.*, p. 83.

Gannett wanted to know what the general thought of America. The reply was revealing:

Thinking men in China hate America more than they hate Japan. Japan talks to us in ultimatums; she says frankly she wants special privileges . . . We understand that and we know how to meet it. The Americans come to us with smiling faces and friendly talk, but in the end your government acts just like the Japanese. And we, disarmed by your fair words, do not know how to meet such insincerity. This is what is behind the anti-Christian movement in China. Your mission-aries write "charity" over their doors, and I do not deny that many of them are good men who do good work. But in the end they make it easier for American policy to follow that of the other imperialist powers. So because we have been deceived by your sympathetic talk, we end by hating you most.[12]

A year later, this same general, Chiang Kai-shek, purged the Communists from the Kuomintang and established his government at Nanking. Shortly thereafter, he became a Christian and, after the Japanese assault on Manchuria, a client of the United States. With the attack on Pearl Harbor, he became a full-fledged ally. Nevertheless, his perceptions of the United States did not change significantly since that first interview in 1926. They emerge quite clearly from his book *China's Destiny,* first published in March 1943, especially since it was written at a time when the United States considered China a staunch ally and a loyal and steadfast friend. The book interprets China's history in the nineteenth cen-tury as the destructive result of Western penetration. The unequal treaties forced upon the Manchu rulers during that time are given as the major cause of decay of all aspects of Chinese life, ranging from politics and law to ethics and psychology. Highly charged phrases, such as "national humiliation" and "the bondage of the unequal treaties," recur constantly.

During the last hundred years, China's national position and the morale of the people deteriorated to such an extent that an unprece-dented situation developed . . . The oppression and bondage of the unequal treaties further undermined the Chinese state and the nation . . . The national decay during the last hundred years reached

---

[12] Chiang Kai-shek, quoted in Harold Isaacs, "Old Myths and New Realities," *Diplomat* (September 1966), p. 45.

a point unequaled in our history . . . until the basis of rebirth and recovery was almost destroyed.[13]

The second chapter of the book is entitled "The Origins of National Humiliation and the Sources of the Revolution." Its opening sentence sets the tone for the rest of the section: "The deterioration of China's national position and the low morale of the people during the last hundred years can be largely attributed to the unequal treaties. The implementation of the unequal treaties constitutes a complete record of China's national humiliation."[14]

America is not singled out for special recrimination, as in contemporary Chinese Communist historiography, but it is nowhere excluded from blame. At times, this omission is quite pointed: "Whenever one country obtained a new privilege from its treaty with China, all the other countries would, *under the evil 'most-favored-nation' clause,* enjoy the same benefits. The special privileges provided in a treaty were often amplified by the foreign interpretation of its terms."[15] It should be remembered that the United States had been one of the chief beneficiaries of the most-favored nation policy in the nineteenth century.

Those who compared Chiang with George Washington and saw him as the West's firm ally might have been disturbed by his statement that "the main objective of the Nationalist Revolution was to escape from the bondage of the unequal treaties and especially to overcome the habits of arrogance, lawlessness, and the attitude of servile dependence upon foreign powers that had been fostered under the unequal treaties."[16] The anti-Western feelings of the author of *China's Destiny* are immediately apparent to the reader. Nor could these feelings be dismissed as the personal idiosyncrasy of Chiang, for the book was made a basic text in the training of all Kuomintang party members, government officials, and officer candidates. Yet after some negative editorial reactions in the United States, the book attracted little, if any, attention, while the myth of a firm Sino-American friendship lived on. Even Franklin D. Roosevelt, who harbored few illusions about the stability of Chiang's regime, retained the conviction that the two nations

---

[13] Chiang Kai-shek, *China's Destiny*, Philip Jaffe (ed.) (New York: Roy Publishers, 1947), p. 42.
[14] *Ibid.*, p. 44.
[15] *Ibid.*, p. 52. Italics added.
[16] *Ibid.*, p. 69.

were united by a traditional rapport. At a private conference on China policy in Cairo on December 6, 1943, he remarked, "Well, now, we've been friends with China for a great many years. . . . They really like us and just between ourselves, they *don't* like the British."[17]

Much of this myth could be attributed to the American people's sincere feelings of good will toward China. We have seen how firmly the United States had come to believe in the benevolence of its historical role in China. And, being allies in a world-wide struggle, the two nations were commonly presumed to be united by bonds of friendship. To admit that the alliance was but a temporary congruence of national interests would have involved a total reconstruction of America's image of her relations with China. Hence, in order to maintain an internal coherence of outlook, it was necessary to presume that the Chinese were not only allies but friends as well. "By projection, this American benevolence toward China was transformed into an exaggerated notion of Chinese friendship for the United States. The extravagant idea of America's popularity in China influenced the estimate of the consequences of a Communist-controlled China for American interests in the Far East."[18]

Yet there were more deliberate elements that helped to solidify the myth. An English translation of *China's Destiny* did not appear in the United States until after the war. The United States State Department had made a translation for its own use but kept the document classified as "top secret" and refused to release it even in 1946, when a group of six congressmen requested to see it in connection with a major congressional debate on China policy. It was not propitious, the State Department said, to release the document at that time.[19] When a translation of the book finally appeared after the war, it was an "authorized" translation, with most of the anti-Western references that might have been offensive to the American reader deleted. Thus, in order to see what Kuomintang officers were reading in their training classes, one had to consult the unauthorized, but accurate, edition.

This official effort to "decontaminate" the real Chiang Kai-shek

---

[17] Franklin D. Roosevelt, quoted in Stilwell, *op. cit.*, pp. 251–252.
[18] Tang Tsou, *America's Failure in China, 1941–1950* (Chicago: University of Chicago Press, 1963), p. 149.
[19] Philip Jaffe, "The Secret of 'China's Destiny,' " in Chiang Kai-shek, *China's Destiny, op. cit.*, p. 18.

and to project an image of the "strong Christian general" to the American public must be understood against the larger background of United States–China relations.

One theme that recurs again and again in American accounts of United States relations with China is the interpreting of events in a strongly moralistic light. Conflicts of interest and hard facts of power are often transmuted into conflicts between good and evil. The world is seen as divided into two camps of which one represents the forces of righteousness and the other the forces of darkness. Thus, Americans since the Open Door and even before, traditionally saw themselves as the benevolent guardians of China. The Chinese were generally seen as the object of American philanthropy, as wards—"devilishly exasperating wards sometimes, but still as wards."[20] The fact that the United States benefited from all the concessions exacted by the European powers was generally glossed over. Nor could it be admitted that the anti-Western passions of the new revolutionary Chinese leadership extended to the United States. Hence, the alliance with Chiang Kai-shek was not perceived in the United States as an arrangement brought about by the power alignments of the period, but rather as an alignment of the forces of justice in a moral battle. It was believed that Nationalists and Communists represented two completely opposite sets of motives and aspirations. Few Americans perceived the complex truth that the Nationalist and Communist revolutions were *both* essentially anti-Western and that the struggle between them was much more a struggle for power between competing forms of authoritarianism than a conflict between radically different ideologies.

A leading historian of American relations with China offers another perceptive insight:

Americans are a funny folk. They applaud moral sentiment but they are rarely ready . . . to take the next step, to make effective the sentiment which they applaud. The time comes when they are asked to put up or shut up. They do neither. They will not put up the force without which sentiments in this wicked world are still sentiments only, but neither will they shut up. They keep talking about the sentiments as if wishes were horses.[21]

---

[20] Isaacs, "Old Myths and New Realities," *op. cit.,* p. 42.
[21] Tyler Dennett, "The Open Door as Intervention," quoted in *Historians and American Far Eastern Policy,* Dorothy Borg (compiler) (New York: Columbia University Press, 1966), p. 20.

A. Whitney Griswold's classic study *The Far Eastern Policy of the United States* reaches similar conclusions. It suggests that American policy toward China had always swung like a pendulum from intense involvement to total lack of concern. Lofty rhetoric and commitments to moral principles were seldom backed up with military or economic sanctions. The Stimson doctrine of non-recognition, proclaimed after the Japanese attack on Manchuria, is cited as one example among many.[22]

In the case of Chiang Kai-shek, the choice of "putting up or shutting up" had to be made during the Chinese civil war in the late 1940s. President Harry S. Truman, true to the form described above, decided to do neither. He did not "put up" the necessary military force to prevent the Communist conquest of China, nor did he "shut up" and accept the fact that the Communists had won the civil war.

Most important for the purposes of this study, American policy, burdened by the Chiang Kai-shek image of the past, found itself unable, after the Communist victory, to make a realpolitik volte-face and deal pragmatically with the new rulers of China. One could not suddenly abandon the pro-American Christian general and engage in commerce with the devil without dire domestic political consequences.

A number of leading American Foreign Service officers strongly urged a shift of policy, but to no avail. Thus, John Service wrote in October 1944: "Any new Chinese government under any other than the present reactionary control will be more cooperative with the United States and better able to mobilize the country."[23] And John Paton Davies wrote:

But we must be realistic. We must not indefinitely underwrite a politically bankrupt regime. We must make a determined effort to capture politically the Chinese Communists rather than allow them to go by default wholly to the Russians. Furthermore, we must fully understand that by reason of our recognition of the Chiang Kai-shek government as now constituted we are committed to a steadily decaying regime and severely restricted in working out military and political cooperation with the Chinese Communists. . . . Power in China is on the verge of shifting from Chiang to the Communists.[24]

---

[22] A. Whitney Griswold, *The Far Eastern Policy of the United States* (New York: Harcourt, Brace, 1938), *passim*.
[23] John Service, quoted in Tsou, *op. cit.*, p. 200.
[24] John Paton Davies, quoted in *ibid.*, p. 201.

According to Tang Tsou, "Service's and Davies' hopes were shared by most of the foreign service officers in China." Nevertheless, the image of Chiang Kai-shek as the bastion of Christian morality and of the Communists as a godless evil ensured the very outcome that these experts in China warned against again and again.

When Chiang was driven to Formosa by the Communists in 1949, most Americans were not psychologically prepared to accept this fact. The forces of evil could not triumph in such a manner. The United States could not be so impotent. Thus, the myth developed that the United States had "lost" China as a result of the work of subversives in the American government. The loss of China was so unthinkable that only treason could explain it.

The rise of the Republican right wing on the American political scene in 1949 and the attacks on the State Department by Senator Joseph R. McCarthy in 1950 were symptoms of this psychological phenomenon. When Mao Tse-tung's armies swept across China toward victory in 1949, a number of American politicians began to mount a furious attack against the administration's China policy. On April 15, 1949, Senator Styles Bridges of New Hampshire demanded a congressional investigation of the State Department and accused Secretary of State Dean Acheson of "what might be called sabotage of the valiant attempt of the Chinese Nationalists to keep at least part of China free."[25] On April 21, Senator William Knowland of California echoed the demand for an investigation and added: "If ever a government has had the rug pulled out from under it, if ever a non-Communist government in the world has reason to feel betrayed, that government is the Republic of China."[26]

When the State Department, in a white paper on China dated August 1949, attempted to present the administration's view of events, four senators immediately denounced the document as a "whitewash of wishful, do-nothing policy which has succeeded only in placing Asia in danger of Soviet conquest."[27] Patrick Hurley, the former United States ambassador to China, described the white paper as "a smooth alibi for the pro-Communists in the State Department who had engineered the overthrow of our ally,

---

[25] Styles Bridges, quoted in Allen J. Matusow (ed.), *Joseph R. McCarthy* (Englewood Cliffs, N.J.: Prentice-Hall, 1970), p. 8.
[26] William Knowland, quoted in *ibid*.
[27] Quoted in *ibid*.

the Nationalist Government of the Republic of China, and aided in the Communist conquest of China."[28] Even Senator Robert A. Taft, known as "Mr. Republican" to millions of Americans and a man famous for his integrity, rose in the Senate to say, "The State Department has been guided by a left-wing group who obviously have wanted to get rid of Chiang and were willing at least to turn China over to the Communists for that purpose."[29] The furor culminated, of course, with the attacks by Senator Joseph McCarthy. For example: "When Chiang Kai-shek was fighting our war, the State Department had in China a young man named John S. Service . . . He sent official reports back to the State Department urging that we torpedo our ally Chiang Kai-shek and stating, in effect, that Communism was the best hope of China."[30]

It is not within the purview of this study to examine the charges of subversion, but it must be noted that underlying these explanations of Chiang's defeat was the assumption that a handful of Americans actually had the power to determine the fate of more than half a billion people in China. The spasm of McCarthyism finally passed, but many Americans continued to believe that China had been betrayed by the forces of evil.

Ironically enough, Chiang Kai-shek, too, felt betrayed by the United States. As late as 1942, after the United States had entered the war against Japan, he repeated his old accusation: "The American attitude toward China is in essence no different from that held by other nations. China is treated not as an equal but as a ward."[31] And, as many visitors to Taiwan have since testified, Chiang Kai-shek continued to see himself in large measure as a victim of American betrayal.

We can only speculate on the exacerbating effects of these distorted images. The record clearly shows that Chiang Kai-shek and the American leadership perceived each other through dark screens that often produced caricatures out of realities. It does not necessarily follow, of course, that, if all these shadows had been cleared away, all the beasts would have become beauties. Objective conditions of conflict were real enough. The thrust of

[28] Patrick Hurley, quoted in *ibid.*
[29] Robert A. Taft, quoted in *ibid.*, p. 23.
[30] Joseph R. McCarthy, quoted in *ibid.*
[31] Chiang Kai-shek, quoted in *ibid.*, p. 46.

the new revolutionary China was anti-Western, and America was a part of the West. But there is little doubt that the opaque screens raised false hopes on both sides that, when shattered, led to only deeper disillusion. Even if Chiang Kai-shek had retained power on the mainland, it is unlikely that he would have remained allied with the United States for long. He might, in fact, have "reverted to type" and become its bitter enemy.

four

CHINA'S INTERVENTION IN THE KOREAN WAR

The victory of the Communists on the Chinese mainland in 1949 ushered in a totally new period in Sino-American relations. Less than a year after the Communist takeover, American soldiers fought Chinese soldiers on the field of battle for the first time in history. This encounter radically changed the American view of China and deeply affected the Chinese view of America.

From the perspective of the United States, the Korean conflict marked the end of America's sentimental attachment to China, the end of the image of the Chinese as the heroic underdog, and the end to paternal interest and avuncular concern. In fact, the post-1950 American image of a hostile, menacing China dates from the Korean War.[1] The events of that period also confirmed the Chinese Communists in *their* view of the United States as an archenemy. These mutual perceptions, in turn, led to policy decisions of the most crucial consequence on both sides.

Let us briefly recapitulate the sequence of events. On June 25, 1950, North Korean troops attacked the Republic of South Korea and began a major campaign down the peninsula. The American response was swift: President Truman ordered American air and naval forces to the assistance of the hard-pressed South Korean armies; the Formosa Straits were "neutralized" by the dispatch of the United States 7th Fleet; and all available American ground forces in Japan were mobilized for action in Korea. At the same time, the United States took steps in the United Nations Security

---

[1] Harold Isaacs, *Images of Asia* (New York: Capricorn Books, 1962), chap. 10, esp. pp. 225–239; Allen S. Whiting, *China Crosses the Yalu* (New York: Macmillan, 1960), p. 167.

Council to place the conduct of the war under United Nations auspices, and so the Korean "police action" was launched.

By late September, the tide of battle had turned dramatically. The North Korean armies, which in the early days of the war had come close to conquering the entire peninsula, were turned back and had been driven back across the thirty-eighth parallel, which marked the boundary between North and South Korea. By early October, the status quo ante-bellum had been restored, fulfilling the objectives announced by the United States at the beginning of hostilities.

At this point, however, the United States shifted its objectives and declared its intention to ensure a unified Korea. Thus, the United Nations forces did not halt their victorious advance at the thirty-eighth parallel. Instead, despite increasing warnings from the Chinese Communists that they would not tolerate the destruction of the North Korean government, South Korean troops crossed the parallel into the North on October 1, followed on October 7 by the United States 1st Cavalry Division.

The Chinese Communists had declared on October 2 that they would intervene if United States troops entered North Korea, but this warning had gone unheeded. The United Nations armies swept steadily northward, taking the North Korean capital of Pyongyang on October 19 and driving onward toward the Yalu River, which marked the international boundary between Korea and mainland China. On November 24, General Douglas MacArthur announced a final offensive: the troops, he declared, would be home by Christmas.

Late in October, however, a new participant entered the war. On October 26, 1950, United Nations troops began reporting contact with Chinese "volunteer" forces, and such clashes occurred more frequently in early November. Simultaneously, the tone of domestic Chinese propaganda became ominously anti-American. Yet the possibility of massive Chinese intervention in the Korean War was steadily discounted in the United States. In the opinion of American policy makers, the Chinese Communists would be foolhardy to intervene in a situation that would strain their resources and expose them to such punishing defeat.[2] Thus,

---

[2] Dean Acheson, "Foreign Policies Toward Asia—A Television Interview with Secretary Acheson," Department of State Bulletin, 23 (September 18, 1950), p. 463.

even the explicit Chinese warning of October 2 went unheeded in Washington until November 26, when the Chinese unleashed a full-scale attack on the United Nations forces. This massive intervention resulted, in the words of General MacArthur, in an "entirely new war."

The Chinese attack was received with consternation in the United States. America had regarded the Korean conflict throughout as a Soviet-directed endeavor—part of the world-wide pattern of deepening tensions between the United States and the Soviet Union that had marked the postwar period. American policy makers had tried to discourage Chinese intervention by repeatedly stressing their benevolent intentions toward China. It was reiterated, for example, that the United States had no aggressive intentions upon the Chinese mainland, that neutralization of the Formosa Straits had been related only to events in Korea, and that the "traditional friendship" of the United States for the Chinese people held as firmly as ever. A report in *The New York Times* was a typical example:

Secretary of State Dean Acheson said today that the United States was trying to discourage the Chinese Communists from entering the Korean war by making it plain in every possible way that this Government felt no hostility toward the Chinese and had no aggressive intentions in the Far East.

The fact that the United States does not have aggressive designs on China . . . has been made repeatedly clear in his own statements, by the Voice of America and by President Truman himself.[3]

Yet these repeated assurances had failed to impress Peking. Instead, they were perceived as only further evidence of duplicity. Scornfully, the Chinese leaders replied that they had heard such rhetoric before. Had not the Americans declared that they would halt at the thirty-eighth parallel, and had they not crossed it? Had not the United States wanted it believed that they would not push their offensive up to the Yalu but would stop short of the river itself, and were not American troops now approaching the river? In the light of such past experience, what credence could

---

[3] *The New York Times*, August 31, 1950.

be lent to the new American assertions that they would not cross the Yalu into Chinese territory?[4]

In analyzing the Chinese decision to intervene, it is difficult, if not impossible, to assess the degree of Soviet influence. In his exhaustive and probably definitive study *China Crosses the Yalu,* Allen Whiting reaches the conclusion that "China entered the war of her own free will":[5]

> It would seem that a Soviet *diktat* was not needed to bring the PRC [People's Republic of China] into the war. There may have been differences between the two allies as to the timing and extent of the move. . . . There undoubtedly were questions of mutual responsibility, some of which may have been resolved to the dissatisfaction of one or both partners. . . . But the final decision to fight appears to have been basically a Chinese decision, conditioned by Russian advice and encouraged by Russian support.[6]

The primary actors in the drama, then, were the United States and China. What, we must ask, was the nature of the misperceptions that led these two nations in the fall of 1950 to misjudge so seriously each other's actions?

The United States–Chinese relationship in late 1950 can be analyzed in terms of four distinctive, yet interrelated, factors: first, each nation's *self-image;* second, each nation's perception of the *character* of its adversary; third, each nation's perception of its adversary's *intentions;* and finally, each nation's perception of the other's *power* and *capabilities.*

In the matter of China's and America's respective self-images, it is important to note that both nations had strongly developed conceptions of their historical missions, and that these conceptions were perceived as antithetical. An atmosphere of conflict, therefore, existed that tended to exacerbate specific incidents. In this connection, one need hardly elaborate upon the United States' conception of itself as the "defender of democracy" or as the "bastion of the free world." Such rhetoric was far more current

---

[4] Editorial from Jen-min Jih-pao, November 6, 1950, quoted in Tang Tsou, *America's Failure in China, 1941–1950* (Chicago: University of Chicago Press, 1963), pp. 582–583. See also Peking's statement of November 17, 1950, *The New York Times,* November 18, 1950.

[5] Allen S. Whiting, *China Crosses the Yalu* (Stanford: Stanford University Press, 1960), p. 154.

[6] *Ibid.,* p. 160.

in the world of 1950, when Stalin was still alive, when the cold war was at its height, and when East-West relations were perceived in terms of the starkest opposition. The outlook was well conveyed by John Foster Dulles in an article for *The New York Times Magazine* of July 30, 1950:

Now we are consciously enlisted in a great cause. We have enlisted voluntarily, as befits free men and women, and we sacrifice voluntarily. We do not work and sacrifice as slaves to any master save truth and righteousness. Our purpose is to join our strength with that of the other free members of the United Nations to preserve such human liberty as remains in the world. . . .

We are engaged in the kind of crusade that Lincoln foresaw when he said, of our Declaration of Independence, that it promised "liberty, not alone to the people of this country, but hope for the world for all future time."[7]

But it is not enough to describe these quasi-religious, crusading elements in the American self-image. This would be too generalized and amorphous an approach. There is more empirical material at hand, and it is to be found abundantly in the personality of General MacArthur. For operational purposes, the perceptions of Douglas MacArthur, so long as he was in command of the Korean theater of war, *were* the American perceptions on which policy was based. Suffice it to say for the moment that MacArthur was frequently acclaimed, and probably believed himself to be, America's greatest living soldier. The startling success of the Inchon landing had made the general's confidence in his own military genius unshakable. Most United States political leaders considered the American cause in Korea to be just and right and America's most honored soldier believed the armed might of the United States to be invincible.

It is equally important to recognize that similar elements existed in Communist China's conception of herself. Where America conceived her mission to be the defense of democracy, Communist China considered herself to be the champion of Marxism-Leninism. The modern Chinese elite saw China as the proper and natural leader of all of Asia and itself as the restorer of China's ancient glories and the redresser of the wrongs inflicted upon her

---

[7] John Foster Dulles, "To Save Humanity from the Deep Abyss," *The New York Times Magazine*, July 30, 1950.

by the West.[8] "He [Mao] . . . felt deeply as a historical thinker the injustices that European imperialism had inflicted on Asia. It seemed to be his view that Europe had unbalanced the life in Asia, and the work of this generation of liberators was to recover the balance."[9]

Mao Tse-tung's liberation image of Chinese Communism was directly linked to his perception of himself as a leading innovator in strategic thought, especially in the field of guerrilla warfare. There is ample evidence to support the view that Mao believed his guide *On Protracted War* to be the definitive work on the subject. The superiority of the peasant guerrilla over the "paper tiger" of American atomic power was relentlessly drilled into new recruits of the Chinese People's Liberation Army. If Mao's image of the new China as a great power dominated his political thinking, the peasant guerrilla constituted his most formidable military weapon against the imperialist West. As General Nieh Jung-chen put it: "They [the Americans] may even drop atom bombs on us. What then? They may kill a few million people. Without sacrifice, a nation's independence cannot be upheld. . . . After all, China lives on the farms. What can atom bombs do there?"[10]

Thus, both the United States and China saw themselves as the foremost proponents of similarly crusading, but deeply divergent, ideologies, both buttressed by weapons that were deemed invincible. On the eve of the Korean War, these self-images created a particularly explosive atmosphere in which incidents could escalate rapidly, signals could easily be misinterpreted; overt conflict became all too possible.

When we compare each nation's perception of the *character* of its adversary, certainly the Chinese image of the United States must make startling reading in America. It was a real devil image, a picture of unequaled malevolence. In the summer of 1950, the Chinese Communists launched an intensive domestic propaganda campaign portraying the United States not merely as the enemy of the moment, but as China's historical archenemy. The deepening Korean crisis was interpreted not as an isolated incident,

---

[8] Tsou, *op. cit.,* p. 563.
[9] K. M. Panikkar, *In Two Chinas* (London: Allen & Unwin, 1955), p. 81.
[10] Nieh Jung-chen, quoted in Samuel B. Griffith II, *The Chinese People's Liberation Army* (New York: McGraw-Hill, 1967), p. 118.

but as one more example of America's longstanding hostility toward China. Jen-min Jih-pao, for example, published a chronology of "American Aggression Against China," which enumerated almost annual examples of aggression—political, economic, and moral—throughout the entire period from 1839 to 1950.[11] To this chronology of overt conflict, there was added the element of moral corruption. The United States was depicted as a

paradise of gangsters, swindlers, rascals, special agents, fascist germs, speculators, debauchers and all the dregs of mankind. This is the world's manufactory and source of all such crimes as reaction, darkness, cruelty, decadence, corruption, debauchery, oppression of man by man, and cannibalism. . . . Here the criminal phenomena that issue forth defy the imagination of human brains. . . . Everyone who does not want the people of his beloved fatherland contaminated by these criminal phenomena is charged with the responsibility of arising to condemn her, curse her, hate her and despise her.[12]

In early November, the Chinese government launched a fierce propaganda campaign under the slogan, "Resist America, Aid Korea, Preserve Our Homes, Defend the Nation." The population was bombarded with anti-American propaganda from loudspeakers, radios, and platforms. Countless mass meetings were organized in every community, school, factory, and commune. At these, the United States, President Truman, and General MacArthur were described as mad dogs, bloodstained bandits, murderers, rapists, and savages. The American leaders were depicted as bloodthirsty or poisonous animals in innumerable cartoons. The virulence of the campaign lashed more than half a billion people into a frenzy of hate and fear.

These were the lurid tones of a Cotton Mather sermon warning of the perils of commerce with the devil. The image projected was one of an opponent with whom there can and must be no compromise, whose very touch brought contamination and defilement. It implied, in short, bottomless hate and contempt.

---

[11] *Hate America Campaign in Communist China* (Washington, D.C.: Department of State, 1952?), pp. 36–43. There are, incidentally, interesting parallels between this interpretation of the history of Sino-American contacts and that of Chiang Kai-shek in *China's Destiny*, Philip Jaffe (ed.) (New York: Roy Publishers, 1947).
[12] "Look, This is the American Way of Life," supplement to *Nan Fung Jih Pao*, CCP official organ, December 1950, in *Hate America, op. cit.*, p. 184.

On the American side, there was also an element of semi-religious ardor. John Foster Dulles referred to the South Korean government as a "moral salient in the otherwise solid Communist despotism of North Asia."[13] General MacArthur wrote in November 1950 that "the Chinese people have thus become militarized in their concepts and in their ideals. . . . This has produced a new and dominant power in Asia, which . . . has become aggressively imperialistic, with a lust for expansion and increased power normal to this type of imperialism."[14]

Despite the fact that MacArthur characterized Communist China as a power lusting for expansion, he had a curious contempt for the Chinese soldier. He equated the highly indoctrinated and well-disciplined Communist soldier of 1950 with the demoralized Nationalist soldier of 1948. To be blunt, he did not respect his enemy, and this disrespect was to cost him dearly.

A nation's perception of its adversary is closely related to its estimation of the adversary's *intentions* toward the nation itself. Here we encounter the most clear-cut divergence in perceptions between China and the United States in 1950. The United States believed that the Chinese Communists neither would nor could intervene in Korea and relied on frequent pronouncements of America's nonaggressive intentions to reassure the Chinese leaders. The Chinese Communists, on the other hand, regarded the United States as the heir to Japan's imperialist ambitions in Asia[15] and became increasingly convinced that only powerful intervention in Korea would prevent the United States from invading China. Two quotations will serve to point up the contrast:

the United States government has taken this series of aggressive actions [in Korea] with the purpose of realizing its fanatical devotion of dominating Asia and the world. One of the master-planners of Japanese aggression, Tanaka, once said: to conquer the world, one must first conquer Asia; to conquer Asia, one must first conquer China; to conquer China, one must first conquer Korea and Taiwan. . . . American imperialism . . . plagiarizes Tanaka's memorandum, and follows the beaten path of Japan's imperialist aggressors![16]

---

[13] Dulles, *op. cit.*, p. 5.

[14] Douglas MacArthur, *Reminiscences* (New York: McGraw-Hill, 1964), p. 367.

[15] Tsou, *op. cit.*, p. 577.

[16] Chinese Communist spokesman in United Nations, Security Council (SC/PV/527), 5th Session, 527th Meeting. (November 28, 1950), pp. 23–24.

I can give assurance that we . . . have never at any time entertained any intention to carry hostilities into China . . . . Because of our . . . long-standing friendship for the people of China we will take every honorable step to prevent any extension of the hostilities in the Far East. If the Chinese Communist authorities or people believe otherwise, it can only be because they are being deceived by those whose advantage it is to prolong and extend hostilities in the Far East against the interests of all Far Eastern people.[17]

Thus, American policy makers chose to view the tension between America and China in 1950 as a passing phenomenon and felt that assurances of good will toward China would suffice to insulate the Korean conflict from Chinese intervention. The Chinese Communists, on the other hand, viewed the Korean conflict as yet another incident in a longstanding pattern of American hostility toward China. These preconceptions helped fashion each side's interpretation of the other's actions. As one scholar of Chinese-American relations has noted:

While Secretary Acheson was talking about the traditional friendship of America, the Chinese Communists were teaching their compatriots that from the early nineteenth century onward the United States had consistently followed an aggressive policy toward China which culminated in her support for Chiang Kai-shek in the civil war and her present actions in Korea and Taiwan. The Chinese people were told to treat the United States with scorn . . . because she was a paper tiger and "certainly" could be defeated.[18]

Operating upon the assumption of longstanding Sino-American friendship, United States policy makers were deeply astonished at the violence of the Chinese response in October 1950. They did not see the intervention coming, either from the specific warning conveyed on October 2 by Chou En-lai to Indian Ambassador K. M. Panikkar in Peking[19] or from the increasingly hostile tone of Chinese domestic propaganda during the two preceding months.[20] That the illusion of a firm Sino-American friendship underlying a Communist veneer persisted in the face of considerable evidence to the contrary suggests that the United States was not yet prepared to take China seriously. Her warnings were not as yet con-

---

[17] Statement by President Harry S Truman, November 16, 1950.
[18] Tsou, op. cit., p. 578.
[19] Whiting, op. cit., pp. 108–109.
[20] Ibid., pp. 84–85, 88–89.

sidered credible. It suggests, in fact, that the United States still tended to look upon China as the immature "ward" it had so long considered her.

A detailed examination of the Chinese warning to Ambassador Panikkar and the American response to it is quite revealing. Chou En-lai clearly told Panikkar on October 2 that, if American troops crossed the thirty-eighth parallel, China would enter the war.[21] Prime Minister Jawaharlal Nehru, in a parliamentary speech, repeated the substance of the Chinese warning in the following terms:

The Chinese government clearly indicated that if the 38th parallel was crossed, they would consider it a grave danger to their own security and that they would not tolerate it. We did, as a matter of fact, convey our views to the governments of the United Kingdom, the United States of America, as well as to some governments in Asia.[22]

Neither President Truman nor General MacArthur took this warning seriously. Truman viewed it as "a bold attempt to blackmail the United Nations" and later observed in his *Memoirs* that "Mr. Panikkar had in the past played the game of the Chinese Communists fairly regularly, so that his statement could not be taken as that of an impartial observer."[23]

On October 7, United Nations forces crossed the parallel and began their sweep toward the Yalu River. On October 10, Chou En-lai repeated his warning and announced that the Chinese people would not "stand idly by in this war of invasion." Once again, it received only passing attention in Washington and Tokyo and was dismissed as just another example of Chinese bombast.

On October 15, Truman and MacArthur met on Wake Island, and the President wanted to know the general's opinion of the possibility of Chinese intervention. MacArthur considered this possibility remote:

Had they interfered in the first or second month, it would have been decisive. We are no longer fearful of their intervention. We no longer stand hat in hand. The Chinese have 300,000 men in Manchuria. Of these, probably not more than 100 to 125,000 are distributed along the Yalu River. They have no Air Force. Now that we have bases for our

---

[21] Cited in, Panikkar, *op. cit.*, p. 110.
[22] Jawaharlal Nehru, quoted in Griffith, *op. cit.*, p. 120.
[23] Harry S Truman, *Years of Trial and Hope, Vol. II: Memoirs* (Garden City, N.Y.: Doubleday, 1956), p. 362.

Air Force in Korea, if the Chinese tried to get down to Pyongyang there would be the greatest slaughter.[24]

Four days later, when MacArthur's forces entered Pyongyang, the State Department also came to the conclusion that Chinese intervention in Korea was "unlikely." In the opinion of one leading authority:

This assessment was by no means confined to the department over which Acheson presided. It was shared alike by the President, the Joint Chiefs of Staff, members of the National Security Council, General Walter Bedell Smith, Director of Central Intelligence, prominent senators, congressmen, and political pundits of all hues. If questioned, that amorphous character "the man in the street" would have expressed the same opinion.[25]

Nevertheless, at the very time that the American leadership, virtually without exception, denied the possibility of Chinese intervention, the Chinese 4th Field Army crossed the Yalu and penetrated the ragged mountain terrain of North Korea.

Truman, MacArthur, and the State Department perceived a China that no longer existed. "The conviction that China would not intervene represented an emotional rather than an intellectual conclusion, an ascription to the enemy of *intentions* compatible with the desires of Washington and Tokyo."[26] This misperception prepared the ground for a military disaster of major proportions.

If the Americans misperceived Chinese intentions by refusing to take them seriously, the Chinese erred in the opposite direction. The world as viewed from Peking presented a picture of implacable American hostility. Not only were American troops marching directly up to the Korean border at the Yalu River, but the United States was protecting the hated Nationalist regime on Taiwan and was aiding the French against the revolutionaries in Indochina. In addition, the United States was rehabilitating and rearming Japan. Hence, the Chinese leadership reasoned, the intention of the United States

(was) to make use of Taiwan as a springboard for the invasion of the Chinese mainland. . . .

---

[24] U.S. Senate, *Military Situation in the Far East,* Hearings before the Committee on Armed Services and the Committee on Foreign Relations, 82nd Congress, 1st sess. (1951), p. 3483.

[25] Griffith, *op. cit.,* p. 124.

[26] *Ibid.,* p. 125.

Her plan is to invade China after her complete occupation of Korea. . . .

The U.S. is now arduously rebuilding and rearming Japan. . . . The aim of the U.S. is to utilize Japanese military force as the U.S. advance guard in the American invasion of the Far East. . . .

Apart from open aggression, the U.S. also tries to work against us from the inside. . . . According to statistics collected in the Southwest, 60% of the principal bandit groups in the Southwest had their training under the U.S. and Chiang.[27]

We Chinese people are against the American imperialists because they are against us. They have openly become the arch enemy of the People's Republic of China by supporting the people's enemy, the Chiang Kai-shek clique, by sending a huge fleet to prevent the liberation of the Chinese territory of Taiwan, by repeated air intrusions and strafing and bombing of the Chinese people, by refusing new China a seat in the U.N., through intrigues with their satellite nations, by rearing up again a fascist power in Japan, and by rearming Japan for the purpose of expanding aggressive war. Is it not just for us to support our friend and neighbor against our enemy? The American warmongers are mistaken in thinking that their accusations and threats will intimidate the people of China.[28]

With this kind of outlook, it was hardly surprising that the Chinese regarded verbal protestations of good will on the part of the United States as a mockery.[29]

---

[27] "How to Understand the United States," in *Hate America, op. cit.,* pp. 50–52.

[28] Quote from Jen-min Jih-pao, September 25, 1950, in Whiting, *op. cit.,* p. 106; see also Tsou, *op. cit.,* p. 577.

[29] It is interesting to note in this respect that hostility toward America and suspicion of its intentions toward China were not exclusively characteristic of the Chinese Communists. The uproar in the Chinese press over the Peiping Rape Case in the winter of 1946–1947 shows how deep anti-Americanism ran in Chinese life well before the Communist victory. See Thurston Griggs, *Americans in China: Some Chinese Views* (Washington, D.C.: Foundation for Foreign Affairs, 1948), pp. 7–15. Later in 1947, some Chinese newsmen were maltreated and insulted by American personnel while covering the withdrawal of United States troops from Tangku. In reporting the incident, the Peiping *Shih Pao,* a Kuomintang paper, remarked on April 23, 1947: "We are led to doubt that such incidents are really isolated and accidental. . . . That these foreigners . . . should build a sense of racial superiority . . . on the grounds of China's weakness and poverty and need for foreign troops . . . is a serious matter." (Quoted in *ibid.,* p. 29). Griggs gives several other illustrations of this current of anti-Americanism in China well before the Communist takeover.

The most crucial category of all, however, is the fourth—that of each nation's perception of the other's *power* and *capabilities*. At no time prior to October 25, 1950, did American policy makers seriously consider the possibility of Chinese intervention in the Korean conflict. The Chinese leaders, it was believed, would not be so foolhardy as to risk their meager resources against the overwhelming military forces of one of the world's superpowers.[30] That Peking might feel so endangered by the Korean action as to believe it had no other course but to intervene was not considered at all likely. Her warnings, therefore, were viewed as mere bluff. The United States' failure to credit these warnings was probably attributable to its having considered China as the "sick man of Asia" for too long to be able suddenly to abandon its paternalistic attitude.

The United States, moreover, had no doubt as to its ability to defeat any military force that the Chinese might send into Korea. General MacArthur expressed his conviction to this effect at the Wake Island Conference.[31] Indeed, one of the major shocks of the Korean War, was America's sudden realization that the Chinese soldier, hitherto regarded with a degree of contempt, was a tough opponent when well equipped and trained.[32] Speaking in this connection of the Korean soldier, Hanson W. Baldwin of *The New York Times,* made some remarks that might as easily have applied to American attitudes toward the Chinese:

We tended prior to Korea, despite the hard lessons taught us by the Japanese in World War II, to look down upon the Koreans as an inferior race. It was with this attitude of patronizing contempt that we went into action in Korea. We quickly discovered that the "gook" was a tough soldier. . . .[33]

This line of analysis, incidentally, casts some light upon General MacArthur's insistence upon crossing the thirty-eighth parallel, for the general, far from regarding the Chinese as equals, insisted that "the pattern of the Oriental psychology [is] to respect and follow

---

[30] Tsou, *op. cit.,* pp. 574, 579.
[31] Leland M. Goodrich, *Korea: A Study of U.S. Policy in the United Nations* (New York: Council on Foreign Relations, 1956), p. 136; see also John Spanier, *The Truman-MacArthur Controversy and the Korean War* (Cambridge: Harvard University Press, 1959), p. 105.
[32] Isaacs, *op. cit.*
[33] Hanson W. Baldwin, *The New York Times,* October 31, 1950.

aggressive, resolute and dynamic leadership, to quickly turn on a leadership characterized by timidity or vacillation . . ."[34] Mac-Arthur's paternalistic and contemptuous view of the military power of the new China led directly to disaster in October and November 1950. The story is worth examining in some detail.

On October 26, to the accompaniment of fierce bugle calls, shrill whistles, and blasts on shepherds' horns, the Chinese launched a surprise attack on South Korean and American forces some fifty miles south of the Chinese border. The results were devastating. Several United Nations regiments were virtually decimated. Nevertheless, Major General Charles A. Willoughby, MacArthur's main intelligence officer, still voiced the opinion on the following day that "the auspicious time for Chinese intervention [had] long since passed" and that "there [was] no positive evidence that Chinese Communist units, as such, [had] entered Korea."[35] On November 1, the Chinese initiated a massive attack against the United States 3rd Battalion and virtually tore it apart. Then, after shattering the United States 8th Cavalry, the Chinese abruptly broke contact and withdrew.

MacArthur's reaction to these events demonstrates how difficult it is for an old, but subbornly entrenched, misperception to yield to the facts. On the day of the Chinese disengagement, his estimate of total Chinese strength in Korea was between 40,000 and 60,000 men.[36] In fact, as of October 31, the Chinese had deployed, in utmost secrecy and within short distances of the American forces they were about to strike, almost 200,000 men.[37] Some of these had crossed the Yalu before the Wake Island meeting between Truman and MacArthur.

The Chinese troops had done what MacArthur had deemed impossible. They had moved by night in forced marches, employed local guides and porters, and used the barren and hostile terrain of the North Korean hills to their advantage. Then they launched their assault on MacArthur's unsuspecting army. When the Chinese temporarily withdrew, MacArthur immediately ascribed this turn of events to the heavy casualties the enemy had sustained. The Chinese needed to rest, in MacArthur's view, and,

---

[34] Douglas MacArthur, Message to Veterans of Foreign Wars, August 28, 1950.
[35] *Military Situation in the Far East, op. cit.,* p. 3427.
[36] Griffith, *op. cit.,* p. 134.
[37] *Ibid.,* p. 129.

hence, a golden opportunity was at hand for a second and victorious American drive to the Yalu.

In retrospect, it is clear that

> The Chinese withdrawal in early November was designed to encourage the enemy's arrogance; to lure the UN forces deeper into North Korea, where their tenuous supply lines could be interdicted and where units separated from one another by the broken terrain could be isolated and annihilated. This was the nature of the deadly trap which P'eng, at his Shenyang headquarters, was setting for the overconfident general in the Dai Ichi Building in Tokyo.[38]

Thus, MacArthur, believing that he was faced with 40,000 instead of 200,000 Chinese soldiers and believing that these soldiers were badly in need of rest after their encounter with the American army, advanced northward again for the "final offensive." The Chinese watched for three weeks and, finally, on November 27, attacked in overwhelming force, turning the American advance into a bloody rout. Thus, a peasant army put to flight a modern Western military force commanded by a world-famous American general. In one bound, China had become a world power, and the image of the Chinese ward, almost half a century in the making, was finally shattered, at a cost of tens of thousands of battle casualties on both sides. MacArthur, incredibly enough, did not learn much from the experience. In the words of his aide-de-camp, Major General Courtney Whitney, the general "was greatly saddened as well as angered at this despicably surreptitious attack, a piece of treachery which he regarded as worse even than Pearl Harbor."[39] The stark truth was that MacArthur had blundered into the trap of his own misperceptions.

The paternalistic attitude of American leaders toward Communist China died hard. It remained extremely difficult for the United States to admit that the new China was growing in power and was fiercely hostile and that this attitude was more than a passing phenomenon. Many rationalizations were invoked to explain this disturbing new presence on the world scene. Communism was viewed as somehow "alien" to the "Chinese character." It would pass, leaving the "traditional friendship"

---

[38] *Ibid.*, p. 134.
[39] Courtney Whitney, *MacArthur: His Rendezvous with Destiny* (New York: Knopf, 1956), p. 394.

between China and America to reassert itself—although the paternalism implicit in this "traditional" relationship was never admitted.[40] At other times, Chinese hostility to the United States was explained as the result of the evil influence of the Soviet Union:

On November 27, immediately following Mr. Vyshinsky's statement of charges of aggression against the U.S., the United States representative in this Committee [one of the United Nations], Ambassador Dulles . . . with a feeling of sadness rather than anger, said one could only conclude that the Soviet Union was trying to destroy the long history of close friendship between China and the United States and to bring the Chinese people to hate and, if possible, to fight the United States.[41]

One of the more bizarre examples of this attempt to maintain old attitudes in the face of bewildering new facts was the brief flurry in the press during December 1950 concerning the possibility of a United Nations military action in China—directed not against the Chinese people, but against the Mao faction, which was presumed to be their oppressor. A headline in the New York *Herald Tribune* proclaimed "Declaration of State of War Against Mao's Faction Urged" and stated in the text that "So far as can be determined now, the action of the UN will not be one of war against China or the Chinese people but against one faction in China, namely the Communists."[42] How this distinction was to be put into effect on the battlefield was never made clear, and apparently the utterly unrealistic nature of the proposal led to its early death. Nevertheless, the distinction between the Chinese people and their Communist leaders persisted for some time. On December 29, 1950, in a statement for the Voice of America, Dean Rusk, then Assistant Secretary of State for Far Eastern Affairs, accused the Chinese Communists of having plotted the North Korean assault. The press reported that "As all American officials have done consistently, Mr. Rusk drew a distinction between the Chinese people, for whom the United States has a long tradition of friendliness, and their Communist rulers."[43] By denying that the

---

[40] See Whiting, *op. cit.*, pp. 169–170.

[41] United Nations, United States Mission, Press Release, No. 1129, February 2, 1951.

[42] "Declaration of State of War Against Mao's Faction Urged," New York *Herald Tribune*, December 6, 1950.

[43] New York *Herald Tribune*, December 30, 1950.

new government of China had a power base and a measure of popular support, the United States tried to maintain intact its old illusions about the historical relationship between the two nations. But that relationship had been a predatory one, and it was precisely this that was never admitted.

Indian Ambassador Panikkar detected this blind spot in the American picture of China. He noted that in the early days of the Korean War, the Western military attachés in Peking had been utterly confident that Chinese troops could not possibly stand up to the Americans. The American defeat in late November, he noticed, came as a profound shock to them, and their attitude thenceforth was very different.[44] In a good summation of the problem, he stated: "China had become a Great Power and was insisting on being recognized as such. The adjustments which such a recognition requires are not easy, and the conflict in the Far East is the outcome of this contradiction."[45]

The Korean crisis provides a good illustration of the practical, operational consequences of divergent perceptions in world affairs. These perceptions are, in effect, definitions of the situation at hand. Once the situation has been defined, certain alternatives are eliminated. One does not conciliate an opponent who is perceived as implacably hostile; hence, the Chinese Communists felt in the end that they had no resort but to intervene in Korea. One does not credit the threats of an opponent whose power one feels to be negligible; hence, the United States perceived even specific Chinese warnings as bluff. One does not compromise with an opponent whose ideology is perceived as antithetical to one's own values; hence, the United States and China remained poised on the brink of potentially disastrous conflict, neither one accepting the other's perception of its world role as legitimate.

Yet, paradoxically, the violent clash between the United States and China in 1950 might in one sense have contributed in the long run to some future improvement of relations between the two nations, for the effectiveness of China's intervention in Korea established her as a power to be reckoned with. It shattered once and for all the attitude of patronization that, until then, had characterized the United States' view of Chnia. To the extent that nations can admit their past mistakes, and are able to learn

---

[44] Panikkar, *op. cit.*, p. 117.
[45] *Ibid.*, pp. 177–178.

from them, the likelihood of war between them will diminish. Verbal threats may continue and various forms of indirect conflict will survive. But to the degree that each remembers the other's power, he will refrain from provocations beyond the point of no return.

five

THE UNITED STATES, CHINA, AND THE WAR IN INDOCHINA: THE FRENCH PHASE

The main thesis of this chapter is that the American perception of Ho Chi Minh underwent profound changes between 1946 and 1954. In 1946, most Americans saw Ho Chi Minh as an ardent nationalist fighting against French colonialism; four years later most Americans perceived him as the front man for Chinese Communism. The point here is that this change was *not* the result of rational analysis or of objective changes in the political character of Ho Chi Minh, but of irrational, largely extraneous perceptions that Americans superimposed upon the situation in Indochina. Similarly, the Communist Chinese leaders superimposed their own perceptual "grid" upon the United States. To them, the world was divided into "imperialists" and "oppressed," and America was viewed as the embodiment of all evil. This devil image on both sides led to operational consequences in the foreign policies of both China and America that in turn made the hostility between them even more implacable.

In 1946, the United States considered itself merely a detached observer in Indochina. Hostilities erupted there, but they were regarded as France's problem. Indeed, many Americans tended to believe that they were just what the French deserved for their colonial ambitions. "Colonial war, then, is back in Indochina," said *The Saturday Evening Post* on November 30, 1946, and the *Christian Science Monitor* on December 24 described Ho Chi Minh's fight as "part of the world struggle of colonial peoples for liberation from foreign influence or control. . . . The peoples of Indochina joined the forward march toward independence more than six years ago and the present clashes are an unpleasant phase of this struggle."

This perception was very much in line with that of President Franklin D. Roosevelt during World War II. Roosevelt had openly opposed the return of French power to Indochina and had advocated some form of international trusteeship for the area.[1] If the fighting in Indochina was a colonial war, it naturally followed that the United States should remain disapproving of France. This was precisely American policy. The United States even urged France to end the war[2] and resisted all appeals for assistance, insisting, for example, that American-produced propellers be removed from the British aircraft given by Britain to the French troops fighting against Ho Chi Minh.[3]

The American view of Ho Chi Minh paralleled the American view of the war as a whole. On February 6, 1946, the *Christian Science Monitor* called him a moderate, and on January 9, 1948, remarked that "Ho Chi Minh's present Government is mixed and does not give the appearance of being Communist dominated." The entire American press showed considerable skepticism toward French claims that Ho was an outright Communist. On the whole, "United States policy decidedly favored Ho Chi Minh."[4] "An American OSS officer who had worked closely with Ho for several months prior to V-J Day had described him as an 'awfully sweet guy' whose outstanding quality was his 'gentleness.' "[5]

When American perception did change, it was not based on actual events in Indochina, but on developments altogether outside the area. In 1948 America's conception of its world role changed profoundly. Crisis followed crisis, in Berlin, in Greece, and in Czechoslovakia. The division between East and West crystallized and hardened. The imagery of the "iron curtain" and of "containment" came to pervade the entire American view of foreign affairs. The chasm between Eastern and Western camps appeared deeper by the day, and the United States, architect of the North Atlantic Treaty, began to see itself as the leader of an

---

[1] Victor Bator, *Vietnam: A Diplomatic Tragedy* (Dobbs Ferry, N.Y.: Oceana Publications, 1965), p. 206.
[2] *The New York Times,* June 17, 1947.
[3] Bator, *op. cit.*
[4] *Ibid.*
[5] Bernard B. Fall, *The Two Vietnams* (New York: Praeger, 1964), p. 82.

embattled "free world" resisting the expansion of a ruthless totalitarianism.

The threat in Europe was undeniably real, and the American response to it was, on the whole, not exaggerated. The ramifications of this new outlook, however, were less rational, for the new definition of the European situation spilled over to encompass the entire globe. Having recognized a mortal threat in the heart of Europe, American leaders soon came to redefine *all* conflicts throughout the world as part of the same struggle.

Inexorably, the United States came to believe that the "frontiers" of the free world included Asia as well. In October 1948, the House Foreign Affairs Subcommittee on World Communism issued a report calling China the active theater in the cold war. The report said the Communists were using China as a testing ground for tactics they might use to take over the world and recommended a "guarantee of territorial and political integrity" to the Chinese Nationalists.[6]

This shift in outlook implied an American redefinition of the "true" nature of Ho Chi Minh as well:

In this country, *it is only now beginning to be understood* that in any Asiatic nationalist movement connected with Moscow through its leadership, the totalitarian-imperialist trend must inevitably kill native nationalism. . . . His [Ho's] Indochinese independence has become a means to another end: Russian conquest of the Southeast Pacific.[7]

The New York *Herald Tribune,* on June 17, 1949, stated flatly that "Ho Chi Minh is a Comintern agent whom the French rate as an authentic political genius." This redefinition did *not* coincide with any *objective* developments in the Indochinese conflict. It coincided instead with an extraneous event: the Communist victory in China. The sense of betrayal that the American public felt over the loss of China intensified the anxieties arising from the cold war. Thus, peril in Europe, compounded by betrayal in China, produced a strongly emotional reevaluation of the United States relationship to Southeast Asia.

Hence, American failure in China was attributed to the machina-

---

[6] U.S. House Foreign Affairs Subcommittee on World Communism, *China and U.S. Far East Policy, 1946–1966,* 80th Cong., 2nd sess. (1967), p. 45.
[7] Andrew W. Green, "Are You a Middle of the Roader?" *Plain Talk,* 3 (April 1949), 35. Italics added.

tions of a world-wide conspiracy. From 1949 onward, the American press reflected an inexorable trend by which the perceptual grid of cold war categories was superimposed upon the older conflict in Indochina. This grid gradually eclipsed all awareness of the nationalist origins of the Ho Chi Minh insurgency. It even erased American recollections of the colonial conditions that had sparked the revolt, until finally, the original disapproval of France as an imperial power disappeared altogether in a redefinition of the French as "defenders of the West."

"Indochina: 'Greece' of 1950?" *U.S. News and World Report* asked on February 24, 1950. "Indochina . . . is in the process of becoming the Greece of Asia, now that the 'cold war' has turned to the East. All of a sudden, with the Communist victory in China to the north, Indochina is out front in the power struggle between Russia . . . and the Western world." On February 2, 1950, the *Department of State Bulletin* asserted that the recognition of Ho Chi Minh by the USSR, China, North Korea, and the Eastern European nations had brought an end to speculation as to the fate of Vietnam under Ho, who was now described as a lifelong servant of world communism.

One by one the ambiguities disappeared. "Nationalist rebels" were steadily amalgamated with the Communist threat. Bao Dai, once referred to as the "nightclub emperor" and as a man irretrievably tainted by his close association with the French colonial regime, was now officially considered as offering "more opportunity to the Vietnamese people to develop their own national life than a leader who . . . must obey the orders of international Communism."[8]

By September 1951, it was considered axiomatic that the rest of Southeast Asia could not be held if Indochina "fell to Moscow-Peiping directed Communist rule,"[9] and by the middle of 1952, the State Department spoke of "the common recognition that the struggle in which the forces of the French Union and the Associated States are engaged against the forces of Communist aggression in Indochina is an integral part of the world-wide resistance by the Free Nations to Communist attempts at conquest and subversion."[10]

---

[8] Policy statement by Ambassador Loy W. Henderson, *Department of State Bulletin*, 22 (April 10, 1950), 565.

[9] *Christian Science Monitor*, September 11, 1951.

[10] U.S. Department of State, "Communique of Talks on Indochina," Press Release, No. 476, June 18, 1952.

Now that the deadly enemy was seen at work in Southeast Asia, the United States was eager to *keep* the French in Indochina. If the United States was to reconcile French presence there with its conception of itself as firmly anticolonialist, however, France's role in Indochina would have to be perceived quite differently. This did in fact happen. "That the French are making a tremendous effort to hold it [Tonking] for the free world is *better understood now than it was a short time ago*," stated *The New York Times* in an editorial on September 24, 1951.[11] The reevaluation was even made retroactive: "A bitter and bloody struggle *between Communist forces and French Union troops* has been racking Indochina for *six years*," declared *Background* in 1951.[12] And in March 1952, a State Department official stated that "In this battle to preserve their country from Communism, France is contributing financially and militarily. . . . French soldiers and resources have borne the brunt of this brutal attack."[13] Thus, what had been regarded as a colonial war was now fully redefined as a brutal attack by an outside enemy, while France was recast as the defender, not the opponent, of Asian independence.

By early 1952, the cold war grid was firmly in place. "The great power struggle in Asia now appears to be moving inevitably and dangerously into a new theatre—Southeast Asia," stated the *Christian Science Monitor* on January 25. No longer was Southeast Asia viewed as the arena of an anticolonial revolt; it had now become part of the East-West power struggle. The same editorial continued that "no one planned that, after a stalemate in Korea, there should be a new trial of strength in the southward projection of Asia," thus implying that the Indochinese conflict had begun *after* the outbreak of the Korean War. The editorial concluded by imposing the cold war dichotomy in full force: "It [Indochina] is a place which is bound to be occupied eventually either by East or West. The strategic prizes are so great that the issue must be joined and eventually settled." Any claim of the Vietnamese to the right to determine their own destiny disappeared in the chasm of East-West divisions.

Thus, the record shows that the American perception of the war

---

[11] *The New York Times,* September 24, 1951. Italics added.
[12] U.S. Department of State, Office of Public Affairs, *Background* (October 1951). Italics added.
[13] U.S. Department of State, statement by Robert E. Hoey, Officer in Charge of Vietnam-Laos-Cambodia Affairs, Press Release, No. 178, March 8, 1952.

in Indochina changed radically in the years between 1949 and 1952. Since the definition of what was going on changed, it was only natural that there should be a related shift in ideas of what should be done. This correlation was, in fact, strikingly close. In May 1950, the Griffin mission recommended an aid program of $23 million in economic assistance and $15 million in military aid to the French in Indochina.[14] In June, the first shipments of aircraft were made to Indochina, and $119 million in military aid was made available to France under the Mutual Defense Assistance Program. This aid increased to $300 million in 1952, then to $500 million in the following year; and by 1954, military assistance had reached the $1 billion mark. By then, the United States was paying over half of the total cost of the Indochinese war.[15]

This policy was rooted in the new American perception of the Vietnamese war, brought strikingly into focus in *Atlantic* magazine in June 1951: "Our support of Bao Dai means the support of a democratically minded native government of the Vietnamese people against a rebellious horde led by known Communists. . . . *On these premises, our present position became inevitable.*" The *New York Times* echoed this sentiment editorially when it stated in February 1953: "the French and the Vietnamese are fighting for the free world in Indochina just as the United Nations force is fighting for it in Korea."

Hence, the American involvement in Vietnam antedates the French defeat at Dienbienphu in 1954. *Material* aid was considerable as early as 1952, and *psychologically* the United States was deeply involved as early as 1950. The American perception of Vietnam, in effect, was "fixed" a full four years before the Geneva Conference. As early as May 14, 1950, *The New York Times* said editorially that "before Indochinese Nationalism can express itself, a real military victory must be won over Ho Chi Minh's regular army and the hard core of his movement either destroyed or driven out of the country. . . . the United States now seems committed to that belief and policy."

It is this emerging sense of *personal* peril that makes American policy in Indochina a case study in United States–Chinese percep-

---

[14] Miriam S. Farley, *United States Relations with Southeast Asia, With Special Reference to Indochina* (New York: Institute of Pacific Relations, 1955), p. 4.
[15] *Ibid.;* see also *Department of State Bulletin,* 28 (January 5, 1953), 13.

tions, for after Mao Tse-tung's victory in 1949, the menace that American leaders saw in Indochina was China herself—a new and threatening China acting as the instrument of Soviet expansionism. China, now lost to the West, had apparently been "won" by the East, and the subsequent reversal of American policy in Indochina was a reaction to what the United States viewed as a sudden and frightening increase in the resources and manpower of international communism.

Large segments of the American public fully *expected* a Chinese military intervention on the side of Ho Chi Minh, especially after Chinese troops had entered the Korean War. Thus, the New York *Herald Tribune* stated editorially on January 3, 1951, that "Ho Chi Minh has either agreed or submitted to a plan of Chinese invasion. The date when the Chinese will move is generally set within this month," and *The New York Times* reported on December 29, 1951, that "observers foresee an increase in participation by Peiping in the Indochina war in 1952."

Most Americans tended to agree with the evaluation of President Dwight D. Eisenhower, who declared that "the struggle . . . began gradually, *with Chinese intervention,* to assume its true complexion of a struggle between Communist and non-Communist forces rather than one between a colonial power and colonists who were intent on attaining independence."[16]

The expectation of a Chinese invasion was so powerful that it defied all evidence to the contrary. Neither the fact that the anticipated invasion failed to materialize nor the lack of evidence that it was actually planned lessened American apprehensions. Instead, the very strength of the expectation produced its own substantiation. Time and again, quite unfounded rumors were accepted as proof of impending intervention. The result was a recurrent pattern of false alarms. Typical of these was a headline in *The New York Times* on April 11, 1951, which reported that a "Chinese Unit [was] said to join [the] Vietminh." Secretary Dulles repeatedly stated that the Chinese were directly engaged in battlefield operations. On April 5, 1954, during the siege of Dienbienphu, he claimed that Chinese troops were actually participating in the battle for the French fortress.[17]

[16] Dwight D. Eisenhower, *Mandate for Change 1953–1956* (Garden City, N.Y.: Doubleday, 1963), p. 167. Italics added.
[17] John Foster Dulles, cited in Bator, *op. cit.,* p. 210.

Thus, American involvement in the Indochinese war in the early 1950s was largely intended to counter an impending Chinese military invasion of Indochina. The towering shadow of Mao Tse-tung was seen by most Americans as hovering over the figure of Ho Chi Minh. The evidence suggests that the threat of Chinese military intervention existed more in the American mind than in reality. The Chinese did aid Ho in the early 1950s but only with light arms and transport vehicles as well as with some technical and advisory personnel.[18] If viewed from the Chinese side, such a level of assistance was certainly no more provocative than the third of a billion dollars given by the United States to France in 1952 for the prosecution of the war.

The hypothesis thus arises that the initial decision to involve the United States in Indochina was based on elements that had little to do with the objective conditions that then prevailed in Indochina. The danger of responding to phantoms in this fashion is that such responses tend to set in motion the mechanism of the self-fulfilling prophecy. A phantom, if endowed in the mind of the beholder with reality, may gradually assume a more concrete shape and ultimately become a real threat. American fear of Chinese aggression led to the United States' aid program to France, which enabled France to continue the war after 1950. Ho Chi Minh, in turn, sought Chinese economic and technical aid, which helped *him* to continue the fight. Thus, the initial American perception dictated a policy of escalation, not accommodation. The United States failed to respond to at least two peace feelers from Hanoi in 1953, because as Secretary of State Dulles remarked, he "never thought there was much sincerity" in them.[19] The same American fear that China stood behind Hanoi militarily brought the United States close to a massive military intervention on the side of France at the time of the French disaster at Dienbienphu in 1954 and helped to persuade the Eisenhower administration to dissociate the United States from the Geneva Accords.[20] In essence, then, the American perception of an expected Chinese intervention prolonged and intensified the war in Indochina.

---

[18] Harold C. Hinton, *China's Relations with Burma and Vietnam* (New York: Institute of Pacific Relations, 1958), p. 18.

[19] *China and U.S. Far East Policy, op. cit.,* p. 66.

[20] For a full account of the events during this period, see John G. Stoessinger, *The Might of Nations: World Politics in Our Time,* 3rd ed. (New York: Random House, 1969), pp. 170–178.

The facts, in all cases, were quite different from the perceptions. First, Ho Chi Minh was neither a Vietnamese nationalist alone nor a Communist alone. He was essentially *both* in equal measure. Second, the relationship between China and North Vietnam was a great deal more complicated and ambivalent than the simplistic American image suggested. And finally, Chinese military intervention on the side of the Vietminh forces never materialized. Instead the Chinese used the Vietminh as their proxy.

Ho Chi Minh is probably one of the most complex political figures of modern times. He was a product of the cross-fertilization of Vietnamese nationalism and European communism. The Vietminh forces that he led were Vietnamese nationalists with Communist leadership cadres. Nationalism and communism were always linked in Ho's mind as mutually supportive, never as mutually exclusive.

Ho Chi Minh's commitment to Vietnamese nationalism is described admirably by Harold Isaacs, one of the few Americans who knew him personally. Isaacs visited Ho when the latter had just become president of the provisional government of the Republic of Vietnam. "My party is my country," Isaacs quotes him as saying, "my program is independence."[21] Neither the Russians nor the Americans could be trusted. In Isaacs' words: "The Annamite Communists I met were men bitten deeply with the bitterness of having been abandoned by their ideological comrades overseas. They had consequently taken refuge in a pure and simple nationalism. Ho Chi Minh was making no idle phrase when he said: 'My party is my country.' "[22]

The Russians were described as being "nationalists for Russia first and above all." As far as the United States was concerned, Isaacs' description of Ho Chi Minh's reaction is revealing:

For the only indication of America's role in their [the Vietminh's] struggle came in the form of lend-lease weapons and equipment being used against them by the French and British, and the stunning announcement of an American deal with France for the purchase of $160 million worth of vehicles and miscellaneous industrial equipment for the French in Indochina. . . . This looked like American underwriting of the French reconquest. The Americans were democrats in words

---

[21] Ho Chi Minh, quoted by Harold R. Isaacs, *No Peace for Asia* (Cambridge: M.I.T. Press, 1967), p. 165.
[22] *Ibid.*, p. 174.

but no help in fact, just as the Russians were Communists in words but no help in fact. "We apparently stand quite alone," said Ho Chi Minh simply. "We shall have to depend on ourselves."[23]

As an exponent of Vietnamese nationalism, Ho Chi Minh was a great deal more persuasive than Bao Dai. In the words of one observer: "Bao Dai's white sharkskin suits, fluent French, clumsy Vietnamese, and corpulent fondness for French cooking contrasted sharply with Ho's wispy frame and plain clothes of black or khaki."[24]

Ho's commitment to communism is equally clear. In 1920, he had become a founding member of the French Communist party by voting with the Communist wing against the socialists. He had worked for the French Communists and, for a time, for the Comintern in Europe. Bernard Fall described him as a "dedicated Communist with Vietnamese reactions."[25]

The basic point here is that, in the American perception, nationalism and communism were regarded as almost mutually exclusive. A man was more of a nationalist *only* if he was less of a Communist. In Ho Chi Minh's mind, however, communism and nationalism were so intertwined that they had become virtually inseparable. This peculiar mixture made Ho Chi Minh's name symbolic for North Vietnam in the same way that the name of Charles de Gaulle had become symbolic for the Fifth Republic of France.

So far as Ho's relations with China are concerned, once again there is a wide gap between the American image and the facts. Ho Chi Minh was always somewhat suspicious of China. In Fall's words, he was "probably equipped with an instinctive Vietnamese fear of Chinese domination," no matter what its political coloration, just as to a Russian, *any* Germany might be slightly suspect.[26] His policy was essentially one of balance, of maintaining the independence and integrity of his movement, vis-à-vis both China and the Soviet Union, while accepting as much aid as could safely be accepted from both.

Chinese aid to Ho Chi Minh was at times considerable, but

[23] *Ibid.*, pp. 174–175.
[24] Claude A. Buss, *Asia in the Modern World* (New York: Macmillan, 1964), p. 596.
[25] Fall, *op. cit.*, p. 90.
[26] *Ibid.*, p. 90.

never decisive. It consisted mostly of light weapons, trucks, and radios, largely of American manufacture, that had been captured from the Chinese Nationalists some years before.[27] In view of economic needs at home and the burdens imposed by the Korean War, China could hardly afford to become a bottomless reservoir of military assistance for the Vietminh forces. The best analysis of the Chinese relationship with Ho Chi Minh has probably been provided by Robert Guillain, the front-line correspondent for *Le Monde* in Indochina: "China adheres to a very simple principle: that the balance of power never inclines in any permanent direction toward the French side. There is no need—and this is the difference from what has happened in Korea—of direct intervention, of an invasion."[28] Thus, when France received more American aid following the outbreak of the Korean War, the Chinese stepped up their own aid program just enough to reestablish a rough equilibrium. As Melvin Gurtov put it: "The Indochina campaign eventually became a crude game in which the French could never permanently regain the high ground."[29]

By 1954, largely as a result of their perceptions, the Americans were fighting a proxy war in Indochina. The battle for Dienbienphu almost changed this into a direct American war of intervention. On March 20, 1954, General Paul Ely, commander of the French forces in Indochina, informed President Eisenhower that, unless the United States intervened, Indochina would be lost. Admiral Arthur W. Radford, chairman of the Joint Chiefs of Staff, recommended military intervention, and Vice-President Richard M. Nixon backed him in a statement on April 16, declaring that "if the United States [can]not otherwise prevent the loss of Indochina, then the Administration must face the situation and dispatch troops."[30] President Eisenhower overruled his Vice-President and the Chairman of the Joint Chiefs of Staff and decided not to intervene. He feared that the French had engendered too much popular antagonism to win the war and also felt that his adminis-

---

[27] Melvin Gurtov, *The First Vietnam Crisis* (New York: Columbia University Press, 1967), p. 14.

[28] Robert Guillain, *La Fin des Illusions: Notes d'Indochine* (Paris: Centre d'Etudes de Politique Etrangère, 1954), p. 39.

[29] Gurtov, *op. cit.*, p. 15.

[30] Richard M. Nixon, quoted in Chalmers M. Roberts, "The Day We Didn't Go to War," *The Reporter* (September 14, 1954).

tration would get little backing from the Congress and from Great Britain for a military intervention. Thus, on the American side the war remained by proxy for a little while longer, but by a narrow margin.

How did China perceive the situation in Indochina and the role there of the United States? The evidence reveals that the Chinese superimposed their own perceptual grid upon the situation. Their dichotomies were as sharp and their expectations of hostile intent as firm as the cold war categories of the United States. The Communist Chinese leadership perceived the entire modern history of China as "nothing but a history of the imperialist invasion of China and of obstruction by it of the path of Chinese independence."[31] It saw itself in deadly peril of renewed imperialist encroachment by the United States from the very beginning. In 1949, for example, Mao Tse-tung told the Preparatory Committee of the New Political Consultative Conference that "the imperialists . . . would not take their defeat in this land of China lying down . . . they may even send part of their armed forces to encroach on China's frontiers. . . . We must decidedly not . . . relax our vigilance toward the wild retaliatory plots of imperialist elements and their running dogs."[32]

It is quite revealing to trace the parallel features in the Chinese and American perceptions of one another. Each pictured the other, a priori, as implacably hostile. Given this axiomatic assumption, the interpretation of each new event was almost predetermined. The American conviction of hostile Chinese intent caused even vague rumors to be taken as hard evidence of an imminent invasion of Indochina. Similarly, the Chinese conviction of hostile American intent caused each American action in the early 1950s to be taken as hard evidence of a concerted American policy of strangulation. In 1951, for example, the Chinese declared that it was

part of the American imperialist plan of aggression to use Vietnam as one of the chief bases for military encirclement and attack on the new China. Having suffered a deplorable fiasco in their invasion of Korea,

---

[31] Quoted from Mao Tse-tung, *On the New Democracy*, in H. Arthur Steiner, "Mainsprings of Chinese Communist Foreign Policy," *American Journal of International Law*, 44 (January 1950), 77 ff.

[32] *China Digest* (June 28, 1949), 4.

the American imperialists are sparing no efforts to carry out disturbances and sabotages against China from different directions.[33]

The Chinese view of American intent imparted a sinister pattern to the entire range of American actions in the Far East. United States intervention in Korea in 1950, the peace treaty with Japan in 1951, the increased military aid to Thailand, the commitment to Chiang Kai-shek on Taiwan, the presence of the American 7th Fleet in the Formosa Straits, and, of course, the deepening involvement in Indochina—all these were seen as a clear-cut pattern of hostile encirclement of the new China. Obviously, the Americans were "now stepping into the shoes of the Japanese,"[34] and "American interventionists would not voluntarily abandon their scheme to conquer Vietnam in preparation for aggression against China,"[35] for they were "intending to usurp the world alone . . . and convert Southeast Asia into a military base for aggression against China and the Soviet Union."[36]

Thus, on both sides a vicious circle was created. Each began with the a priori assumption of the other's implacable hostility; the power of this conviction caused actions to be interpreted as confirming the validity of the original assumption; hence, the adversary was found to be hostile a posteriori as well, since his actions had "proved" that the original assumption was correct. The very actions that the Chinese perceived as an American plot to encircle them were perceived by the Americans as necessary measures to forestall Chinese aggression. Confronted by a series of American policies that appeared to prove American enmity, the Chinese embarked upon an increasingly virulent Hate America campaign that the United States in turn took as proof of implacable hostility. What seemed patently provocative to one appeared obviously defensive to the other. In this tragic spiral of reciprocally negative reinforcement, the border line between real and imagined threats tended to blur and finally to disappear altogether.

It is easy to see why political accommodation would be almost impossible under such conditions. On a deeper psychological

---

[33] Survey of China Mainland Press, No. 47 (Hong Kong: American Consulate General, January 12, 1951), p. 5.
[34] Survey of China Mainland Press, No. 166 (September 2–4, 1951), p. 18.
[35] Survey of China Mainland Press, No. 236 (December 14–15, 1951), p. 10.
[36] Survey of China Mainland Press, No. 334 (May 13, 1952), p. 25.

level, such mirror devil images are the stuff that holy wars are made of, for to each side in the conflict, the enemy is not quite human and it becomes difficult, if not impossible, to identify with any part of him. Hence, each adversary is left with his fears and terrors, which are in no way allayed by their failure to materialize. But such fears can call forth a reality as terrible as the most anguished nightmare. This was the peril of the encounter between China and America during the first decade of the war in Indochina.

six

THE UNITED STATES, CHINA,
AND THE VIETNAMESE WAR:
THE AMERICAN PHASE

The Chinese-American encounter in Vietnam during the presidency of Lyndon B. Johnson never exploded into armed conflict. It is the thesis of this chapter that this was the result of valuable lessons that the two antagonists drew from the Korean War. In that conflict, misperceptions on both sides played a significant role in hastening the day of Chinese intervention. In Vietnam, on the other hand, the Chinese initiated specific military moves in order to signal Washington of their intentions, rather than relying entirely on verbal warnings and diplomatic channels. Similarly, the United States not only announced to China that American goals did not include the destruction of the Hanoi government or an attack on China, but also refrained from military actions such as amphibious landings or large reconnaissance raids into North Vietnam that might have triggered a Chinese response in the way the American crossing of the thirty-eighth parallel in Korea had done. Thus, two nations that had suffered grievously as a result of policies based on misperception were capable of learning and growing from the experience.

The Geneva Conference of mid-1954 and the formation, a few weeks later, of the Southeast Asia Treaty Organization (SEATO) marked the end of French military involvement and the beginning of an American military presence in Indochina. The Geneva Conference resulted in the signing of several agreements to cease hostilities in Indochina and to establish three independent sovereign states: Laos, Cambodia, and Vietnam. The accords on Vietnam provided for a "provisional military demarcation line" at the seventeenth parallel. Vietminh forces were to regroup north of the line, while the forces of the French Union were to regroup to the south. The line was to have military significance only, and the political unification of Vietnam was to be brought about through a general election two years hence under the supervision of a neutral three-power International Control Commission consisting of Canada, India, and Poland.

France had little choice, but her exit was made somewhat more graceful. Ho Chi Minh's Vietminh forces were dominant in more than three-quarters of Vietnam and were poised to overrun considerably more. To Ho, the terms of the accords were acceptable, since he was convinced that the general election of 1956 would win him all of Vietnam. From his point of view, the certainty of a military victory was simply replaced by the certainty of a political victory. Both the Soviet Union and Communist China, reflecting their recently adopted line of "peaceful coexistence," applied pressure on Ho to accept the terms of the accords, reassuring him that his victory at the polls was certain.

The United States never signed the Geneva Accords. But, in a unilateral declaration at the end of the Geneva Conference, the United States government pledged to "refrain from the threat or the use of force to disturb" the settlement and added that it would view any violation of the accords with grave concern.

The general American position at the conference remained ambivalent, since on the eve of a congressional election campaign, the maintenance of Eisenhower's domestic appeal as peace maker in Asia was of great importance. Moreover, to block a peaceful settlement of the Indochina war would also have jeopardized French participation in European defense plans. These conflicting considerations led the Eisenhower administration to dissociate the United States from the Geneva Accords and to seek another solution that would prevent any further territory in Asia from falling under Communist control. The answer was the creation of SEATO. Secretary of State Dulles declared that now that the war had ended, the United States could make arrangements for collective defense against aggression and build up "the truly independent states of Cambodia, Laos, and South Vietnam." On the day the treaty was signed at Manila, in an additional protocol, its eight members designated the states of Cambodia and Laos and "the free territory under the jurisdiction of the state of Vietnam" to be under SEATO protection. The United States thus created

SEATO to offset the results of Geneva. It also decided to consider South Vietnam as a separate state.

The Vietminh, on the other hand, regarded SEATO as a clear
violation of the spirit of the Geneva Accords. Ho Chi Minh saw
the American position as an effort to deprive the Vietminh in the
political arena of what it had gained militarily on the battlefield.
Nevertheless, Ho withdrew his forces from the South, assuming
that he would get enough votes there in 1956 to emerge with a
clear national majority at election time. His election in the North
would be a certainty, and if only a minority would support the
Vietminh in the South, his election would be assured. President
Eisenhower, too, thought that elections, if held on the basis of
the Geneva Accords, would lead to a Communist victory. As he
put it in 1954, "Had elections been held as of the time of the
fighting, possibly 80 percent of the population would have voted
for the Communist Ho Chi Minh as their leader rather than Chief
of State Bao Dai."[1]

In the meantime, Ngo Dinh Diem, an American-backed Roman
Catholic from a Mandarin family, began to challenge Emperor Bao
Dai in the South. The United States strongly supported Diem in
his bid for power, and in October 1955, Diem proclaimed the
establishment of a Republic of Vietnam, with himself as president.

Hence, Geneva and the SEATO treaty meant the end of French
power in Indochina and the beginnings of the American effort to
enter the struggle with its own military presence. As yet, there
were no significant military encounters between Vietminh and
American forces. But the issue was joined. The Vietminh saw the
Americans as following the path of French imperialism, and the
Americans perceived Geneva as a well-laid Communist trap to
engulf all of Vietnam. The end of a colonial war merely signified
the beginnings of a war between Americans and Communists.

As the East-West conflict superseded the colonial war, the pace
of battle gradually intensified. A pattern of escalation emerged in
which every diplomatic failure to achieve negotiations paved the
way for yet another upward step on the scale of violence.

The first such discernible moves after Geneva were the American effort between 1954 and 1956 to strengthen President Diem's
military establishment and Ho Chi Minh's visit to Moscow and

---

[1] Dwight D. Eisenhower, *Mandate for Change* (Garden City, N.Y.: Doubleday,
1963), p. 372.

Peking in 1955 to negotiate aid and friendship treaties with the two Communist powers. Diem declared in July 1955 that, since South Vietnam had not signed the Geneva Accords, he was not prepared to permit elections under the conditions specified by them. He also added that there was no freedom in the North to campaign for any opposition to Ho Chi Minh. The American government supported this view, and July 1956, the date scheduled for general elections in the accords, passed without elections being held. Ho, in retaliation, began to train Communist cadres for guerrilla warfare in the South. He also became the recipient of aid from the Soviet Union and China for the purpose of shoring up the economic base of the North Vietnamese state.

On December 20, 1960, a National Liberation Front (NLF) was created in South Vietnam. The front announced a ten-point program calling for the overthrow of the incumbent Saigon government and the removal of American military advisers.

During the remaining years of the Eisenhower administration, the United States continued to support the increasingly unpopular President Diem with military advisers. The second level of escalation was reached in January 1961, when Hanoi announced its endorsement of the National Liberation Front in South Vietnam.

The three years of the Kennedy administration were years of gradually deepening, though always limited, American involvement. By the time of President John F. Kennedy's death, the United States had approximately 17,000 advisers in Vietnam, though there was no direct American participation in actual combat. The situation was further complicated by the increasingly oppressive nature of Diem's regime, which was ultimately overthrown by a military coup in November 1963. Kennedy always tried to draw a distinction between American assistance to South Vietnam and Americanization of the war. "In the final analysis," he said, "it is their war. They are the ones who have to win it or lose it."[2] In the meantime, Communist insurgency in the South was growing rapidly. The resurrected Vietminh, now called Vietcong by the Americans, infiltrated the South in increasing numbers. The National Liberation Front built a highly efficient network of political cadres, which began a campaign of terror and assassination in South Vietnamese villages. By late 1963, both sides had raised the stakes and the United States, though not yet directly involved in

---

[2] *Department of State Bulletin,* 49 (September 30, 1963), 498–499.

combat, began to establish the necessary logistical base for further action.

Another threshold was crossed in the summer of 1964. In July, the new South Vietnamese prime minister, General Nguyen Khanh, delivered a major address, the keynote of which was "to the North." Two days later, Nguyen Cao Ky, the commander of the South Vietnamese air force, announced that he was prepared to bomb North Vietnam at any time. In early August, North Vietnamese torpedo boats allegedly launched attacks on two American ships in the Gulf of Tonkin. President Johnson retaliated by bombing oil depots and other facilities in North Vietnam. On August 10, the President secured the passage of the Tonkin Gulf Resolution in Congress, which authorized him "to take all necessary measures to repel any armed attack against the forces of the U.S. and to prevent further aggression." The air war had gone north of the seventeenth parallel for the first time.

The next step in the escalation was reached in February 1965. On February 7, the Vietcong staged a night raid against American barracks at Pleiku, killing 8 Americans and wounding 126. Twelve hours later, American jets attacked North Vietnam in what was to be the first of an almost uninterrupted series of daily air attacks against the North. In the South, marines were introduced into the ground war, which was now rapidly becoming Americanized. By 1966, United States fighting units were frequently suffering higher casualty rates than were their South Vietnamese allies. The National Liberation Front responded to these events with its harsh five-point manifesto of March 1965, in which it refused to enter into negotiations until after American troops had been withdrawn. Three weeks later, however, Hanoi published its own four-point program, in which it did not rule out the possibility of negotiations. In mid-May, the United States stopped bombing the North for five days, but no talks ensued—and the air attacks were resumed.

In February 1966, President Johnson met with the South Vietnamese leader, Air Marshal Ky, at Honolulu, where the two men underlined their solidarity against "the aggression from the North." In mid-1966, Johnson announced that guerrilla infiltration from the North had increased at an alarming rate and that further American retaliatory action might be necessary. In June, the United States bombed the North Vietnamese capital of Hanoi and its largest port, Haiphong. In the South, American manpower had risen from 17,000 to 500,000 by 1968. There was no evidence, however, that this policy of "strategic persuasion" had deterred the Hanoi regime from sending more guerrillas to the South or the National Liberation Front from attempting to infiltrate the countryside. The war had escalated in ever more violent bursts, but no decisive change had occurred in the balance of power among the main belligerents.

By this time, a deep division had occurred within the United States over the American commitment in Vietnam and the future course of American foreign policy in Southeast Asia. The administration defended its policy in Vietnam on the following grounds: first, the air attacks were strategic persuasion of the North to leave its neighbors to the South alone. Moreover, the bombing raids raised the costs of aggression and made it more difficult to send guerrillas to the South via the Ho Chi Minh Trail. Second, a withdrawal would signify a tremendous victory for the Chinese view on wars of liberation, reinforcing a view of the United States as a paper tiger and encouraging stepped-up aggressive moves by communism elsewhere in the world. Third, "aggression must be stopped at the source"—Hanoi stood behind the National Liberation Front, and China stood behind Hanoi; hence, China had to be contained on her periphery as the Soviet Union was twenty years earlier. A withdrawal, on the other hand, would produce a "row of falling dominoes" and bring to an end the American presence in Southeast Asia.

Critics of the administration pointed to the experience of 400,000 French troops in Indochina and wondered whether the United States could fare better in a counterinsurgency war in which a ten-to-one troop ratio in favor of the United States might be necessary for victory over the Vietcong. Opponents of the war also accused the United States of destroying the social fabric of South Vietnam—the very nation it had set out to save from communism—through air bombardments and ground warfare. In addition, the danger of Chinese or Soviet intervention on Hanoi's side took a prominent place in the view of most critics. Finally, opponents asserted that the United States still behaved as if communism were a monolithic force that had to elicit an American response whenever a Communist regime appeared. Communism, the argument continued, was now much more diffuse, and each such regime should be evaluated in a specific and pragmatic manner by the United States, rather than seen automatically as an attempt to extend the design of world communism. Thus, while the American involvement in Vietnam would have made sense twenty years earlier, as did the formation of NATO in Europe, in the 1960s a strategic United States commitment in Southeast Asia was at best an anachronism and, at worst, a catastrophe. These differing perceptions of the nature of communism lay at the heart of the dialogue between "hawks" and "doves" in the United States.

In North Vietnam, too, there was division over the war. North Vietnamese hawks tended to resist the prospect of negotiations with the United States, arguing that the one time negotiations had taken place—at Geneva—the Vietminh had lost at the diplomatic table what they had almost won on the battlefield. Moreover, they argued, the American will to fight would collapse, as did that of France on the home front in 1954. On the other hand, there were influential forces arguing in favor of accommodation. They asserted that the air attacks had hurt the economy badly and, moreover, that North Vietnam could not rely too heavily on aid from China and the Soviet Union because of the continuing rift between those two major Communist powers. Hence, negotiations with the Americans might become necessary after all.

By early 1968, the impasse over negotiations among the main belligerents—the National Liberation Front and North Vietnam, on one side, and the United States and South Vietnam, on the other—had crystallized into a single issue: the bombing of North Vietnam. Hanoi and the NLF demanded the cessation of bombings as a precondition to talks; the United States and South Vietnam demanded an end to Communist infiltration into the South as a prerequisite to the cessation of air attacks on the North. On March 31, 1968, President Johnson decided to stop all bombings north of the nineteenth parallel. Shortly thereafter, peace talks began in Paris between the United States and North Vietnam. At these talks, the North Vietnamese negotiators insisted on a total halt to the bombings; the United States in turn insisted on the simultaneous reduction of guerrilla infiltration into South Vietnam as an act of reciprocity. On October 31, President Johnson ordered the complete cessation of the bombings. The Paris peace talks were broadened to include South Vietnam and the National Liberation Front. But as in Korea, the peace talks did little to mitigate the ferocity of war.

The Chinese-American relationship during the Korean War had

suffered from distortions in each of our four main analytical categories: self-image, perception of the other's character, perception of the other's intentions, and perception of the other's power and capabilities. In Vietnam, a considerable degree of distortion was evident in the first three categories, but there was little, if any, in evidence in the last. Both nations had a realistic assessment of each other's power, and this realism prevented a direct military clash between them. Let us first recall the sequence of events in Vietnam that affected United States–Chinese relations during the Johnson administration.

The first significant Chinese action to counter American operations in Vietnam reflected the experience of the Korean War in 1950. At that time, diplomatic warning to the United States not to cross the thirty-eighth parallel had proved ineffective. Peking then ordered the dispatch of troops across the Yalu to stop the advance of the United Nations forces. In the autumn of 1964, however, the Chinese response to American attacks on North Vietnamese PT boat bases was to make a specific military gesture. The Chinese quietly deployed several units of MIG jet fighters, 50,000 railroad construction troops, and some antiaircraft detachments to North Vietnam and began to construct military air bases in South China. This was a clear signal to Washington that China would not remain unengaged in hostilities directed specifically against North Vietnam.[3] There had been no such military "signal" in Korea. During the next few months, no major escalation took place either on the American or the Chinese side. In February 1965, however, the United States began the bombardment of North Vietnam and committed an increasing number of troops to combat operations in South Vietnam. As the number of American ground forces in South Vietnam rose steadily during 1966 and 1967, tensions with China increased as well. On April 26, 1966, an aerial dogfight took place between two American F-4C Phantom fighters and a Chinese MIG-21 fighter. The United States denied a Chinese assertion that the MIG was shot down over China. On May 27, 1966, the State Department chose "not to challenge" a Chinese report of May 12 that five American aircraft had crossed the

---

[3] This was first revealed publicly by Dr. Allen Whiting, former Director of Intelligence and Research for East Asia, U.S. Department of State, in an article entitled "How We Almost Went to War with China," *Look* Magazine (April 29, 1969).

Chinese border and had shot down a MIG-17. In August 1966, American bombs fell within ten miles of China, and "American, North Vietnamese and Chinese fighters flew ever closer to each other, with Communist planes relying on the sanctuary of bases in China."[4] These events marked the high point of United States–Chinese brinkmanship during the Vietnamese war. Even during these tense months, however, when the number of American ground troops crept up toward the half million mark, considerable prudence and restraint characterized the policies of both sides. President Johnson was reliably reported to have said that "Russia doesn't want war, China doesn't want to get into a war, and you know damned well that we don't want to get into the big war."[5] On the other side, Chou En-lai stated repeatedly that "China [would] not take the initiative to provoke a war with the United States."[6]

The cessation of the American bombing of North Vietnam and the beginning of the Paris peace talks also reduced tensions between China and America. The Chinese leadership, while continuing its verbal attacks on the United States, reduced its manpower commitments in Vietnam. During 1969, the 50,000 railroad construction troops that had been sent to North Vietnam in 1964 and 1965 were quietly pulled back to China.

The American *self-image* during the war in Vietnam retained most of the features that had characterized it during the Korean War. Once again "defender of democracy" and "bastion of the free world" were phrases that appeared regularly in President Johnson's speeches. In addition, honor and the sacredness of a commitment were frequently hailed as American ideals in the war. The image of the United States as "world policeman" emerged with even greater force in Vietnam than it had in Korea. In his address at Johns Hopkins University in 1965, for example, President Johnson justified the American involvement in Vietnam in the following terms:

We are also there to strengthen world order. Around the globe, from Berlin to Thailand, are people whose well-being rests, in part, on the

---

[4] *Ibid.*

[5] Lyndon B. Johnson, quoted in Hugh Sidey, *A Very Personal Presidency* (New York: Atheneum, 1968), p. 238.

[6] Chou En-lai, "Four-Point Statement on China's Policy Toward the United States," *Peking Review* (May 13, 1966).

belief that they can count on us if they are attacked. To leave Vietnam to its fate would shake the confidence of all these people in the value of American commitment, the value of America's word. The result would be increased unrest and instability, and even wider war.[7]

And even more clearly, he said: "History and our own achievements have thrust upon us the principal responsibility for the protection of freedom on earth."[8]

Similarly, on the Chinese side, many of the self-images that prevailed during the Korean War, carried over to the Vietnamese experience. Once again, Peking spoke of its revolutionary mission and the need to make China a "secure base for world revolution." The split with the Soviet Union that had developed since the Korean War, of course, deeply colored Peking's view of itself. The self-image of China as the true and only torchbearer of militant communism injected a Messianic zeal into the statements of the Chinese leadership that far exceeded those that had been made during the Korean War. Marshall Lin Piao, in an article published in September 1965, conceived of China as the revolutionary base of the "world countryside" of Asia, Africa, and Latin America, as it prepared to surround and ultimately defeat the "world cities" of Europe and North America.[9] The practical operational consequences of this article have been the subject of much discussion. Some scholars saw it as a blueprint for world conquest, while others interpreted it in a much more modest light. In any case, the article no doubt projected a self-image of China as the last stronghold of militant, unspoiled communism and the world's last hope of obtaining communism's universal ideals.

Thus, the self-images of both major powers had changed somewhat since the Korean War. Both China and America saw themselves as even more on the side of right, truth, and justice than they had fifteen years earlier. A greater degree of rigidity and self-righteousness had begun to color their perceptions of themselves. And each now harbored an almost passionate sense of mission to spread its truth and justice beyond its borders.

---

[7] Speech by President Lyndon B. Johnson at Johns Hopkins University, April 7, 1965, cited in *The Vietnam Reader,* Marcus G. Raskin and Bernard B. Fall (eds.) (New York: Vintage, 1967), p. 345.
[8] Lyndon B. Johnson, quoted in *The New York Times,* February 13, 1965.
[9] Lin Piao, "The International Significance of Comrade Mao Tse-tung's Theory of People's War," *Foreign Language Press* (Peking, September 1965), pp. 42–59.

The mirror devil image that had characterized each nation's perception of its adversary's *character* during the Korean War was even more intensely manifest in Vietnam. The Chinese viewed the Americans as "aggressors and imperialists," and the United States leadership regarded China as "aggressive and expansionist." Each side compared the other's character to that of Hitler's Germany. China was the first to make the comparison in an editorial published in the *Peking Review* on April 30, 1965, entitled "Escalation Means Getting Closer and Closer to the Grave:"

The tactics used by the Johnson Administration are very similar to Hitler's gradual expansion of aggression before World War II. The aim is nothing less than to slacken the vigilance of the world's people, so that they will be faced with a 'fait accompli' by the US aggressor before they know it.[10]

In the United States, Marshall Lin Piao's article was seen by numerous high officials as the Chinese blueprint for world conquest, comparable to Hitler's *Mein Kampf*. Secretary of State Dean Rusk stated repeatedly that the aggression in Vietnam was backed by China, that it was similar to Hitler's aggression in Europe, and that appeasement in Vietnam would have the same consequences as appeasement in Munich. President Johnson struck the same note when he said: "Retreat leads to retreat, just as aggression leads to aggression in this still primitive international community."[11] The American image of China's character conjured up a predatory beast poised to unleash hordes of faceless millions bent upon overrunning first Asia then, possibly, the rest of the world. In fact, numerous statements made by leading American statesmen brought to mind Kaiser Wilhelm's view of the "yellow peril." The racist "yellow" had yielded to the ideological "red," but otherwise all the old devil images remained intact. The Chinese view of the United States was equally one-dimensional and uncompromising. America was still the old imperialist nation bent upon trampling underfoot the yearnings of the peoples of Asia for independence. Driven by an economic engine that fed upon others like a parasite and powered by a vast military and industrial establishment that hungered for ever further conquest, the United States was the aggressor incarnate.

---

[10] Cited in Marvin Gettleman (ed.), *Vietnam* (New York: Fawcett, 1965), p. 428.
[11] Lyndon B. Johnson, *The Choices We Face* (New York: Bantam, 1969), p. 27.

Perceptions of the *intentions* of the adversary were complex and ambivalent on both sides. Although the Chinese press repeatedly described the American purpose in South Vietnam to be the enslavement of that nation and later an invasion of China, this was not the only view expressed. In January 1965, Mao told Edgar Snow that domestic pressures would soon precipitate an American withdrawal, but Anna Louise Strong, an authoritative voice from Peking, wrote that "The further the US escalates the more it will be entangled. Even now it is hard to tell whether the US ruling class really wants the long war which the experts say it will take to subdue South Vietnam, or whether they are on a tiger and cannot dismount."[12] Thus, at times the United States was portrayed as intent upon the conquest of Vietnam and a subsequent attack on China; at other times, the United States was depicted as about to withdraw and later to collapse internally from the domestic pressures and bewilderment over its involvement in the Vietnamese war. This ambivalence over American intentions characterized Chinese perceptions during the entire term of the Johnson administration.

On the American side, a dual image of Chinese intentions prevailed as well. The more widespread view was frequently articulated by elected officials and the mass media. It envisioned a militant and aggressive China actively seeking to conquer its Asian neighbors and, ultimately, to dominate all nonindustrial nations of the world. This view was reinforced by Rusk, who frequently asserted his belief that the war in Vietnam was directed from Hanoi and inspired from Peking. This "militant China" school saw confirmation of its views in the previously mentioned article by Lin Piao. The following passage served as evidence: "Everything is divisible and so is this colossus of US imperialism. It can be split up and defeated. The peoples of Asia, Africa, and Latin America, and other regions can destroy it piece by piece, some striking at its head and others at its feet."[13] Parallels to Hitler's *Mein Kampf* were repeatedly drawn from these lines.

A second school viewed Lin Piao's article as clever rhetoric masking Peking's unwillingness or fear to intervene directly in the Vietnam war. Limited MIGs, antiaircraft weapons, construction

---

[12] "When and How Will China Go to War?" "Supplement to Letter from China, 38, on 25 April 1966."

[13] Lin Piao, *op. cit.*, quoted in *The New York Times*, January 19, 1966.

workers, and supplies would be the extent of China's tangible involvement in the Vietnamese struggle. This view was suggested in an analysis by the Rand Corporation in November 1965, entitled "People's War, China Takes a Second Look at Vietnam." A similar interpretation of Lin's article was given by Donald S. Zagoria in *Vietnam Triangle*.[14] Zagoria argued that the article was in reality a veiled exhortation to Hanoi to do the job of national liberation itself, without military assistance from China. Thus, Lin Piao's article provided the raw material for both the *Mein Kampf* and the "do-it-yourself" images of China's intentions. The Rorschach ink blot quality of the article suggests that, in the absence of hard information about the adversary's intentions, Americans tended to perceive what they wanted to perceive. But the view that ultimately prevailed among the policy-making elite during the Johnson administration was that of a militant China.

There is no doubt that for China and the United States the crucial difference between the Korean and the Vietnamese encounters lay in the two nations' *perceptions of each other's power and capabilities*. Despite the extremity of the perceptions described above, Korea remained a restraining memory for both sides. President Johnson had a high respect for China's military power. He said, "We know there are about 200 million in the Chinese Army. . . . Think about 200 million Chinese coming down those trails. . . . No, Sir, I don't want to fight them."[15] This was a far cry from Douglas MacArthur's view of the Chinese army in 1950. In addition, the explosion of nuclear bombs in October 1964 and in February 1965 helped to alter the American view of Chinese military "backwardness."

A similar process of reevaluation went on in China after the Korean War. Despite China's self-image of virtual invincibility and countless references to the United States as a paper tiger, a good measure of respect for American power often showed through the rhetoric. For example, in 1967, *People's Daily* warned that "the United States is very powerful; it is the strongest country in the world."[16] The Chinese leadership also paid close attention to American statements on the disposition of combat forces and the

---

[14] Donald S. Zagoria, *Vietnam Triangle* (New York: Pegasus Press, 1967), *passim*.

[15] Lyndon B. Johnson, quoted in Philip Geyelin, *Johnson and the World* (New York: Praeger, 1966), p. 197.

[16] *People's Daily* (Peking), April 5, 1967.

dispatch of arms and strategic aircraft, and it seems that most such statements were believed and taken at face value. Peking in fact exercised a great deal of caution. Mao's policy seems to have been to provide as much Chinese aid as possible to North Vietnam and to act as its rear area of support, but to avoid any involvement that might provoke American attacks on China. The possibility of the use of nuclear weapons no doubt acted as an additional deterrent.

Of course, the Korean War was not the only reason that a greater degree of realism entered Sino-American views of each other's power. The international constellation had changed dramatically since the conclusion of the Korean War. The most momentous change, of course, was the rift in Sino-Soviet relations. During the Korean War, the Soviet Union and China were on friendly terms and had just concluded a formal alliance in which they had agreed that, in case of attack on one, the other would use all means available to provide immediate military assistance. By 1966, the hostility between them had become so intense that Peking accused the Soviet Union of having "aligned [itself] with US imperialism in a holy alliance against China."[17] Moreover, the Vietnamese war, far from healing the Sino-Soviet rift, had tended to exacerbate it further.[18] In addition to the Sino-Soviet split, both China and the United States had to face internal traumas during the course of the Vietnamese war that made them doubly anxious to avoid a military clash. In the United States, a wave of violence was rampant, and the pressures against the war in Vietnam finally became so powerful that they drove President Johnson from office in 1968. China not only was wracked by her "cultural revolution," but her foreign policy suffered severe setbacks in Indonesia, on the Asian rimland, and in Africa. All these changes in the balance of world power tended to inject a greater degree of caution into the policies of China and the United States vis-à-vis each other.

A comparison of the Korean and Vietnamese encounters between China and America permits a number of suggestive conclusions. The extreme images of self and of adversary that were evident during the Korean War persisted during the Vietnamese experience. In the latter case, they were even more extreme and one-dimensional. Images of the adversary's power, however,

---

[17] *Associated Press*, March 24, 1966.
[18] Zagoria, *op. cit., passim.*

which had been seriously distorted in the Korean War, exhibited a remarkable degree of realism in the Vietnamese war. The conclusion is inescapable that the Korean experience served as an important corrective during the Johnson presidency. Thus, even when extreme images of one's own country's rectitude and the enemy's evil character and intentions continue to persist, disastrous consequences can be avoided if images of the enemy's power and capabilities tend to conform roughly to reality. One cannot, of course, answer with certitude the question of whether China and America would have gone to war over Vietnam in the 1960s if they had not fought in Korea. But in a broader sense, the melancholy answer that this analysis suggests is that the most efficient corrective to war may continue to be the memory of war itself.

part two

the role of perception in russo-american relations

seven

CZARIST RUSSIA AND THE
UNITED STATES

There is a strange sense of paradox about the relations between Russia and America during the eighteenth and nineteenth centuries. The two peoples saw little of one another and their systems of government were radically different; yet the two nations almost always encountered each other with intensity. Relations between them at different times ranged from affection through ambivalence all the way to hostility and hatred. Russians and Americans were rarely indifferent to one another. Most of the time, these intense emotional reactions rested on images, fictions, and legends rather than on facts. Policy decisions with the most serious consequences often flowed from these legends, particularly on the American side.

This chapter will examine four significant Russo-American encounters during the eighteenth and nineteenth centuries: Catherine the Great and the American War of Independence; the role of the Russian fleet during the American Civil War; the purchase of Alaska; and the role of the United States during the Russo-Japanese War. Each of these vignettes illuminates a different side of the multifaceted Russo-American encounter. In addition, each shows the dramatic power of perception in the relations of states.

CATHERINE THE GREAT AND THE AMERICAN WAR
OF INDEPENDENCE

Legends about international relationships are usually born in times of stress and danger. They are burned into the national consciousness under the impact of crisis and then live on tenaciously, often developing a life all their own, quite independent of events. Such a legend developed in America during the War of Independence about Catherine the Great. It was to dominate the thinking of most Americans for several generations.

The simple facts were that in 1775 King George III asked Catherine whether he could hire 20,000 Russian soldiers in order to crush his rebellious subjects in the American Colonies. The czarina turned down the request, and no cossacks appeared on American soil during the War of Independence.

The legend that grew out of this episode became the basis of the traditional friendship between Czarist Russia and the young American republic. The czarina was perceived as the "Mother of Independence." Americans were brought up to believe that she had spurned the call for help from her fellow sovereign out of love and sympathy for the American revolutionaries.

American historians who were given access to the Czarist archives were forced to destroy this myth. The archives revealed that Catherine took an interest in the American Revolution because it affected British and European politics. The empress, from the very beginning, had decided not to interfere on behalf of Britain because a weakened Britain was in Russia's national interest. She had also decided as early as June 1775 that America would become independent in her own lifetime and that "the colonies [had] told England good-bye forever."[1] In her private correspondence, Catherine did not hesitate to say that she believed the Colonies to be right and that England had provoked a useless quarrel that was bound to weaken her and, thus, redound to Russia's advantage. The best course for Russia under the circumstances was neutrality. In her letter to George III, Catherine stated that she had just finished an exhausting war with Turkey and that she deemed it unwise to send 20,000 troops so far from Russian soil.

The conclusion that must be drawn from the above is that the Russian empress dealt with the American question on grounds of pure realpolitik. She neither liked nor disliked the Americans and probably never met an American in her entire life. The only question that concerned her in connection with the American Revolution was the primacy of the Russian national interest.

The American revolutionaries, on the other hand, perceived the Russian empress as a personal friend and explained her refusal

---

[1] Catherine II, quoted in Frank A. Golder, "Catherine II and the American Revolution," *American Historical Review* (October 1915), p. 92.

to help King George as the high-minded act of an unselfish ruler. In essence, they confused personal motives with political consequences. The traditional friendship between the people of Russia and America was born out of this confusion.

When in 1780, Catherine II organized the neutral nations of Europe into an alliance called the Armed Neutrality, the young American republic once again hailed her as the Mother of Independence and assumed that, without question, the Russian empress had formed the league out of sympathy for the struggling Colonies.

The facts, again, were quite different. By forming the Armed Neutrality, the empress hoped to force Britain to acknowledge the rights of neutral shippers and, thus, to benefit Russian commerce. She also hoped to be a mediator in Britain's war with Spain, France, and the Netherlands and, thus, to establish herself as the arbiter of the destiny of Europe.

The news of the Armed Neutrality reached America just after the disastrous defeats of Charleston and Camden. There is evidence that the good tidings lifted American morale and strengthened the determination of the colonists to fight on to Yorktown and beyond. Another legend now sank roots: the Armed Neutrality won the war for the embattled colonists. As late as 1905, *Harper's Weekly* declared, "The surrender of Cornwallis at Yorktown did not bend the inflexible will of George III; what broke the King's stubborn heart was the adhesion of Catherine II to the League of Neutrals by which British commerce was exposed to a process of strangulation."[2]

The truth was that the Armed Neutrality was not a decisive factor. Catherine ultimately referred to it as the "Armed Nullity." But the American legend about Catherine's role in the American Revolution persisted and became an objective morale factor to be reckoned with in the War of Independence.

American perceptions of Catherine, ironically enough, underwent a volte-face in the years from 1793 to 1795, when the Russian empress divided Poland with Austria and Prussia. By that time the American republic had won its independence from Britain and no longer had need of Russian help. American sympathy now went out to the Polish "underdog," fighting for its life. Thaddeus Kosciuszko, the Polish patriot, became the "Washington of Poland." Catherine

---

[2] *Harper's Weekly* (September 23, 1905).

suddenly became a she-wolf and a ravenous she-bear. When she died in 1796, Philip Freneau, "the poet of the American Revolution," wrote a poem completely reversing the legend of the czarina's denial of troops to George III:

> She would have sent her Tartar bands
> To waste and ravage gallic lands,
> She would have sent her legions o'er,
> Columbia! to invade your shore![3]

The early Americans saw what they needed to see and acted on it. But their perceptions bore little resemblance to reality. After the partition of Poland had become a memory, the legend of Catherine the Mother of Independence surfaced again and dominated American thinking for a long time to come. Neither the positive nor the negative view of Catherine had much to do with reality. But both became the basis of policy and outlook for the young American republic.

THE RUSSIAN FLEET AND THE CIVIL WAR

Perhaps the most amazing and yet most durable legend in Russo-American relations was born during the Civil War. The time for such a legend was ripe, for when the guns began to boom at Fort Sumter in 1861, the governments of Czar Alexander II and of President Abraham Lincoln had similar problems and the same European enemies.

First, for more than half a century, Czarist Russia had encouraged the growth of the United States as a commercial and naval counterweight against Britain and France. Hence, on the eve of the Civil War, Alexander II's sympathies clearly were with the cause of the Union. For precisely the opposite reasons, Russia's European enemies, Britain and France, were hoping that the Union would founder. Britain remained coldly neutral, and France openly supported the South. Second, both governments were fighting insurrections. Lincoln was determined to put down the Southern rebellion; Alexander was facing rebellion by the Poles. Significantly enough, this time the majority of Americans favored the Russian, rather than the Polish, cause. The London *Punch* ran

---

[3] Fred L. Pattee (ed.), *The Poems of Philip Freneau* (Princeton: Princeton University Press, 1907), Vol. III, p. 136.

a sardonic cartoon in which Lincoln said the following to Czar Alexander:

> Imperial son of Nicholas the Great
> We are in the same fix, I calculate
> You with your Poles, with Southern rebels I,
> Who spurn my rule and my revenge defy.[4]

Lastly, Alexander had freed the serfs, and Lincoln was trying to free the slaves. Thus, it was only natural that "Lincoln the Emancipator" and "Alexander the Liberator" should feel friendly toward one another.

It was against this background that, during the autumn of 1863, two Russian fleets appeared in the United States. Without any explanation, six Russian vessels dropped anchor in New York harbor and another six entered San Francisco Bay. The Russian minister in Washington, when queried about the presence of the vessels, merely stated that they had come for "no unfriendly purpose."

The timing of the arrival of the Russian ships could not have been more dramatic. The battles of Gettysburg and Vicksburg had just been fought, and much terrible fighting still loomed ahead. The rumor immediately swept the North that two "splendid" Russian fleets had "swept" into the ports of New York and San Francisco in order to serve notice to both Britain and France that, should they dare to intervene on the side of the South, they would have to reckon with Russian guns on the side of the North.

The Russian fleet commanders neither confirmed nor denied these rumors, and their enigmatic silence gave further momentum to the growth of a new legend. The fleets had dropped anchor, the legend went, in order to demonstrate that Russia and the United States were about to conclude an alliance against Britain and France. Lincoln and Alexander would unite in order to repel Anglo-French intervention. "God bless the Russians!" exclaimed Secretary of the Navy Gideon Welles, and this sentiment was echoed throughout the entire North.

This legend led to a spontaneous outburst of enthusiasm for the somewhat bewildered Russian visitors. Elaborate balls were held for them in most of the northern cities. Innumerable toasts were

---

[4] *Punch* (October 24, 1863).

drunk to Lincoln the Emancipator and Alexander the Liberator. General Hiram Wallbridge declared in New York that "There shall be two great hemispheres, one the Eastern and the other the Western. The one shall be represented by Russia, and the other by the United States."[5] The Russians tactfully spoke of Russo-American amity but gave no specific reasons for their presence in the two American ports. There was only a single lapse from this pattern. During a disastrous fire in San Francisco, some 200 Russian volunteers helped fight the blaze, and the grateful citizens of the city staged an elaborate ball for the Russian volunteers. Toward morning, the rumor swept the city that two Confederate destroyers were about to sail into San Francisco Bay and bombard the city. The Russian Rear Admiral Popov, probably under the spell of the enthusiastic reception given him and his men, was so carried away that he issued an order to repel the Confederates should the need arise. Upon hearing of this move, the Russian Minister of Foreign Affairs in St. Petersburg, Prince Gorchakov, sternly countermanded Popov's order. This move, however, in no way dampened the enthusiasm of the Americans for their Russian visitors. Before the Russians departed in 1864, they were lavishly entertained in Washington by leading members of the Cabinet and the Congress. They were widely perceived in the United States as the allies of the Northern cause.

The conviction that the presence of the Russian fleet in American waters had helped to save the Union lived on tenaciously for many years. When Alexander II was assassinated in 1881, Secretary of State James G. Blaine dispatched the following note of condolence to his successor:

The Emperor [had] sent a large and powerful fleet of war vessels as a proclamation to the world of his sympathy in our struggle and of his readiness to strike a blow on the side of the Union if any foreign power should strike a blow in aid of the insurrection.[6]

Blaine concluded by saying that the United States deeply appreciated the czar's act "even at the risk of plunging his own empire into war."

---

[5] General Hiram Wallbridge, quoted in the London *Times*, October 15, 1863.
[6] U.S. Department of State, *Papers Relating to the Foreign Relations of the United States, 1881*, (Washington, 1882), p. 1014.

The truth about the visit of the Russian fleet to America did not come to light until 1915, when an American historian, Dr. Frank A. Golder, was given access to the official Czarist records. Drawing on these primary sources, Golder concluded that the Russian visit "had nothing whatever to do with American affairs" and was to be explained solely in terms of the Russian national interest.[7]

In 1863, the French and British threat to Russia was very real. In case of war, the czar reasoned, the Russian fleet would be trapped in the Baltic Sea by the British. Hence, the fleet was given orders to drop anchor in a friendly neutral port. Every available harbor in the Pacific was in the hands of England, Holland, Spain, Portugal, or France, none of whom could be trusted. Taking these factors into consideration, the choice of American ports was logical. The Russians would be sure of a friendly reception there, and when the time came, their ships could leave port to prey on the vulnerable merchant ships of the British. New York and San Francisco were ideally suited as temporary bases for the Russian fleet. Indeed, when the danger of war had passed in 1864, the Russian commanders were ordered home. Upon their arrival in Kronstadt, the czar thanked them for their service and promoted nearly all of the sailors to higher ranks in the navy. He looked at this cruise as "one of the great practical achievements in the history of the Russian navy and one of the noteworthy pages in the history of his reign."[8]

Research into the Russian archives also revealed that the Russian fleet hardly swept into New York and San Francisco. The condition of the twelve vessels was far from splendid. All the ships were wooden, and although some of them had engines, the principal propellant was wind. Moreover, the sails did not fit properly; the sailors were inexperienced; and scurvy broke out on board during the long voyage. Two vessels had to be left behind as unseaworthy, and one was wrecked some thirty miles off San Francisco. Both Britain and France had ironclad ships in their navies, and any one of them could have made short shrift of the Russian ships in a hostile encounter. It is quite probable that in case of a naval engagement, the entire Russian fleet would have been annihilated.

Yet the legend of the selfless Russians continued for half a

[7] Frank A. Golder, "The Russian Fleet and the Civil War," *American Historical Review* (July 1915), p. 805.
[8] Czar Alexander, quoted in *ibid.*, p. 811.

century after the event. Most Americans stubbornly believed that the Russian ships had come to America for the single purpose of helping the Union in its darkest hour. At the time it was born, the legend boosted the morale of the United States when it needed such boosting most, and Secretary of State W. H. Seward was encouraged to deal more boldly with Britain and France than he might have otherwise. For purposes of national policy, the myth of the Russian fleet became as important as if it had been a fact. In the words of a leading diplomatic historian: "The realization that the United States had one firm friend in Europe who was restraining its enemies bolstered faltering Northern morale, and— although this can never be proved—may have spelled the difference between quitting and continuing on to victory."[9]

THE PURCHASE OF ALASKA

In 1867, three years after the Russian fleet left American shores, Russia sold Alaska to the United States for $7,200,000. When Secretary Seward asked the Congress to approve the purchase that he enthusiastically endorsed, the debate was heated and even bitter. What finally secured congressional approval was American gratitude for Russian assistance to the United States during the Civil War. In short, "Seward's Icebox" or "Walrussia," as Alaska was referred to derisively, was purchased as a debt of gratitude to Czar Alexander II.

As it became apparent over the years that the new American possession was valuable and as its vast natural resources increasingly became an enormous asset to the United States, the legend gradually took hold that the czar had sold his huge possession to his American "ally" for a pittance, out of sentimental regard for the traditional Russo-American friendship. Like the fleet legend, the Alaska purchase legend became the basis of policy, even though it had little to do with the actual facts of the transaction.

The unadorned facts are that Russia decided to dispose of Alaska in her own national interest. First, Russian America, as Alaska was then called, had become a burdensome economic liability to the czar. The Russian-American Company, which had a monopoly over the territory, was bankrupt, and the Russian government was in no

[9] Thomas A. Bailey, *America Faces Russia* (Ithaca: Cornell University Press, 1950), p. 80.

mood to act as a receiver in bankruptcy. Second, should Britain wish to annex Alaska, the Russians, with their weak navy, would be in no position to defend the territory. Thus, Alaska was a permanent hostage to Britain. Third, the Russians were aware of the growing spirit of Manifest Destiny then on the upsurge in the United States. The Americans had taken over west Florida and Texas. A gold rush had brought them to British Columbia. The czar was aware of gold deposits in Alaska. In view of the possibility of an American gold rush, this knowledge was an additional incentive to sell. Under such conditions, it might be difficult, if not impossible, to defend the territory. Thus, while many Americans later believed that the Russians had sold Alaska because they had no knowledge of the gold deposits, the opposite was the case.[10] Finally, the friendship of the Americans was of importance to the czar, especially in the light of continuing tensions with Britain. Thus, the decision to sell was reasonable; the alternatives seemed to be the possible loss of both the territory and the friendship of the United States.

When Edouard de Stoeckl, the Russian minister in Washington, hinted that the emperor might be persuaded to sell Alaska, Secretary Seward avidly rose to the bait. Seward was a convinced advocate of Manifest Destiny and his eagerness to purchase Alaska made him a poor bargainer. He quickly settled for a purchase price of $7,200,000, even though the Russian archives revealed that the czar would have sold the territory for as little as $5,000,000.[11]

Seward's real battle was not with the Russian negotiators but with the American Congress. Senators and congressmen alike, burdened with the problems of Reconstruction, were shocked at Seward's decision to spend such a large amount of taxpayer's money for what appeared to be an almost worthless piece of real estate. The secretary of state had to launch an educational campaign in order to convince the reluctant legislators. He pointed out the vast economic resources of Alaska, the improvement in America's strategic position, the imperatives of Manifest Destiny, the commercial advantages that Alaska yielded in the competition

---

[10] A. G. Mazour, "The Prelude to Russia's Departure from America," *Pacific Historical Review* (September 1941), pp. 311–319.
[11] F. A. Golder, "The Purchase of Alaska," *American Historical Review* (April 1920), pp. 419–420.

with Britain, and, finally, the necessity of preserving and strengthening Russo-American amity. He enlisted the enthusiastic support of Charles Sumner, the powerful chairman of the Senate's Committee on Foreign Relations, and one of the leading orators of the time, for his cause. Sumner gave a three-hour speech advocating the Alaska purchase. He cited all the economic and commercial benefits that would accrue to the United States, but the climax of his speech was a reminder to the senators that Russia had been the only real supporter of the North during the Civil War. Czar Alexander, out of his deep regard for the United States, had decided to sell Alaska for very little money. Under the circumstances, it would be shabby behavior indeed to throw it back in his face. Besides, his good will might be needed again in the future. Thus, influenced by Sumner's effort, and with the memory of the Russian fleet still fresh in their minds, the senators approved the Alaska purchase on April 9, 1867, by a vote of 37 to 2. Most of the legislators agreed with Senator Cameron of Pennsylvania that the purchase was "an act of recompense to a tried friend."

The House of Representatives presented a much more difficult hurdle than the Senate. Many congressmen dwelt at length on the worthlessness of Alaska. The territory was referred to in the most uncomplimentary terms as "the country of short rations and long twilights." While most congressmen were mindful of the need to preserve Russo-American friendship and made grateful references to the Russian fleet, doubts were expressed as to whether friendship called for the sacrifice of taking over "Walrussia" for a price of several million dollars. Representative Benjamin F. Butler argued that if it was necessary to pay $7,200,000 to retain the czar's good will, then the United States should pay the amount and refuse to take over Alaska.

The prolonged debate in the House so upset Russian Minister de Stoeckl that he suggested at one point that the emperor offer Alaska to the United States as a gift in order to shame the Americans into paying. Alexander II vetoed this suggestion, whereupon de Stoeckl hired prominent lobbyists in Washington to get the House to pass the appropriation. Even some bribery of congressmen seems to have been involved. What finally won the day for Seward was a combination of factors. First, many congressmen were reluctant to "haul down Old Glory" from Alaska. As Congressman William Orth of Indiana stated: "Shall that flag which waves so proudly there now be taken down? Palsied be the hand that would dare remove it! Our flag is there, and there it will remain."[12] Second, Seward's educational campaign about Alaska's potential economic wealth had made a deep impression in the House. And finally, the legend of the Russian fleet still cast a powerful spell. Most congressmen were reluctant to vote against "the only true friend of America." Thus, the appropriation for the Alaska purchase passed the House on July 14, 1868, by a vote of 113 to 43. The deal was consummated, but not without a bitter aftertaste. The Americans believed that they had paid in full their debt of gratitude for the Russian fleet. Minister de Stoeckl, on the other hand, was so unnerved by the congressional debate that he requested the czar for another assignment in order to "breathe for a while a purer atmosphere than that of Washington."

As the years passed, the value of Alaska, of course, became increasingly apparent. Americans began to read back into the past the mood of the moment. A feeling of gratitude for the czar's apparent generosity developed retrospectively. As relations with Russia slowly began to worsen toward the turn of the century, as George Kennan revealed the horrors of the Siberian exile system to Americans for the first time, as pogroms and clashing power objectives began to poison the traditional friendship, the memory of Czar Alexander's "selflessness" in ceding Alaska for a pittance still remained a bond in Russo-American relations. As the objective dictates of power and national rivalry drove the two nations ever further apart, as the differences in the two systems of government became more and more dramatically apparent, the legends of the generosity of Czar Alexander, myths though they were, still exercised a remarkable influence, especially on the American side, in delaying for some time the decline of Russo-American relations into suspicion and hostility.

THE DEATH OF A LEGEND: THE RUSSO-JAPANESE WAR AND THE UNITED STATES

Alexander II was killed by an assassin's bomb in 1881, and with his passing the golden age of Russo-American relations came to an end. Under the heavy hand of his successor, Alexander III, ominous events took place that gradually eroded the American

---

[12] Congressman William Orth, quoted in Thomas A. Bailey, *A Diplomatic History of the American People* (New York: Appleton-Century-Crofts, 1950), p. 401.

legend of Russia like so many drops of corrosive acid. A violent wave of anti-Jewish pogroms that followed the assassination of Alexander II swept across Russia and brought large numbers of immigrants to the United States. The horrible tales of these pogroms outraged many Americans and made them turn away from Russia. When in 1891 the distinguished American publicist George Kennan[13] exposed the truth about the conditions of prisoners in Siberia, in his classic *Siberia and the Exile System,* the legend was shattered almost beyond repair. Thus, on the eve of war between Russia and Japan, American sympathies were definitely with Japan, to the incredulous surprise and consternation of Czar Nicholas II and the entire Russian press. Even the able and gifted Russian diplomat Count Sergei Witte, who represented his country at the Portsmouth peace talks, was unable to reverse the anti-Russian tide in America. Theodore Roosevelt had only unkind words for the Russians. They were perceived by him as stupid, insincere, treacherous, and corrupt. Czar Nicholas was seen as "a preposterous little creature."[14] A legend had died, and another had risen to take its place.

The anti-Jewish pogroms in Russia from Kiev in 1881 to Kishinev in 1903 turned large segments of American public opinion against Russia. In 1882, Representative Samuel S. Cox of New York City in demanding action listed 167 places where there had been riots, burnings, pillagings, rapes, and murders.[15] The number of Jewish families reduced to beggary was estimated at 100,000. The pogroms continued during the 1880s and 1890s and culminated in the frightful orgy of Kishinev, which seemed to many Americans to be condoned by the bureaucracy of Nicholas II.

The outcry of horror in the United States was not limited to the Jews alone. But the State Department was too embarrassed to protest vigorously, primarily because of the American Negro problem. As one Berlin cartoon had President Theodore Roosevelt remark to the czar: "You cut up your Jews, I'll burn my Negroes."[16] Some Americans argued that out of gratitude for past favors, the United States should not now criticize Russia too harshly. But

---

[13] A distant relative of the scholar-diplomat George Frost Kennan.

[14] H. F. Pringle, *Theodore Roosevelt* (New York: Macmillan, 1931), p. 385.

[15] U.S. Congress, House, *Congressional Record,* 47th Cong., 1st sess. 1882, pp. 651–658.

[16] *Review of Reviews* (September 1903), p. 269.

leading American Jews, such as Oscar S. Straus, began to undermine the basis of Russo-American friendship by casting serious
doubts on the fleet legend.[17]

Perhaps no one single person did more to bury the American
legend of Russia than George Kennan. To most Americans of
1880, Siberia was a frozen wasteland to which convicts were
banished by edict of the czar. Kennan was the first American ever
to visit Siberian prisons, and his exposé, published in 1891, became
a classic of thoroughness and dramatic power. The conditions he
found were horrible beyond belief. Victims were banished without
trial; torture was commonplace; starvation was the rule of the
day; and the callousness of prison officials was barbaric. Kennan,
a gifted writer and lecturer, brought countless American audiences
to the verge of tears with his forceful and evocative descriptions.
And for the first time, he delineated a distinction that was increasingly perceived by the Americans—between the Russian government and the Russian people. "As for me," Kennan wrote, "my
sympathies are with the Russia of the people, not the Russia of
the Tsars."[18] This distinction increasingly dominated American
perceptions of Russia and exercised a profound influence on
American policy toward Russia during the Bolshevik Revolution.

When the Japanese fleet attacked Russian naval units at Port
Arthur in a surprise attack and without any declaration of war,
most American newspapers praised the clever and courageous
Japanese who were not afraid of Russian bully tactics and were
resourceful enough to catch the Russians off guard.[19] Kennan, now
a distinguished war correspondent, wrote that the Japanese were
superior to the Russians and that Russian prisoners of war were
better off in Japanese prison camps than they would have been
as Czarist exiles in Siberia. Even though Japan had fired the first
shot, most Americans were on the side of the Japanese "underdog"; it seemed like a contest between David and Goliath. President Roosevelt convinced himself that Japan was "playing our
game." If Russia won, she would presumably close the door for
the United States in Asia while Japan would keep it open for

---

[17] Oscar S. Straus, "The United States and Russia: Their Historical Relations,"
North American Review (August 1905), pp. 244–245.
[18] George Kennan, *Century Magazine* (July 1893), p. 472.
[19] The parallels to the attack on Pearl Harbor are remarkable, but few Americans
drew them in 1941.

American commerce. Even though there was little evidence to support this claim, it permeated the thinking of most American government officials and business interests.

The Russian response to this American about face was one of shock and anger. The Russian press during the Russo-Japanese War was full of references to American ingratitude for past favors. Moreover, Russia was a white Christian nation, and in times of threat from the yellow peril, white Christian nations should stand together. Finally, the Japanese aggressors had clearly struck the first blow, while Nicholas II was a man of peace who had initiated the Hague Peace Conference. The American attitude was both stupid and incomprehensible to most Russian officials.

A new debate began in the United States about the role of the Russian fleet during the Civil War. Serious doubts were cast on the old legend. Especially after the disastrous defeat of the Russian fleet at the Tsushima Strait, many Americans began to question just how useful the fleet would have been to the Americans if it had been engaged in naval battle by Britain or France. So far as Alaska was concerned, cash had been paid and no debt was involved. Pogroms and Siberian prisons had brought into being a far less generous, even a cynical, reaction to Russian claims on American gratitude for favors received in the past.

By 1905, both Russia and Japan were exhausted from the war. Russia's navy was crippled, and she faced the possibility of revolution at home. Japan was near the end of her manpower and economic resources. The story of Theodore Roosevelt's mediation at Portsmouth is well known and will not be recounted here. What is important is that the changed attitudes of the United States and Russia toward each other became painfully clear to both sides during the negotiations.

Czar Nicholas II was badly shaken by the new American hostility. In 1905, near the end of the war, he asked the following of the American ambassador: "Say to your President I certainly hope that the old friendship which has previously existed and united the two nations for so long a period will be renewed."[20] The czar knew that the ancient friendship had been shattered, and he was eager to rebuild it. He sent to Portsmouth the brilliant diplomat Count Witte, who did his best to swing American public opinion

---

[20] Czar Nicholas II, quoted in Bailey, *America Faces Russia, op. cit.,* p. 205.

away from Japan back to Russia. But a careful analysis of American press attitudes during the Portsmouth negotiations demonstrates that "the great majority of the press remained unswervingly pro-Japanese on the specific issues which divided the Portsmouth delegates."[21]

A new image had taken hold: the Russian government was a group of blundering despots and liars; the Russian army was inept; the navy was beyond hope; and the people were the abject victims of a brutal and mindless tyranny. "It is the system that has failed, not the men," explained the American *Review of Reviews*. While during the reigns of Catherine and Alexander, the Russians could do no wrong, under Nicholas they could do little that was right.

THE BIRTH AND DEATH OF LEGENDS

Perhaps the most remarkable conclusion to be drawn about American perceptions of Russia during the pre-Bolshevik period is how violently they swung from one extreme to the other, while Russia, the object of these perceptions, changed relatively little. For an entire century, Russia was America's trusted friend. Catherine's refusal to lend troops to King George, Alexander's dispatch of the Russian fleet to American ports, and Alexander's sale of Alaska, all were perceived as selfless and generous acts and uncritically accepted as such. The legend of Russia, the "trusted ally," was born in these events, and policy decisions of far-reaching importance were based on the assumption that all the legends were true.

Russia, under both Catherine and Alexander, had acted purely in accord with the dictates of her national interest. Though somewhat surprised by the effusive gratitude of the Americans, the czars did little to dispel it. When the pendulum of American perceptions swung to the other extreme, Nicholas II was bewildered and shocked. He tried to appeal to the ancient friendship, but the old American image of Russia, once dead, could not be resurrected. Americans saw prisons and pogroms in Russia, where formerly they had seen only good will and benevolence. This perception, equally one-sided as its predecessor, led to policies that helped estrange America from Russia.

---

[21] Winston B. Thorson, "American Public Opinion and the Portsmouth Conference," *American Historical Review* (April 1948), p. 454.

One cannot help but note the unevenness of the American attitudes. Russian views of America were fairly accurate, and Russian
policy was cold and selfish, but steady and fairly predictable. The
young American republic tended to see the Russians either as
angels or as monsters. Personal factors such as trust and friendship
were read into policy; personal motives were perceived as national
objectives; and finally, romanticism yielded to bitterness and
disillusion.

Perhaps legends grow more easily in young nations than in old.
Young America had to supplant one legend with another, equally
distorted. Czarist Russia, nearing its end, did not indulge in
legends. Only with the advent of the Bolshevik Revolution did the
new Russian leadership fashion legends of its own.

eight

THE BOLSHEVIK REVOLUTION AND THE UNITED STATES

The shattering events that changed the face of Russia in 1917 also had a profound impact on the United States. The reaction of the American public-at-large to the Russian Revolution and its aftermath was marked by wide swings of emotion. The events of March 1917 were widely perceived as the triumph of democracy in Russia. Most Americans believed that Russia, having thrown off the Czarist yoke, would fight even harder on the Allied side against Germany. After all, Russians would now be fighting for themselves, and not for a cruel tyranny that had been imposed on them for centuries.

When Russia signed a separate peace treaty with Germany, however, and left the war in March 1918, the American public was swept by a sense of outrage and betrayal. The Bolsheviks who had been seen as liberators from Czarism were now perceived as German agents and as a threat to civilization in general and to American democracy in particular. The attitude of the American public now swung to the opposite extreme. The greatest danger to mankind was no longer the German "Hun," but the Bolshevik "Red." The Bolsheviks, most Americans believed, were not really Russians at all. If Lenin and his clique could only be removed, the true democratic spirit of Russia would at last assert itself.

Little wonder then that there were powerful popular pressures in the United States in 1918 favoring armed intervention in the Russian civil war. This intervention did indeed take place in the summer of 1918; not until after the end of the war were American troops withdrawn from Russia. Still the bitterness toward the Bolsheviks remained. It manifested itself in the "Red Scare" that swept the United States in 1919 and resulted in the deportation of many Americans with Communist sympathies. Romanticism had turned to cynicism, disillusionment, and bitter hatred.

President Woodrow Wilson had been deeply affected by the Russian Revolution. Eager to "make the world safe for democracy," he quickly welcomed the new "democratic Russia" as a "fit partner for a league of honor."[1] Wilson retained a favorable disposition toward the Soviet Union, even after the new Soviet government left the war. Indeed, he resisted the popular pressures for armed intervention in the civil war until the summer of 1918. What finally prompted him to intervene was not so much the hope of overthrowing the Bolsheviks as the desire to come to the rescue of a contingent of anti-Bolshevik Czechoslovaks who were fighting their way westward through the Russian interior. Wilson did not really perceive the new Soviet government as the "Red Terror" poised to engulf the Western world. But he intervened because the lives of sons and brothers and husbands were at stake. In this sense, American policy was not based on distorted perceptions or unrealistic expectations, but on a relatively sober military calculation in which the cruder perceptions and motivations of the American public appear to have played a fairly minor role. A year later, however, when the popular fury against the Bolsheviks had hardened, America endured the short-lived but intense Red Scare at the instigation of Attorney General A. Mitchell Palmer.

On the Bolshevik side, the two leading figures with sustained interest in the United States were V. I. Lenin and Leon Trotsky. Although their attention was largely focused on Europe, they nevertheless had very definite views of the United States during the turbulent years of world war and revolution. These perceptions were deeply influenced by Marxist ideology. Even before the United States entered the war, America was seen as a nation in which a few self-seeking capitalist monopolists were imposing their control on the large masses of exploited workers. When the United States joined the struggle against Germany and the Central Powers and thus became an ally of the Czarist regime, Lenin pronounced his scorn for both sides in the war. Lenin's triumph in November 1917 brought this loathing to the surface. It was perfectly clear to him that he should take Russia out of the war at

---

[1] Woodrow Wilson, War Message to Congress, April 2, 1917, *Papers Relating to the Foreign Relations of the United States*, Supplement I: *The World War*, 1918, p. 200.

the earliest opportunity. Let the imperialists devour each other while Russia maneuvered, bided her time, and slowly grew in strength. Not even President Wilson's Fourteen Points speech of January 1918, with its conciliatory comments about the new Soviet government, changed the Soviet leader's view. Several weeks later and one month before the Brest Litovsk Treaty of March 1918 which took Russia out of the war, Lenin had the following to say:

The war with England and America will go on for a long time; the aggressive imperialism of both groups has unmasked itself finally and completely. Under such conditions a socialist Soviet Republic in Russia will be a model for all other peoples and excellent material for propaganda purposes. On the one side there will be the bourgeois system engaged in a strife between two coalitions of confessed plunderers, and on the other side a Socialist Soviet Republic living in peace.[2]

While some Bolsheviks flirted briefly with the idea of regarding the United States as the lesser evil, Lenin firmly rejected such an attitude. The Allied military intervention in the summer of 1918 only hardened Lenin's convictions. His perceptions of the United States at that time were set forth with great clarity in his "Letter to American Workingmen from the Socialist Soviet Republic of Russia," written in August 1918. In this remarkable document, the United States was seen as a house divided between a few greedy plutocrats, on the one hand, and the mass of destitute workers, on the other. Lenin said, "America has become characteristic for the depth of the abyss which divides a handful of brutal millionaires who are stagnating in mires of luxury, and millions of laboring, starving men and women who are always staring want in the face." It was only a question of time, in Lenin's view, until the revolution would come to America. "The American working class will not follow the lead of the bourgeoisie," Lenin predicted confidently, "it will go with us against the bourgeoisie." On August 30, 1918, the day he was shot and seriously wounded, Lenin gave a speech in Moscow in which he once again revealed his view of the United States: "A handful not of millionaires but of billionaires takes over everything, and the entire population remains in slavery and subjection."[3]

---

[2] Lenin, quoted in *Pravda*, February 24, 1918.
[3] Lenin, quoted in George F. Kennan, *The Decision to Intervene* (Princeton: Princeton University Press, 1958), p. 462.

The evidence suggests that Lenin's policy toward the United States was derived directly from this ideological model. While Wilson's policies toward the new Bolshevik government were based on a number of interrelated factors of which the American perception of the Soviet Union was only one—and by no means the most important one—the Bolshevik leader perceived the United States almost completely through the prism of Communist ideology and fashioned his policy accordingly.

The essential thesis of this chapter, then, is that Lenin and, to a lesser extent, Wilson saw what they expected to see. Wilson, before the Allied intervention, saw a Russia that was largely fictitious, and Lenin saw the same in the United States. Thus, the two men often talked past each other and their statements about each other's countries frequently took on an exasperating air of irrelevance. Their policies unfortunately followed suit. George F. Kennan, in describing these early Soviet-American encounters, recounts the hoary anecdote about two cross-eyed men who bumped into each other. The one said, "Why in hell don't you look where you are going?" To which the other replied, "Why in hell don't you go where you are looking?"[4]

AMERICA VIEWS RUSSIA: 1917–1920

The great majority of Americans from the President down to the rank-and-file saw the overthrow of Czarist Russia as the triumph of freedom and democracy, American style. The unanimous reaction of statesmen, businessmen, labor leaders, editors, and politicians to the events in Petrograd was truly extraordinary. Elite and public alike shared this view virtually without dissent. George Kennan, then widely regarded as the leading authority on Russia, proclaimed "the complete triumph of democracy" in March 1917.[5] Other commentators were equally enthusiastic. *The New York Times*, referring to the government of Prince Lvov, stated editorially that "democracy [was] the very soul of the Russian revolution, the sustaining principle of the new Government."[6] President Wilson, in his war message to Congress on April 2, 1917, not only

---

[4] George F. Kennan, *Russia and the West Under Lenin and Stalin* (Boston: Little, Brown, 1961), pp. 10–11.
[5] George F. Kennan, "The Victory of the Russian People," *Outlook* (March 28, 1917), p. 546.
[6] *The New York Times*, March 16, 1917.

pronounced the new Russian government as "a fit partner for a league of honor," but despite Russia's Czarist past, continued to describe that nation as "democratic at heart, in all the vital habits of her thought, in all the intimate relationships of her people that spoke their natural instinct, their habitual attitude towards life."[7] Religious groups were lavish in their praise. The reaction of *Zion's Herald*, a Boston Methodist weekly, was typical: "Autocracy has received its death blow; democracy has triumphed. All of America rejoices in the dawn of the new day for Russia."[8] And the Washington *Star* editorialized: "A free people naturally wants all the other peoples of the world to be free."[9] Russia was thus perceived as a Slavic version of the United States and Russian "democracy" as a replica of the American model.

The facts, well known in retrospect, were quite different. Prince Lvov and his government were wealthy landowners with strongly aristocratic tastes. The majority of the population were peasants with little or no experience in self-government, who harbored bitter resentments against the landholding classes. The political situation in Russia in the spring of 1917 was hardly ripe for democratic government.

In most of America, the wish inspired the thought. In March 1917, the United States was about to declare war on Germany and help to "make the world safe for democracy." It would have been embarrassing, to say the least, to be allied with the Czarist autocracy in this crusade. The Russian Revolution was nothing less than providential. It removed the embarrassing czar just in time for Wilson's war message and, in the view of most Americans, reinstated the Russian people as fellow belligerents in the democratic cause against the German Kaiser and the Central Powers. Russia had not only become a democratic nation, she would now also become a formidable military ally. In the American mind, democracy in Russia and continuing the war were inextricably linked. This misperception of the March Revolution was destined to bear bitter fruit when the real nature of the revolutionary process in Russia began to reveal itself.

The American ambassador to the Provisional Government was a

---

[7] Wilson, *Foreign Relations, op. cit.,* p. 200.
[8] *Zion's Herald,* March 21, 1917.
[9] Cited in Leonid I. Strakhovsky, *American Opinion About Russia* (Toronto: University of Toronto Press, 1961), p. 6.

sixty-seven-year-old former grain merchant from Missouri, David R. Francis. Francis, who was almost completely out of touch with the realities in Russia, sent back glowing reports about the prospects of the new government. In June, Wilson dispatched Elihu Root, a conservative and wealthy elder statesman, on a good will mission to Russia. Root was to encourage the Russians to keep up the fight against Germany. While walking through a Siberian village in June 1917, however, Root stated: "I am a firm believer in democracy, but I do not like filth."[10] He was not equipped to understand the Russian Revolution; nor were most Americans at the time.

When the Bolsheviks seized power in November 1917, most Americans reacted as if the impossible had happened. And since it was impossible, it would soon cease happening. Again, a distinction was drawn in the American mind between the Russian people and the "usurping gang" of Bolshevik leaders.[11] The American missionary spirit asserted itself in the pages of the influential New York *World:* "Russia cannot be abandoned, either to Germany or to anarchy."[12] The predominant belief in the United States was that the Bolsheviks were a small minority whose crazy ideas would soon topple them from power, whereupon the democratic instincts of the Russian people would again rise to the surface. *The New York Times,* according to a study made by Walter Lippmann during the period from November 1917 to November 1919, predicted the fall of the Bolsheviks from power no fewer than ninety-one times.[13] It also reported four times that Lenin and Trotsky were planning flight and three times that they had already fled. Three times it announced Lenin's imprisonment and once even his death.[14]

The separate peace of Brest Litovsk convinced the United States that the impossible might last a little longer than had been anticipated. The *North American Review* confessed: "We have optimistically—and somewhat credulously—called Russia free, a republic, a democracy. Russia has not, for a single day, been either a

---

[10] Elihu Root, quoted in Philip C. Jessup, *Elihu Root* (New York: Dodd Mead 1938), Vol. II, p. 361.
[11] *Literary Digest* (December 8, 1917), p. 15.
[12] Cited in *ibid.*
[13] Cited in *The New Republic* (August 4, 1920).
[14] *Ibid.*

republic, a democracy, or free."[15] Most Americans reacted to Brest Litovsk as an act of Bolshevik perfidy and regarded the Russians as cowardly quitters at best or German agents at worst. Trotsky was awarded the "ignoble peace prize" by several American newspapers, and one paper, the Kansas City *Star*, with a strong suggestion of sour grapes, stated: "Well, if Russia is lost to us, all right. We never did want to make the world safe for the Bolshevik kind of democracy anyway."[16]

The cycle of President Wilson's perceptions of Russia swung within narrower confines than that of the American public-at-large. The President had been critical of the czar but not violently so. The victory of the Bolsheviks disappointed him but did not outrage him. He even made some conciliatory gestures toward the new Soviet government in early 1918, although he decided to withhold formal recognition. Some contemporary American observers of the Russian scene have claimed that this American reluctance to recognize the new regime and the decision not to have any dealings with it precipitated Brest Litovsk and Lenin's determination to pull Russia out of the war. Raymond Robins, for example, the head of the American Red Cross Mission to Russia in 1918, maintained that "the bitter anti-Bolshevism of his government was to blame for the separate peace."[17] He recounted a dramatic scene according to which Lenin, just before the meeting of the Fourth All-Russian Congress of Soviets on March 16, 1918, asked him whether he had heard from Washington about the possibility of recognition. When Robins replied in the negative, Lenin mounted the rostrum and convinced the delegates to ratify the Brest Litovsk Treaty. The inference here is that the United States was responsible for Brest Litovsk.

The historical evidence does not bear out the Robins thesis. George Kennan in his *Russia Leaves the War* has demonstrated conclusively that Lenin was determined to take Russia out of the war regardless of American policy toward the new Soviet government.[18] The Bolshevik slogan of "an end to the war" was an

---

[15] *North American Review* (February 1918), p. 186.
[16] Cited in *Literary Digest* (January 12, 1918).
[17] U.S. Senate, *Hearings Before a Subcommittee of the Committee on the Judiciary*, 65th Cong., 3rd sess. (1919), pp. 800–807.
[18] George F. Kennan, *Russia Leaves the War* (Princeton: Princeton University Press, 1956), pp. 487–517.

integral plank in the platform that had swept Lenin to power. It was not contingent on what the Americans would or would not do. Nevertheless, Robins testified before the Senate Judiciary Subcommittee in March 1919 and convinced a number of influential opinion shapers of his views, among them, Arthur Bullard, who was Colonel Edward M. House's representative in Russia in 1918, and Professors Edward A. Ross and Samuel N. Harper. President Wilson, significantly enough, ignored the suggestions of Robins and his circle. Wilson's attitude toward the new Bolshevik regime was essentially one of aloofness—one does not engage in commerce with the devil. On the occasion of the Brest Litovsk Treaty, the American President sent the following statement to the Soviet government: "The whole heart of the people of the United States is with the people of Russia in the attempt to free themselves forever from autocratic government and become the masters of their own life."[19] But he added, regretfully, that the United States would not be able to offer either economic aid or recognition.

The All-Russian Congress replied to Wilson's message in kind, thanking "the toiling and exploited classes of the United States of North America" and expressing

> its warm sympathy and its firm confidence that the happy time is not far distant when the toiling masses of all bourgeois countries will throw off the yoke of capitalism and will establish a socialist order of society, which alone is capable of assuring a firm and just peace as well as the cultural and material well being of all the toilers.[20]

In the words of a leading scholar of the period, "Suddenly, Americans were hearing their own gospel, in Bolshevik translation, returning to them like an ironic and ominous echo. Two missionaries were now competing for the souls of the peoples of the world."[21]

Even after Brest Litovsk, most Americans still believed that the Russians were democratic at heart and anxious to defeat the German autocrats. The myth of the Bolsheviks as a transient, German-inspired phenomenon died hard. Lenin, after all, had

---

[19] Acting Secretary of State Polk to Consul-General Summers at Moscow, March 11, 1918, *Foreign Relations, op. cit.,* pp. 395–396.
[20] Quoted in Kennan, *Russia Leaves the War, op. cit.,* pp. 512–513.
[21] Peter G. Filene, *Americans and the Soviet Experiment, 1917–1933* (Cambridge: Harvard University Press, 1967), p. 37.

been spirited into Russia in a train provided by the German general staff, and Trotsky's real name was Bronstein. *The Saturday Evening Post* told its two million subscribers that Germany practiced despotism by an elite, but Lenin represented a "despotism by all the lowest."[22] The Bolsheviks were an evil that the Wilson administration boycotted diplomatically and the vast majority of Americans opposed vehemently. Thus, when Japan, Britain, and France prepared for intervention against the Bolsheviks in April 1918, and when the counterattacks of the Whites at the same time had reduced the areas under Soviet control to the size of medieval Muscovy, the demand for American military intervention mounted. Wilson resisted these pressures for several months, even though he had come to believe that "the new dictatorship in Russia was just as selfish, ruthless, and pitiless as that of the Czars, and his heart went out to the ill-starred masses."[23] During May and June, the public clamor grew in vehemence, and numerous high officials, both in the Wilson administration and in elective office, demanded intervention, either for anti-Bolshevik or anti-German reasons or a combination of both. As Senator James Reed of Missouri told the Senate: "If Russia rises against the entering troops, that would prove that Russia is already Germanized."[24] Many of the President's diplomatic advisers joined the interventionist tide. What finally forced Wilson's hand, as we have seen, was a marooned contingent of some 45,000 Czechoslovak soldiers in eastern Russia who caught the popular fancy and whose thousands of relatives in America put additional pressure on Congress and the President. A force of 9,000 Americans was sent to Russia, and the resulting loss of lives in battles with Bolshevik contingents embittered both sides even further.

New myths about Bolshevik Russia sprang up in the United States during the interventionist phase. The Bolsheviks now became veritable monsters who had ordered the nationalization of Russian women. In October 1918, *The New York Times* reported that, in certain Russian provinces under Soviet control, every eighteen-year-old girl had to register at a "bureau of free love"

---

[22] *The Saturday Evening Post* (July 6, 1918).
[23] R. S. Baker and W. E. Dodd, *The Public Papers of Woodrow Wilson, 1917–1924* (New York: Harcourt, Brace, 1927), Vol. II, p. 70.
[24] U.S. Congress, Senate, *Congressional Record*, 65th Cong., 2nd sess., August 22, 1918, p. 9348.

and was then given a husband without her consent.[25] Senator Lawrence Sherman of Illinois delivered a lengthy speech on the subject in the Senate in January 1919. Such reports appeared in numerous American papers until late 1919.

After the Allied armistice with Germany in November 1918, American intervention simply no longer made sense. The Czechoslovaks had been evacuated; the war was over; and the parents of the American soldiers in Russia brought great pressure to bear on their representatives in Congress to bring their sons home. Enthusiasm for intervention turned to bitterness that Americans were still suffering and fighting in Russia despite the armistice in Europe. The public clamor against the intervention was now as vociferous as it had been six months earlier in favor of it. But not until June 1919, after hundreds of casualties, were American troops withdrawn from northern Russia, and the last troops did not leave Siberia until April 1920.

During the intervention, the American attitudes toward Russia froze into an almost bizarre hostility. As one observer put it: "Bolshevism means chaos, wholesale murder, the complete destruction of civilization."[26] According to *Current History*, the issue was "Bolshevism Against Civilization." As late as November 1919, Secretary of State Lansing was still in favor of extending diplomatic recognition to the White General Kolchak, and Senator William A. Smith of Michigan asserted that "the Russian people, God bless them, [were] anxious to overthrow the Bolsheviks and to fulfill a noble destiny."[27] When the Bolsheviks had clearly won the civil war, Americans finally despaired about the "democratic spirit" of Russia. There now developed considerable support for making Russia a trusteeship under the League of Nations and thus to supervise her gradual entry into civilization.[28] William Allen White concluded bitterly in October 1919: "Let the thing fry in its own grease. So far as interior Russia is concerned, the whole trouble with Russia is Russia."[29]

---

[25] *The New York Times*, October 26, 1918.

[26] Lincoln Steffens to Allen H. Suggett, *Letters* (New York: Harcourt, Brace, 1938), Vol. I, p. 466.

[27] U.S. Congress, Senate, *Congressional Record*, 65th Cong., 3rd sess., January 24, 1919, p. 1081.

[28] *The New York Times*, January 12, 1919.

[29] William Allen White, quoted in Filene, *op. cit.*, p. 61.

The Red Scare of 1919 exposed the darker side of the missionary spirit. The emotions of the two crusades against Germany and Bolshevism, not yet dissipated, frantically sought new objects. Vindictiveness and xenophobia now took command. Strikes in Seattle and Boston and a Communist coup in Hungary provided additional fuel for the mounting hysteria. In November 1919, Attorney General Palmer arrested 450 supposed Communists in 12 cities and one month later seized 4,000 more suspects in 33 cities. On December 21, 1919, 249 persons were actually deported on the "Soviet Ark" to the Soviet Union. As one supporter of the attorney general put it, "My motto for the Reds is S.O.S.—ship or shoot. I believe we should place them all on a ship of stone, with sails of lead, and their first stopping place should be hell."[30] The Red Scare, in the words of one thoughtful observer, was "Wilsonianism turned inside out, confident messianism become paranoid, intolerant Americanism seeking to purify the nation of alien and disturbing elements."[31]

Thus, most Americans by 1920 perceived a Russia that had merely changed chains. After a few brief glimpses of liberty, she was now enslaved by a despotism far more diabolical and cunning than that of the czars. Czarism, though objectionable, was at least content to oppress its own people. The Bolsheviks, however, were determined to impose their fearful philosophy beyond their own borders on the rest of the world.

THE BOLSHEVIKS VIEW THE UNITED STATES: 1917–1920

Lenin's empirical knowledge of the United States was quite slender. He seemed to have had little interest in it and probably identified it with the England he came to know during his period of exile in London. America seemed to have been just another capitalist country and not a very important one at that. The Decree on Peace, which Lenin drafted personally in the fall of 1917, referred to England, France, and Germany as "the three mightiest states taking part in the present war." The United States was not even mentioned, though she had entered the war in April 1917.

---

[30] Quoted in Foster R. Dulles, The Road to Teheran (Princeton: Princeton University Press, 1944), p. 164.
[31] Quoted in Filene, op. cit., p. 63.

Trotsky had visited the United States from January 13 to March 27, 1917. During this brief stay he lived on New York's upper eastside—on 162nd Street—in what he described as a "working-class district." He spent most of his working day in the editorial offices of the Russian-language socialist newspaper *Novy Mir* near Union Square. In his autobiography, he relates that he studied American economic life in the New York Public Library and adds that his "only profession in New York was the profession of a revolutionary socialist."[32] Before leaving New York, Trotsky urged his followers to keep on organizing in order "to overthrow this damned rotten capitalistic government."[33] The evidence suggests that the rich variety of American life, the "flesh-and-blood America . . . remained for him—fortunately for the peace of his brilliant but dogmatic mind, unfortunately for the course of Soviet-American relations—a closed book."[34]

Hence, even while Lenin and Trotsky were still fugitives from Russia, they regarded the United States as an intrinsic part of the capitalist world, which they hated with every fiber of their deeply political natures. The fact that this hatred was transferred from its primary objects—England, France, and Germany—made it no less real. But what they hated was not the real America of 1917, but a fictitious America, one that had been created half a century earlier by the pen of Karl Marx.

Both Lenin and Trotsky had been taken completely by surprise by the March Revolution. As good Marxists, they had expected the revolution to strike first in Germany or in England. When it occurred in one of the least industrialized countries in Europe, the two Bolshevik leaders happened to be in exile but were galvanized into action at once. As is well known, Lenin was permitted by the German government to traverse Germany in the famous sealed train. He entered Russia in April. A few weeks later, he and Trotsky were hard at work to turn the March Revolution into a full-fledged victory for the Bolshevik cause.

When the Bolshevik Revolution struck in mid-November, the first policy statement, issued on the very day of the revolution, was the Decree on Peace. In this document Lenin proposed an

---

[32] Leon Trotsky, *Mein Leben* (Berlin: S. Fischer Verlag, 1930), p. 259.
[33] Leon Trotsky, quoted in Thomas A. Bailey, *America Faces Russia* (Ithaca: Cornell University Press, 1950), p. 238.
[34] Kennan, *Russia Leaves the War, op. cit.,* p. 32.

immediate armistice and also called on the class-conscious workers of England, Germany, and France to liberate the toiling masses of the world. The document was aimed at "peoples," rather than governments and, to some extent at least, was meant to encourage social revolution in the three European countries. The United States was not mentioned even once.

The first Soviet policy statement regarding the United States directly was made by Trotsky, at a meeting of the Central Executive Committee of the Soviet of Workers' and Peasants' Deputies, held four days after the promulgation of the Decree on Peace. His statement sums up the view of the early Bolshevik leaders very well:

The United States began to intervene in the war after three years, under the influence of the sober calculations of the American Stock Exchange. America could not tolerate the victory of one coalition over the other. America is interested in the weakening of both coalitions and in the consolidation of the hegemony of American capital. Apart from that, American war industry is interested in the war. During the war American exports have more than doubled and have reached a figure not reached by any other capitalist state. Exports go almost entirely to the Allied countries. When in January Germany came out for unrestricted U-boat warfare, all railway stations and harbors in the United States were overloaded with the output of the war industries. Transport was disorganized and New York witnessed food riots such as we ourselves have never seen here. Then the finance capitalists sent an ultimatum to Wilson: to secure the sale of the output of the war industries within the country. Wilson accepted the ultimatum, and hence the preparations for war and war itself.[35]

An analysis of this statement reveals the tragic gaps between perception and reality that dominated Trotsky's thinking on the matter of the United States. First, he dismissed American democracy as a preposterous sham and saw the real rulers of American political life in the monopoly capitalists of Wall Street. Second, he accused the United States of desiring to weaken the Allies in order to profit from the economic disaster of both sides. Third, Wilson's decision to enter the war was seen as a capitulation to monopoly capital. And finally, Trotsky painted a picture of hunger and deprivation far worse than anything that had been

---

[35] Leon Trotsky, cited in *ibid.,* p. 88.

seen in Russia. To what extent Trotsky really believed these things and to what extent he consciously used them to advance the Bolshevik cause may never be precisely known. But it is a safe assumption that he believed *some* of the things he said. And his experience in the drab interior of an obscure Russian paper in New York probably did little to correct these stereotypes; perhaps it even reinforced them.

Lenin's writings before the 1917 revolution are replete with references to the United States. In *Imperialism, the Highest Stage of Capitalism,* written in exile in 1916, Lenin first developed the thesis that the war then in progress was "imperialist" on both sides. England, Germany, and Japan had already reached the highest stage of capitalism that made a nation inexorably imperialist. The nation about to reach that stage, according to Lenin, was the United States, whose economic expansion had recently been "even more rapid than in Germany and for this very reason the parasitic features of American capitalism stood out with particular force."[36] Such was the vigor of this new American imperialism that it was "actually beating Great Britain" and would soon clash with the expansionary drives of the other capitalist powers. In Lenin's view, therefore, the United States as a capitalist nation was inescapably committed to the imperialist exploitation of other countries. Its trusts, monopolies, and cartels would make sure of that.

Lenin, like Trotsky and the other Bolshevik leaders, regarded American entry into the war with cynicism. Wilson's assertion that the motive was to "make the world safe for democracy" was dismissed with utter contempt. The United States, in Lenin's view, was "infected with the same flame as Germany" and would go to the "same savage and insensate lengths" to attain its sinister objectives. Only the proletarian revolution could save the United States from ultimate self-destruction.

It is safe to assume that these convictions remained with Lenin until his death. The little contact he had with America and Americans did nothing to shake them. Not even President Wilson's conciliatory gesture toward the new Bolshevik government, made in January 1918 in his Fourteen Points speech, was able to jar the

---

[36] V. I. Lenin, *Sochineniya (Complete Works),* 4th ed. (Moscow: State Publishing House for Political Literature, 1950), Vol. XXVII, p. 553.

consistency of Lenin's world view. Even though—according to one eyewitness of Lenin's first reaction to the speech—the Bolshevik leader "was as joyous as a boy over the President's humanly understanding words toward Russia and his recognition of the honesty of Bolshevik purpose," Lenin's attitude quickly reverted to the old hostility.[37] Several days later, Lenin gave his first diplomatic reception to the various "bourgeois" ambassadors then residing in Petrograd, including the American Ambassador David R. Francis. Lenin's own description of this event is striking:

After live, real Soviet work, in the midst of workers and peasants who are occupied by real things, by the cutting of the forest and the tearing out of the roots of the landowners' and capitalist exploitation— one was suddenly obliged to be carried into a "strange world," to be brought face to face with some sort of arrivals from a new world, from the camp of the bourgeoisie and its voluntary and involuntary, conscious and unconscious servants, dependents, lackeys, and defenders. . . .

As though history has inadvertently or mistakenly turned the clock back and we had before us, instead of January 1918, May or June 1917! It is a terrible thing! To fall from the midst of living people into the company of corpses, to breathe the smell of corpses . . . this is something unbearable![38]

In light of the above, Lenin's iron determination to take Russia out of the war, even at the price of the harsh peace terms imposed by Germany at Brest Litovsk, is hardly surprising. It is true that the Bolsheviks, in their quandary, inquired, just before signing the peace treaty, about possible aid from the Allies, including the United States. Lenin, in response to a question posed by the other members of the Central Committee as to whether capitalist aid against Germany was acceptable, penned the following message on a piece of paper: "I request that my vote be added in favor of the acceptance of potatoes and arms from the bandits of Anglo-French imperialism."[39] Thus, Lenin did proclaim that aid could be accepted, but only if the very life of the Bolshevik government was at stake. Actually, nothing ever came of this feeler, since Lenin threw his enormous prestige behind the Brest Litovsk settlement.

---

[37] Cited in Kennan, *Russia Leaves the War, op. cit.,* p. 260.
[38] Lenin, *Sochineniya, op. cit., Vol. XXII,* p. 182.
[39] *Ibid.* Vol. XXVII, p. 520, n. 13.

We have referred above to the hypothesis that the Soviet government might have decided to continue the war against Germany in exchange for diplomatic recognition or some tangible evidence of friendliness from the United States. Not only did Raymond Robins defend this view at the time of Brest Litovsk, but so have some recent historians, claiming that the United States—swayed by the fear and prejudice of American capital—had needlessly estranged the Soviet leaders in the early days of their power. Not only has George F. Kennan's meticulous study of Brest Litovsk punctured this thesis decisively, but a study of Lenin's role in the October Revolution makes it seem inconceivable that Lenin could have done anything *but* take Russia out of the war after his seizure of power. After all, that was the main reason why he had come to power in the first place. It would have been suicidal for the Bolshevik leaders to do anything else but sue for peace, and it was no accident that the Decree on Peace was Lenin's first official proclamation. With Lenin's accession to power, the departure of Russia from the war was a certainty. It was consistent with the pragmatic political realities of the hour, and it flowed logically from Lenin's profoundly held conviction that both sides in the war were evil. Brest Litovsk, then, was seen as a precious breathing spell during which Soviet power could be consolidated and strengthened.

It should be noted in passing that the Soviet perceptions of the United States were not limited to Russians alone. A number of Americans who were caught up in the fever of the March and October revolutions shared these views. The most prominent of them, no doubt, was the young Harvard intellectual John Reed, author of the poetic and evocative *Ten Days that Shook the World*. Reed saw his own country so much through Bolshevik eyes that Trotsky, in January 1918, took the incongruous step of appointing "Citizen John Reed" as consul-general of the Soviet government in New York. Needless to say, the United States government found Reed's credentials wanting, but the episode illustrates the atmosphere of unreality that dominated relations between the two countries during this period.

With the beginning of the American intervention, first in northern Russia and then in Siberia during the summer of 1918, Lenin's anger at the United States mounted to extreme hatred and fury. Both he and Trotsky believed that the Allies, including the United States, had been responsible for the uprising of the Czechs in Siberia, which in turn had precipitated the Wilsonian intervention. Soviet historians have held to this view down to the present day. In September 1957, for example, *Pravda,* in connection with the fortieth anniversary of the October Revolution, offered the following interpretation of the intervention:

In the effort, to throttle the young republic of the Soviets, the imperialists, led by the leading circles of England, the U.S.A., and France, organized military campaigns against our country. From all sides—from north and south, east and west—the attacking hordes of interventionists and White Guards poured onto our territory. . . . For over three years the Soviet Republic was obliged to fight off the mad armed attack of the combined forces of the imperialist beasts of prey. . . .[40]

Lenin's policy was to fight all the interventionist forces with equal ferocity. On one occasion, this undifferentiated view of all capitalists cost him a measure of power. During May and June 1918, the northern port of Murmansk was occupied by Allied contingents including some American troops. Even though Murmansk was threatened by the Germans, Lenin absolutely refused to strike a bargain with the Americans stationed there. A review of this episode affords a fascinating glimpse into the subtle relationships between ideology and power. The head of the Murmansk Soviet, A. M. Yuryev, was a practical man who favored a Soviet détente with the Allies at Murmansk. As a result, Lenin dispatched a stern warning to him: "If you still refuse to understand Soviet policy— a policy equally hostile to the English and to the Germans—you have yourself to blame."[41] To which Yuryev replied: "It is all very well for you to talk that way, sitting there in Moscow. We ourselves know that the Germans and the Allies are imperialists, but of the two evils we have chosen the lesser."[42] Lenin, in turn, decided to purge Yuryev from the party. But the price that he paid for ideological purity was that Murmansk was turned into what might be called an anti-Soviet Soviet.

If one looks at the American intervention in perspective, the conclusion is inescapable that this ill-starred adventure embittered Soviet-American relations for decades to come. In fact, the leaders

---

[40] *Pravda,* September 15, 1957.
[41] V. I. Lenin, cited in Kennan, *The Decision to Intervene, op. cit.,* p. 374.
[42] A. M. Yuryev, quoted in *ibid.,* p. 374.

of the Soviet Union have never permitted their citizens to forget it. Soviet historians for the last half century have portrayed the intervention as a concerted and major military effort by the Western governments, mustering all the force they could, to bring down the Soviet government.

Lenin, holding fast to his Marxist convictions, composed his "Letter to American Workingmen" in August 1918, at the height of the intervention. He believed, it seems, deeply and sincerely that the working classes in America would oppose the interventionist policies of their capitalist masters and ultimately overthrow their tormentors altogether. As it turned out, the intervention did end, but its aftermath, rather than a Communist uprising, was the Red Scare.

The tragedy of the early Bolshevik-American encounters is that the deepening mirror devil images became more and more one-dimensional as time went on, until virtually all reality was lost.

When the United States entered the war in April 1917, it saw itself as an embattled democracy engaged in the struggle to make the world safe. The problems of Russia were seen in American terms. As George F. Kennan put it:

There is nothing in nature more egocentrical than the embattled democracy. It soon becomes the victim of its own war propaganda. It then tends to attach to its own cause an absolute value which distorts its own vision on everything else. *Its* enemy becomes the embodiment of all evil. *Its* own side, on the other hand, is the center of all virtue. The contest comes to be viewed as having a final apocalyptic quality.[43]

Similarly, the Bolsheviks regarded the October Revolution as the most important phenomenon on earth. With equally tenacious egocentricity, they believed that they were the bearers of all virtue and that it was the sole ambition of the Western European powers and of the United States to crush them. If one studies the accounts of Soviet historians of the period, one sees almost no evidence that a world war was in progress. The Americans regarded this war as a holy crusade; the Bolsheviks regarded it as a squabble among rival imperialists. Each side perceived itself as the sole purveyor of the good life on earth.

---

[43] Kennan, *Russia and the West Under Lenin and Stalin, op. cit.,* p. 5.

These self-images, of course, determined the perceptions of the adversary's character. The Americans came to view the Bolsheviks with gradually deepening horror. At the time of the Red Scare, Bolshevism had become the devil incarnate. Lenin and Trotsky, in turn, regarded the United States with increasing contempt, which, by the time of the intervention, had developed into a bitter and relentless hatred. Most Americans viewed the Bolsheviks as more wicked in their intentions than the old Czarist regime. The czar, after all, had harbored no global ambitions. The Bolsheviks, however, preached world revolution and had established the Comintern in order to subvert the noncommunist part of the world. Similarly, Lenin believed that the United States, by virtue of its capitalist nature, would be driven inexorably to expansion and imperialism.

Finally, Wilson and most of his fellow-Americans viewed the Bolsheviks as a transitional phenomenon. There was the hope that they would be overthrown and that the intervention might speed the process. Lenin, too, saw the United States as a house divided and its power built on sand, ready to collapse under the determined onslaught of its workers.

This was the way in which two great peoples collided in the cauldron of world war and revolution. And this was how they started on a road that was to lead them to the brink of war. Neither Wilson nor Lenin was able to transcend his experience or to expand his vision. Each remained within his universe, and neither developed a sense of empathy for the other's destiny. Thus, neither could teach his people to reach out across the gulf that was to separate Americans and Russians for generations.

Concrete policy decisions flowed from these perceptions. On the American side, the March Revolution was seen as the triumph of democracy and the birth of a powerful new ally in the war. This linkage between democracy and war proved fatal; it led to the American insistence that Russia continue the war even though her people were desperately longing for peace. The price that the United States paid for having Russia in the war for one more year was the victory of Bolshevism.

On the Soviet side, Lenin and Trotsky viewed the United States through the lenses of Marxism. The empirical reality of America remained largely inaccessible to them. This peculiar perception led to a policy of a priori rejection of America as a political presence in the world. Any meaningful modus vivendi or partnership was foreclosed by both Lenin and Trotsky. There was simply not enough room for both systems in the world for very long.

Thus, each side came to perceive the other as its mortal enemy. And since both sides believed this with growing intensity and deepening conviction, by 1920 they had come very close to being right.

nine

THE ESTABLISHMENT OF DIPLOMATIC RELATIONS BETWEEN THE UNITED STATES AND THE SOVIET UNION

Perception played a particularly interesting role in United States–Soviet relations during the decade preceding the establishment of diplomatic relations. In a curious and subtle way, each nation used the other as a flattering mirror of itself. At different times, the failure of one became proof of the success of the other.

In the Soviet Union, the turmoil of revolution was soon followed by the ravages of famine. When Lenin introduced the New Economic Policy (NEP) in 1921, however, and defined his new initiative as "state capitalism," most Americans perceived this move as a capitulation to the "natural forces" of capitalism. The prosperity that marked the United States economy during the 1920s made it easy for American capitalists to indulge in self-congratulation.

Ten years later, the tables had turned dramatically. By the early 1930s, the success of the first Soviet Five-Year Plan presented a striking contrast to the withering depression that was holding the American economy in its grip. To the Soviet leadership, this contrast was a convincing demonstration of what it had been claiming all along: capitalism carried within itself the seeds of its own destruction and communism constituted the wave of the future. The horror at the impoverishment of the American masses that was now expressed by many Russians paralleled the sentiments that Americans had expressed about the Soviet Union a decade earlier. As the debates over the need for greater state controls and discipline in the United States began to crystallize with the emergence of Franklin Delano Roosevelt's New Deal, Russians enjoyed pointing out its socialist inadequacies in much the same way that

Americans had earlier identified the capitalist shortcomings of Lenin's New Economic Policy. As Americans had used Russia to mirror their own achievements in the 1920s, so did Russians now use America as a yardstick of their successes in the 1930s. And both sides saw in themselves and in each other essentially only what they wanted to see.

These images still prevailed on the eve of diplomatic recognition in 1933. The establishment of diplomatic relations was a response to the dictates of *raison d'état* in both the political and the economic spheres. This chapter will present an analysis of the complex manner in which negative perceptions had to be reconciled with the need, based on realpolitik considerations on both sides, to take positive steps toward rapprochement.

AMERICANS VIEW THE NEW ECONOMIC POLICY AND RUSSIANS VIEW THE DEPRESSION

American views of Soviet Russia between the end of the war and the onset of the Great Depression tended to combine defensive outrage with arrogant self-righteousness. The material values of the prosperous "new era" of the twenties permeated most of American life and also conditioned perceptions of the Soviet Union. The views of most Americans, from the President down to the laborer, were a mixtue of prejudices and stereotypes that had been formed during the turbulent years of the Bolshevik Revolution. These attitudes lived on with a remarkable tenacity. Contradictory evidence and even dramatic new developments in the Soviet Union did little to change them. Rather, new facts were arranged into old categories. Only the profound and traumatic effects of the Great Depression forced Americans to look at themselves, and also at Soviet Russia, in a new and somewhat less one-dimensional light.

The election of Warren G. Harding to the presidency in 1920 marked the "return to normalcy" in the United States. In Soviet-American relations, President Harding continued the nonrecognition policy of his predecessor. His secretary of state, Charles Evans Hughes, insisted that he would have nothing to do with the Bolsheviks who had repudiated their lawful debts, refused to make reparations for confiscated American property, and fomented revolution abroad.

Most American public officials in the twenties praised themselves and attacked the Soviet system with equal vigor. Henry Ford was known at home and abroad as the spokesman for the new era's efficiency, innovation, and prosperity. The president of the National Association of Manufacturers stated in 1922: "Ours is a land of undreamed of opportunity such as none but a Christian civilization and the genius of democratic institutions could create."[1] Economic pride became synonymous with patriotism, and the United States was frequently referred to interchangeably with civilization. The American businessman ruled the new era with supreme confidence. His values guided government, defined success, and even affected religion. They were intensely material values, but with powerful Messianic overtones.

Bolshevik Russia was perceived as the antithesis of civilization. Senator Henry L. Myers of Montana, in a speech to the Senate on April 28, 1920, expressed quite accurately the views most of his countrymen held of the Bolsheviks:

They have utterly destroyed marriage, the home, the fireside, the family, the corner stones of all civilization, all society. They have undertaken to destroy what God created and ordained. They defy alike the will of God, the precepts of Christianity, the decrees of civilization, the customs of society. It is hard to realize that such things exist and are tolerated by the civilized world.[2]

Civilization, in the American view, had become a verbal basket into which all good things were thrown, while Bolshevism had come to connote the incarnation of all evil. Most Americans wanted to have nothing to do with such a brutal government, but many continued to hope, as they had done in Wilson's day, that the Russian people would get rid of their Bolshevik masters. As the Baltimore *Sun* editorialized in 1920: "The less we meddle, the sooner Russia will throw her pirates overboard." A small minority entertained the hope that capitalism would succeed where intervention had failed. Thus, the *Review of Reviews* suggested that "With outside pressures removed, and with opportunities restored for selling Russian wheat, flax, and other products and buying manufactured goods, Russia may become a sane country within a few years."[3] The dollar, it was hoped, would convert those who had been impervious to words and armies.

In March 1921, the Soviet Union abruptly changed direction.

---

[1] National Association of Manufacturers, *Proceedings of NAM*, Twenty-Seventh Annual Convention, May 8–10, 1922, p. 115.
[2] U.S. Congress, Senate, *Congressional Record*, 66th Cong., 2nd sess., April 28, 1920, p. 6208.
[3] "The Menace of Russian Propaganda," *Review of Reviews*, 61 (February 1920), 121.

Confronted with the threat of total economic breakdown, Lenin adopted the New Economic Policy, confessedly a "strategic retreat" from the radical economic programs of war communism. The Soviet premier instituted some capitalist incentives in order to rescue the economy from disaster. Among these were a measure of private trade, private property, and the abandonment of wage fixing. Lenin described the NEP in the famous formula "one step backward in order to take two steps forward."

Americans immediately saw in NEP the death of communism. As Senator Joseph I. France told *The New York Times* after a four-week tour through the Soviet Union: "Russia is reverting to capitalism inevitably, by the play of relentless natural forces."[4] Walter Duranty, the correspondent for *The New York Times,* reported the end of communism in the fall of 1921.[5] The *World's Work* declared that "Lenin has an astonishingly open mind for a fanatic and so he may learn the necessity for production by capitalistic methods."[6] Typical of this volte-face in American perceptions was the reaction of William H. King, Democratic senator from Utah. In 1919, he had told the Senate that "any man who support[ed] Bolshevism [was] an enemy of civilization." After returning from Russia in 1923, he informed the Senate that the Communists were firmly in power, but were rehabilitating the stricken nation with extraordinary success by resorting to good capitalist methods.[7] On the whole, Americans suddenly saw the birth of a new capitalist Russia. The Soviet leaders were succeeding because they had surrendered to capitalism and to American methods and values.

Shortly after the launching of NEP, a terrible famine descended on Russia which threatened more than 30 million people with a lingering death. Conditions became so desperate that Maxim Gorky, the world-renowned Russian writer, appealed to "all honest people" in Europe and America for aid. Encouraged by the NEP experiment and eager to help the new Soviet version of capitalism, the American people responded with enthusiasm. Secretary of Commerce Herbert Hoover was authorized to organize a massive relief program under the auspices of the American Relief Administration (ARA). Thus, in mid-1921, Hoover, a leading

---

[4] Joseph I. France, quoted in *The New York Times,* August 1, 1921.
[5] Walter Duranty, *The New York Times,* October 5, 1921.
[6] "For a Talk With Lenin," *World's Work* (February 1922), pp. 348–349.
[7] U.S. Congress, Senate, *Congressional Record,* 68th Cong., 1st sess., December 13, 1923, pp. 256–276.

spokesman for individualism and capitalism and a severe critic of the Bolsheviks, was directing a relief mission to the Soviet Union. The paradox resolves itself when one takes note of Hoover's statement made in 1921 that "American charity had planted the American flag in the hearts of all those little ones and it is a greater protection to the United States than any battleship."[8] In Hoover's opinion, the American dollar would succeed where Allied armies had failed in rescuing Russia from the Bolsheviks. Toward the end of the massive American relief effort, Colonel William N. Haskell, reporting to Hoover, said the following: "To the mind of the Russian common people, the American Relief Administration was a miracle of God which came to them in their darkest hour, under the Stars and Stripes. It turned the corner for civilization in Russia."[9] The American missionaries brought bread together with their creed. It was Manifest Destiny with a dollar sign.

Not surprisingly, the Bolshevik leaders regarded American charity with extreme ambivalence. The foreign loaf was feared almost as much as the foreign sword. Lenin had difficulty understanding why the United States would dispense charity to the Russian people while refusing to recognize their government. At frequent intervals during the relief program, Lenin accused the Americans of giving food to anti-Communist elements. The suspicion that the United States might have ulterior motives never left the Soviet leader's mind.

When Lenin died in 1924, America exulted. American editors described him as "another scourge of God," "the Judas of the real Russian revolution," and "one of the great wreckers of history." The *United Presbyterian* exclaimed: "The great beast has gone down into the pit! Glory be to God!"[10] Communism was dead. Capitalism and civilization had triumphed.

Americans were utterly unprepared for the eventuality that one day the tables might be turned, that the Soviet Union might be an economic success and that the United States might come close to economic disaster. The business spokesmen of the new era of the twenties overlooked the dangers in their basically economic definition of American success and Soviet failure. Julius H. Barnes,

---

[8] Herbert Hoover, in *The Saturday Evening Post* (April 30, 1921).
[9] Haskell to Hoover, August 28, 1923, cited in ARA, *Bulletin*, No. 41 (October 1923), 2–3.
[10] Quoted in Peter G. Filene, *Americans and the Soviet Experiment, 1917–1933* (Cambridge: Harvard University Press, 1967), p. 87.

president of the Chamber of Commerce in 1925, found it incredible that "a nation living just above the verge of utter barbarism attempts to instruct orderly America, busy with its expanded economic life and social opportunities, typified by its eighteen million automobiles and its towering skyscrapers."[11] The assumption was, of course, that until the Soviet Union had an equal number of automobiles and skyscrapers, it had no right to criticize the United States. But what if the Soviet Union should begin to approximate American material standards? What if the skyscrapers housed empty offices and no customers could be found for the automobiles? What if the boom of the twenties should bust? And what if the Soviet planned economy should boom?

By 1930, this was exactly what had happened. Herbert Hoover, now President, tried desperately to pull the United States out of the quicksands of depression. Unemployment was rampant. American government officials and business leaders began to look at the Soviet Union with fear. Russia was driving ahead to complete her first Five-Year Plan. The United States had no plan, but it had millions of unemployed. The United States–Soviet relationship, as if by some cruel trick of fate, had been turned upside down. America, the "New World," had suddenly become old and decadent, and the "new civilization" of the Soviet Union, inspired by Marxism-Leninism, was bestriding the world like a colossus. Many Americans began to demand economic planning and looked with envy at the Soviet Five-Year Plan. Others felt that the Soviet Union might be able to rescue American industry by placing large orders in the United States. The irony of the new situation was not lost on anyone.

The Soviet leadership now viewed the United States with new contempt. The Soviet press mocked Hoover's efforts to salvage the corpse of capitalism with traditional capitalist methods. Stalin referred to the 3 million unemployed in the United States as "the first swallows of an impending spring." In a speech to representatives of the American Communist party, he declared that the moment was not far off when a revolutionary crisis would develop in America that would be the beginning of the end of world capitalism. In an interview with Walter Duranty of *The New York Times* in late 1930, he predicted that the economic crisis in America would become much more severe. The depression had finally and fatally exposed capitalism's great weaknesses and inher-

---

[11] Julius H. Barnes, quoted in *Nation's Business* (November 1925). p. 20.

ent contradictions. Capitalism could not exist without markets. The mutual rivalry among capitalist states had created a situation in which each country endeavored to exclude all others from its own markets while gaining access to theirs. Militarization and war were bound to arise from this rivalry and finally bring about the self-destruction of the entire system.

Only one power, according to Stalin, stood aloof from this frenzied and violent competition for world markets. The Soviet Union did not have to resort to devious stratagems or armed force to maintain the growth of its economy, since it was independent of the contradictions of capitalism. By virtue of its example, the Soviet Union was showing the world that socialism was not only possible, but was the only way in which orderly progress could be achieved. As Stalin declared in his interview with *The New York Times*: "We will show the foreigners and the whole world that socialist production is possible and is growing and will succeed."[12]

Other Communist leaders echoed Stalin and showered the United States with their disdain. Politbureau member Lazar Kaganovich, in an address to the Ninth Congress of the Communist Youth League in 1931, reviewed the depression in America and compared it with progress in the Soviet Union. Bringing his audience "to the verge of hysterical laughter," he illustrated the capitalist contradictions of American life with the following words:

Even rich America, which thought it had found perpetual prosperity, is now so embarrassed by unemployment that a certain town recently decided to clear snow from its streets by men with shovels instead of with big machinery—to provide work for the unemployed. Whereupon one of the newspapers suggested that if providing work was what mattered, why not remove the snow with teaspoons and employ thousands more?[13]

One year later, Vyacheslav Molotov, in a speech delivered before the Seventeenth Party Congress, described as a "pillar of bourgeois society the famous American capitalist Al Capone." It was a mistake, Molotov insisted, to regard the Chicago gangster merely as a renegade and a criminal within a peaceful and law-abiding society. Capone was, rather, a major capitalist in his own right and a powerful figure in the American establishment. He was a criminal only by Communist, not by capitalist, standards:

---

[12] Joseph Stalin, quoted in *The New York Times*, December 1, 1930.
[13] Lazar Kaganovich, quoted in *The New York Times*, January 17, 1931.

Al Capone is a big capitalist, one of the pillars of bourgeois society, possessing numerous enterprises, and drawing huge revenues. From the American and European press, we learn that despite his relative youth—32 years—Al Capone has already made more than $700 million. In a word, this Chicago bandit is not one of the small fry of the capitalist world but one of the biggest capitalist sharks in the United States.[14]

Molotov concluded with the conviction that capitalism, with its Al Capones, was doomed, while the Soviet Union, with its shock brigades of socialism, was marching to complete victory.

The Soviet leadership did not confine its contempt to the American economy. No less emphatically, it held that American capitalism engendered a spiritual and cultural decay, of which the alleged toleration of criminals like Al Capone was only a symptom. Perhaps the most scathing indictment of the United States came from Maxim Gorky in 1932, who a decade earlier had appealed for American charity. In an open letter "to American intellectuals," Gorky described the "bourgeois intelligentsia" as "the nurse of the capitalist class." "The philosophical and ecclesiastical vestments of the bourgeoisie," Gorky declared, "that old and filthy fabric [was] thickly besmirched with the blood of the toiling masses. The intelligentsia has patched up with white stitches the soiled garment of capitalism." The doctrines of Marx and Lenin, in Gorky's view, were the only salutary antidotes against the poison of selfish Philistine American thought.

Gorky went on to criticize general American values with equal savagery. Americans, he pointed out, were fond of collecting "postage stamps and tramway tickets" rather than serious art. Science existed only insofar as it was able to serve the objectives of crass self-enrichment or to increase the sexual energies of bourgeois libertines. "Rotten bourgeois society, mad with hatred and panic [was] undermining culture in order to produce a rich crop of idiots who [would] be too stupid to recognize the monstrosity of the capitalist system."[15] In conclusion, the Soviet writer invited American intellectuals to join in the great task of creating a new proletarian way of life.

---

[14] V. Molotov, *The Second Five-Year Plan,* Speech to the Seventeenth Party Congress of the Communist Party of the Soviet Union (Moscow: Moscow Publishing House, 1932), p. 6.
[15] Maxim Gorky, quoted in Alexander Kaun, *Maxim Gorky and His Russia* (New York: Macmillan, 1931), *passim.*

As can be seen from the above, there was little that was tentative about Russian perceptions of the United States in the early 1930s. At the core, there was a profound contempt for decadent American values coupled with an orgy of self-congratulation on the occasion of the success of the Five-Year Plan. America, for most Russians, remained during her period of adversity a symbol for all that was evil and hostile to the advance of civilization. Similarly, the Soviet Union served as a mirror for the prejudices and fears of American capitalists. On both sides, the mirror was terribly distorted, reflecting only selected facts. The businessmen of the new era and the "social engineers" of the early thirties refused to see anything in it that they did not wish to see. The same was true of their Soviet counterparts. Thus, two missionaries with two mutually exclusive visions competed for the hearts and minds of their peoples. Little room for accommodation remained where two Manifest Destinies collided.

THE DECISION TO ESTABLISH DIPLOMATIC RELATIONS

"In the long run facts will control," said Henry Ford in June 1930.[16] These were prophetic words. Despite bitterly hostile perceptions on both sides, the United States and the Soviet Union decided to establish diplomatic relations in 1933. On each side, negative perceptions had to contend with hard, objective political and economic facts that clearly pointed in the direction of diplomatic recognition. Finally, after agonizing debate and self-examination, both sides decided to be on speaking terms with one another. Realpolitik had won.

In the United States of the early thirties, a vigorous debate raged over the issue of recognition. In almost every case, those who argued against recognition rested their case on distorted perceptions of the kind that we have described. Those who favored recognition, on the other hand, generally permitted new empirical evidence to influence their views.

First, there was the issue of the Bolshevik repudiation of debts amounting to approximately $650 million, and the Bolshevik seizure of private properties owned by American corporations and businessmen, amounting to $300 million. Many Americans felt that recognition would place the seal of approval on Soviet flouting of

---

[16] Henry Ford, "Why I Am Helping Russian Industry," *Nation's Business* (June 1930), p. 22.

contracts that were recognized under international law. "Soviet lies have made Russia's word as good as her bonds," observed the New York *Herald Tribune.* The Communists should recognize their financial obligations to the United States and begin to make some payments. If they showed no such evidence of good faith, the argument ran, continuation of the policy of nonrecognition was fully justified.

By 1933, however, the image of the Soviet Union as a "deadbeat debtor" nation no longer tallied with the facts. Actually, the Soviet government had recognized its legal obligations to the United States at a conference held in Genoa in 1922 but had made a counterclaim based on the damages caused by American troops during the military interventions in Siberia and northern Russia. The Genoa conference broke down because no agreement could be reached. By 1933, the depression had forced several nations, including France, to default on their debt payments to the United States, while Italy and Great Britain were making only token payments. There was the further problem that, if the Soviet Union would agree to reimburse the United States in full, it would then be haunted by other creditors to pay sums far beyond its capacity. Most important, during the twenties, the Soviet government had established an excellent reputation for honoring its financial obligations, and a number of American corporations, in negotiating new contracts for exports, had privately worked out reasonably satisfactory adjustments of their confiscation claims.

Second, there was the problem of Communist propaganda and subversion. The Communist party in the United States was viewed with extreme fear by many Americans. To extend formal recognition to the Soviet Union would enable it to open embassies and consulates from which to disseminate its subversive ideology. Supporters of recognition admitted that the presence of Communist propaganda in the United States was undesirable, but pointed out that nonrecognition would not stop such propaganda. The Communist party in the United States was in fact weak and torn by internal dissension. Moreover, even though a wide chasm of differences continued to persist in the political systems of the two societies, a degree of convergence had taken place between them in their economic forms of organization. After all, Russia had moved toward state capitalism under the NEP, and even under Stalin some private property and quasi-capitalist incentives continued to exist. In the meantime, under the New Deal, the United States had begun to move away from laissez-faire capitalism toward planning and a larger measure of governmental controls. Moreover, advocates of realpolitik pointed out that the rising danger of Nazism in Germany and of militarism in Japan were in themselves potent arguments for recognition. Russia and America might have to learn to live together in order to defend themselves against Germany and Japan.

Third, the image of the "godless" Bolshevik persisted. The official atheism of the Soviet government continued to shock millions of religious Americans. The *Literary Digest,* for example, reported in 1923 that, during atheistic celebrations in Moscow, young men dressed as devils danced around burning effigies of Jesus, Moses, and Mohammed.[17] Related to the image of the godless Bolshevik was that of the "free-loving" Bolshevik who had abolished the sacrament of marriage and nationalized Russian womanhood to satisfy his degraded lust.

The facts again were quite different. While it was true that atheism was the official dogma of the Soviet Union, this dogma had lost much of its militancy by the thirties. The Russian Orthodox Church was not persecuted by the government. Rather, it was used by it as an additional vehicle of political control. While there were still considerable outcroppings of anti-Semitism, there was little evidence of persecution of Christians and Moslems who chose to practice their faith. So far as the government's attitude toward the family was concerned, the days of free love were definitely over by Stalin's time. If anything, Russia of the thirties had become almost Victorian in its sexual mores and laws governing marriage and divorce. Few Americans of the "jazz age" of the twenties would have felt comfortable in the Soviet Union at the time of the first Five-Year Plan.

Fourth, the distinction between the Russian people and their Communist masters persisted with remarkable tenacity in the minds of many Americans. The point was frequently made that the Soviets had established not a dictatorship *of* the proletariat, but a dictatorship *over* the proletariat. The Bolsheviks had never permitted a free election, and to recognize them would blast the hopes of Russian liberals who might be the torchbearers of true democracy. The assumption here was that the Communist regime was transient and unstable; to establish diplomatic relations with it would bestow a legitimacy on it that might well give it a permanence it did not deserve.

---

[17] *Literary Digest* (April 14, 1923).

The facts again presented a different picture by 1933. The Soviet government, despite intervention, famine, and catastrophe, had nevertheless been able to maintain itself in power. Not only had it weathered terrible storms but it was well on the way toward making Russia into one of the leading industrial powers of the world. While it was true that the Soviet Union was a dictatorship that had used extremely oppressive methods, especially during the years of forced collectivization, by the early thirties many Soviet citizens exhibited great national pride and a measure of genuine loyalty to their government. In 1930, approximately 10,000 Americans visited the Soviet Union.[18] Most of them, upon their return, talked about the vigor of the Soviet state and the impressive advances made under the Five-Year Plan. As the *Ohio State Journal* put it rather plaintively: "One of the most annoying things about Soviet Russia is that she is still managing to get along."

Finally, there was the question of trade. Many leading Americans accused the Soviets of using forced and convict labor in their production system and of then dumping their products on the American market in order to destroy the economy. In July 1930, for example, Assistant Secretary of the Treasury Seymour Lowman prohibited the entry of a shipment of Soviet paper pulpwood, claiming that it had been made by convict labor. To protect the American economy, the assistant secretary banned the pulpwood and proposed an investigation of Soviet manganese ore, coal, and timber on similar grounds.[19] In September 1930, Secretary of Agriculture Arthur M. Hyde accused the Soviets of selling short 7.5 million bushels of wheat in Chicago in order to depress American wheat prices and thereby sabotage the market. Hyde's announcement provoked a near panic. The charge turned out to be completely false. In a Senate bill proposing an embargo on all Soviet goods produced by convict labor, the following phrase appeared: "We see the beautiful structure of our civilization built so lovingly by those who made our great nation blasted, torn apart, and consumed by the collective labor of the USSR."[20]

On the other hand, trade was a powerful argument in favor of recognition for those who looked at the facts. The Soviet Union

---

[18] *Fortune* (March 1932).
[19] *The New York Times,* July 26, 1930.
[20] U.S. Congress, Senate, *Congressional Record,* 71st Cong., 3rd sess., February 27, 1931, p. 6231.

offered a huge potential for American markets. In 1933, the Soviet foreign minister talked of placing orders abroad for $1 billion. Obviously Britain and France, who had extended recognition, would receive the major share of these orders unless the United States followed suit. Not only would manufacturers and merchants benefit from such increased trade, but new jobs would be created for tens of thousands of unemployed Americans languishing on government relief rolls. As the El Paso *Herald* quipped in 1931: "A dangerous Red is any Russian who appears in America without placing an order for machinery." In short, recognition would be mutually profitable: the United States needed the Russian market, and Soviet Russia needed American goods.

A survey of opinion polls in the United States during the early thirties showed a sharp trend toward recognition. A State Department analysis of editorials in 183 newspapers undertaken in March 1931 revealed only 13 percent in favor of recognition and 63 percent against any change in diplomatic policy. In October 1933, just before recognition, the Committee on Russian-American Relations of the American Foundation published the results of a questionnaire that had been sent to more than 1,100 newspapers. In this questionnaire 63 percent of the editors favored, and only 27 percent opposed, recognition. The evidence suggests that, during the two-and-a-half-year interval between the two surveys, a drastic change in American opinion had occurred.

Any analysis of this dramatic shift must remain impressionistic. It is highly probable, however, that the bitter opening years of the thirties made most Americans more receptive to new facts and more critical of old prejudices and misperceptions. Men do not abandon stereotypes through rational analysis but through trauma and catastrophe. The Great Depression was such a catastrophe.

On the Soviet side, old cliché-ridden perceptions of the United States also vied with the dictates of realpolitik, but in their own peculiar way. On the one hand, few official statements emanating from the Soviet Union that referred to the United States failed to invoke the usual epithets. The American "ruling classes" were variously described as imperialists, Wall Street sharks, oppressors, plunderers, and criminals. On the other hand, the Soviets wanted American capital, provided they could get it on favorable terms. They wanted trade in order to import those goods that Russia desperately needed. They wanted diplomatic recognition in order to facilitate the extension of credits and the development of

Soviet-American trade and—amazingly and paradoxically enough —for prestige in the community of capitalist states.

This curious ambivalence had been typical of the Soviet government's attitude since 1917. Neither Lenin nor Stalin ever had anything good to say about the United States, but both consistently worked toward, in fact demanded, diplomatic recognition from a regime they had vowed utterly to destroy. Both the negative perceptions as well as the objective needs for diplomatic relations persisted over the years. The resulting schizophrenic attitude of the Soviet government on the matter of recognition has been captured by George F. Kennan in his own paraphrase of Soviet policy toward the United States:

We despise you. We consider that you should be swept from the earth as a government and physically destroyed as individuals. We reserve the right, in our private if not in our official capacities, to do what we can to bring this about: to revile you publicly, to do everything within our power to detach your own people from their loyalty to you and their confidence in you, to subvert your armed forces, and to work for your downfall in favor of a Communist dictatorship. But since we are not strong enough to destroy you today—since an interval must unfortunately elapse before we can give you the *coup de grace*—we want you during this interval to trade with us; we want you to finance us; we want you to give us the advantages of full-fledged diplomatic recognition. . . . An outrageous demand? Perhaps. But you will accept it nevertheless. You will accept it because you are not free agents, because you are slaves to your capitalistic appetites, because where profit is involved, you have no pride, no principles, no honor. In the blindness that characterizes declining and perishing classes, you will wink at our efforts to destroy you. . . . Driven by this competition which you cannot escape, you will do what we want you to do until such time as we are ready to make an end of you. It is in fact *you* who will, through your own cupidity, give *us* the means wherewith to destroy you.[21]

In addition to the economic facts, some hard political facts convinced Stalin that rapprochement with the United States had become a necessity by the early thirties. The Japanese seizure of Manchuria in 1931 threatened Soviet Russia on her eastern flank. The memory of Japanese intervention during the civil war made

---

[21] George F. Kennan, *Russia and the West Under Lenin and Stalin* (Boston: Little, Brown, 1961), pp. 184–185.

the Soviet leadership doubly apprehensive. In addition, the rise of Hitler in Germany and his repeated anti-Bolshevik utterances posed an ever more menacing threat from the West. Russia had to de-emphasize, perhaps even postpone, the export of revolution and, like any other national state, had to seek allies. In the emerging power balance of the thirties, America seemed a logical nation with which a partial détente might be both desirable and profitable.

Thus, by 1933 the stage was set for mutual recognition, even though negative perceptions persisted on both sides and continued to live on in a twilight world of their own. Most Americans continued to hate the Soviets for what they thought they *did;* and most Russians continued to hate Americans for what they thought they *were.*

While reality thus triumphed over misperception, distorted images continued to have a residual effect. They made it very difficult for a genuine modus vivendi to develop between America and Russia during the thirties. Had one been achieved, it might have made possible a common front against the Axis powers *before* the cataclysm of World War II forced the two superpowers to become close—though temporary—allies.

One cannot help but wonder how different the world might have been if the Soviet Union and the United States had been able to work together effectively during the 1930s to stem the rise of the Axis powers and thereby to prevent the calamities that followed. Undoubtedly, the residual spillover of the old clichés worked to prevent such genuine collaboration. Even during the "grand alliance" of World War II, there never was complete trust between Americans and Russians. There never emerged a supreme command as under Marshal Foch in 1918. The Soviet Union and the United States essentially waged two separate wars against the Axis. Each fought the common enemy in its own way. They were quasi-allies, rather than full-fledged allies. Thus, the old misperceptions still took their toll. They compounded the difficulties besetting the grand alliance and contributed to its eventual disintegration. No doubt they hastened the coming of the cold war and the tragic confrontations of the postwar world.

ten

THE COLD WAR SPIRAL: GERMANY AND THE DIVISION OF EUROPE

The victory of the Allies over Nazi Germany also marked the beginning of a new conflict: the cold war. Much has been written about this tragic development and of the manner in which the positions of the two superpowers gradually hardened and ultimately congealed into a posture of relentless hostility. But little has been done to ascertain how much of this process was determined by the power realities of the times and how much by the images that the two superpowers held of themselves and of each other. These perceptions had powerful operational consequences in the policies that led directly to the cold war.

In order to analyze Soviet perceptions of the United States at the end of the war, we must first ascertain the role played by ideology in the overall Soviet cognitive view of itself and of the United States. Then we must determine the degree to which these ideological "lenses" yielded a distorted picture.

There is no doubt that Stalin's perception of the United States at the end of the war was colored, to some extent, by Marxist-Leninist ideology. But a perusal of his policies suggests that ideology alone did not prompt him to join or to break any alliance that he would not have joined or broken on the grounds of pragmatic considerations of national interest. There are indications, however, that in some cases ideology retarded or speeded up the change. Certainly Marxism-Leninism compounded the difficulties besetting the grand alliance during World War II and contributed to its disintegration; no Communist nation could conceive of a permanent alliance with the leading capitalist power. This residual quality of ideology no doubt hastened the coming of the cold war.

One leading scholar of Soviet foreign policy has expressed this well:

The Marxist-Leninist tradition has made it very difficult to reach a *modus vivendi* with the Soviets which the Americans have been genuinely anxious to do. A belief in the inherently aggressive tendencies of modern capitalism obviously excludes any agreement except an armed truce of undetermined duration. Likewise, the acceptance of the Leninist theory makes it almost impossible to believe in the friendly intentions of American leaders.[1]

To Stalin, then, Marxism-Leninism was an instrument for ordering and comprehending reality, but it was not the *only* instrument. There were also considerations of realpolitik. After all,

In the Second World War the Soviets could scarcely have permitted their Anglo-American partners to extend Western influence into all sections of the power vacuum created by the Axis defeat. American expansion in both Europe and Asia has often been hesitant and reluctant. Nevertheless the war ended with an American general in Berlin and another in Tokyo. This the Soviets could hardly afford to neglect.[2]

On balance, it is likely that the residual effect of Communist ideology was powerful enough to preclude in Stalin's mind more than a transitory alliance with the United States.

It is tempting to explain American policy toward the Soviet Union during and after World War II purely in terms of reaction to the ideologically conditioned expansionary moves of the Soviet Union. Yet here again we must beware of the pitfall of the single-factor analysis. No doubt there is much truth in such an interpretation of American policies, but it explains only part of the picture. It is quite clear, for example, that World War II had broadened the United States' definition of its strategic interests. Soon after hostilities had ended in Europe, the entire North Atlantic, from the Azores to Iceland and Greenland, had come within the sphere of American influence. And as a result of the occupation of Japan, the Pacific was transformed into what was virtually an American strategic lake. Indeed, World War II had created several power vacuums that the United States had decided to fill long before the cold war actually crystallized.

---

[1] Barrington Moore, Jr., *Soviet Politics—The Dilemma of Power* (Cambridge: Harvard University Press, 1950), p. 392.
[2] *Ibid.*

However, it is nevertheless clear that the United States' reaction to Stalin's perception of America as a predatory capitalist power contributed to the coming of the cold war. President Roosevelt had remarked at Yalta that two years would be the limit for keeping American troops in Europe. But shortly before his death, on March 24, 1945, when handed a cable from Stalin, "he banged his fists on the arms of his wheelchair and said: "Averell [Harriman] is right; we can't do business with Stalin. He has broken every one of the promises he made at Yalta."[3] Roosevelt, and Truman after him, were quite bewildered by the Soviet portrayal of the United States as an inherently aggressive nation. So deep was the disparity between the image and reality that the American leaders could only conclude that Soviet ideology could not possibly represent a truly held conviction. It must be a screen for political cynicism and a deliberate distortion of reality by men who lusted for world domination. In short, ideology, which for the Soviet leaders served as an instrument for comprehending reality, was perceived by the Americans as a deliberate smokescreen for Soviet imperialist ambitions. As President Truman put it at the signing of the North Atlantic Treaty in 1949:

We are like a group of householders . . . who decide to express their community of interests by entering into a formal association for their mutual self-protection. . . . We have no purpose of aggression against others. To suggest the contrary is to slander our institutions and defame our ideals.[4]

Thus, the impasse had become complete. By 1949, the cold war had begun to assume the proportions of a struggle between two competing theologies. It had passed out of the realm of ambiguity into a period of moral clichés based on absolute definitions of good and evil that were to blight relations between the superpowers for over a decade. Out of the syndrome of forces responsible for the origins of the cold war, perception played a major role. Stalin no doubt perceived the United States as more hostile toward the Soviet Union than it actually was, and the United States, failing to grasp this fact, reacted to Soviet actions first with misgivings, then with anxiety, and finally with outright hostility. Thus, perception and counterperception clearly had

---

[3] Franklin D. Roosevelt, quoted in Arthur Schlesinger, Jr., "Origins of the Cold War," *Foreign Affairs* (October 1967), p. 24.
[4] Harry S Truman, White House Press Release, April 4, 1949.

operational consequences on policy. The effects of these perceptions on policy, however, were different in the Soviet Union and the United States. President Roosevelt believed, at least until early 1945, that a long-range accommodation with the Soviet Union was possible. Stalin, on the other hand, partially conditioned by his ideological views, believed in no more than an armed truce of fairly short duration.

The impact of perception on policy became particularly pronounced, of course, after the reciprocal cold war images of mutually hostile intent had become firmly embedded in the minds of American and Soviet leaders. This had occurred by the late 1940s. Hence, to highlight the perception factor, our case study is drawn from the cold war period itself: United States–Soviet interaction over the rearmament of Germany between 1949 and 1955.

In 1949, both superpowers were still apprehensive about their former enemy. For both, Germany had been a formidable antagonist, defeated only recently and at great cost; and at Potsdam, both had solemnly agreed that under no circumstances was Germany to be rearmed.

The original American commitment to the North Atlantic Treaty Organization (NATO) called for no German participation, nor did it envisage a major commitment of American resources. NATO only "formally registered a widespread belief . . . which had crystallized during the Berlin blockade, that Soviet encroachment could be prevented only if the United States associated herself . . . *before* the outbreak of war, with the efforts of Western European nations to defend themselves."[5] Official United States policy held that the Western European nations in NATO, given a moderate degree of additional American aid, had time to create the necessary defensive forces on their own. German participation was considered neither necessary nor desirable.

Within American policy circles, however, this stance was viewed with serious misgivings. By 1949, the Soviet threat already appeared great in the eyes of many American leaders. Secretary of State Dean Acheson, for example, was privately convinced that German military participation in NATO would ultimately be necessary. So, too, were key American military leaders. The Army Joint War

---

[5] Robert Osgood, *NATO: The Entangling Alliance* (Chicago: University of Chicago Press, 1962), p. 28.

Plans Branch had already drawn up a plan for Western defense in which the incorporation of several German divisions in NATO was regarded as essential.[6] Not until late in 1950, however, was the United States government able to act publicly upon its private convictions, for to have done so earlier would have been to risk wrecking the NATO alliance itself.

In 1950, the Western European nations still perceived the Soviet threat quite differently from the United States. Germany still ranked high, or even higher, on the scale of perceived threats than did the Soviet Union. For the United States, however, the Soviet threat had well outdistanced that of Germany. This "perceptual deadlock" was only broken by the outbreak of the Korean War. Korea united the alliance in its collective assessment of the Soviet threat, for the United States was not alone in its belief that the North Korean invasion had been Soviet-inspired or in its fears that Korea might be a herald of Soviet aggression in Europe. Most NATO Allies agreed. Korea thus "precipitated the first—and only serious attempt to create the forces . . . for withstanding a Soviet attack in Europe."[7]

The United States seized the opportunity to press the other NATO nations to agree to a new policy toward Germany. At the Three-Power Foreign Ministers' Conference in New York in September 1950, the United States offered to comply with two of the Europeans' most pressing demands: to assign an American as the Supreme Commander of an integrated NATO command, and to increase substantially its troop commitment to Europe. In return, the Europeans were to consent to the incorporation into the NATO command of some ten or twelve armed German divisions.

This proposal was greeted with considerable ambivalence by the European NATO members, now caught in a painful conflict between old fears of Germany and newly enhanced fears of the Soviet Union. The effort to resolve this conflict gave rise to the ill-fated plans for a European Defense Community (EDC). While the long debate over the EDC delayed the rearmament of Germany for five years, the Allies did agree in 1950 to the principle of German military participation in NATO and to the relaxation of restrictions on German industrial production.

---

[6] Lawrence W. Martin, "The American Decision to Rearm Germany," in Harold Stein (ed.), *American Civil-Military Decisions* (Birmingham: University of Alabama Press, 1963), pp. 648–649.

[7] Osgood, *op. cit.*, p. 68.

If, from the American point of view, the new German policy was dictated by the necessities of self-defense, the Soviets saw the proposal in a radically different light. By ending the state of war with Germany without Soviet consent, the United States had clearly violated the Potsdam agreement, and by proposing the rearmament of Germany, it had shown its true intent: to "use Western Germany, its manpower and material resources . . . behind which are the aspirations of the USA ruling circles for world supremacy."[8] The decision to lift the limits on German steel production only proved the point in the Soviet view: "The true meaning of the New York communiqué is that now the heavy industry of the Ruhr is openly being adjusted to meet the Western Powers' military strategic war tasks."[9] So obvious was this motivation, the Soviets concluded, that NATO statements of purely defensive objectives were an insult to their intelligence. If the United States really sought to demonstrate good faith, it ought to return to the German policy decided upon in 1945 at Potsdam. The USSR then proposed a new Four-Power Conference to discuss such a return, but the United States, convinced of *Soviet* bad faith, opposed it unless the agenda also included the problem of East-West tensions in general. The Soviets took the rejection as the expected endorsement of their original conviction. Both sides were thus entrenched in their belief of the other's insincerity.

It is fruitless to ask at this point whether either side was sincere in its offers, either before or after 1950. The tragedy of the cold war lay precisely in the fact that its defining characteristic was so total an attitude of distrust that any serious diplomatic effort at a compromise was rendered impossible. The attitude itself, to be sure, was intangible and subjective. Out of it, however, grew the concrete reality of a divided Germany.

The hardening process took some five years from beginning to end. In December 1950, the NATO Council agreed to the principle of German participation in an integrated European military force. On July 9, 1951, the United States, Britain, and France formally

---

[8] Statement by the foreign ministers of the USSR, German Democratic Republic, Poland, Czechoslovakia, Hungary, Rumania, Bulgaria, and Albania in Prague, October 21, 1950, in Beate Ruhn von Oppen (ed.), *Documents on Germany Under Occupation 1945–54* (London, New York, Toronto: Oxford University Press, Royal Institute of International Affairs, 1955), p. 523.
[9] *Ibid.*

ended the state of war with Germany. In May 1952, the Bonn Convention was signed between the three Western powers and the Federal Republic of Germany, revoking the Occupation Statute and abolishing the High Commission. Simultaneously, the Pleven Plan for the European Defense Community was inching forward to ratification. EDC's inception, it was hoped, would create a European army of mixed nationalities, including German officers and troops.

Each of these steps was seen from the Soviet side as a confirmation of the USSR's worst expectations. The "imperialist warmongers" were proceeding on schedule, increasing the "aggressive" North Atlantic Treaty's military capability, absorbing Western Germany into their sphere of influence, and recreating a German army—all in the name of "defense." The Soviet Union tried several times to stop these developments. Its diplomatic overtures, however, were unable to satisfy what the United States regarded as the basic requirements for European security. In American eyes, these efforts appeared cynical plays for time by the Soviets and were accordingly rejected.

On the issue of German reunification, the United States insisted on free all-German elections as a prerequisite. The Soviet Union rejected this proposal for fear of losing East Germany. Its counteroffer, embodied in the Grotewohl Proposal of November 1950, called for the establishment of an all-German Constituent Council with equal representation from East and West Germany. This council was then to prepare for the formation of a provisional all-German government to consult with the four powers on a peace treaty. Only then was it to organize all-German elections.[10]

The United States in turn rejected the equal representation proviso in the Soviet proposal, for should only a few of the Western representatives vote with those of East Germany, the East would have been able to control the entire council. In September 1951, the Soviet Union dropped this proviso and offered to give free elections priority over a peace treaty in the council's tasks. The new Soviet condition stipulated that "all democratic parties and organizations" were to have the right to submit lists of candidates and to form election blocs.[11] The United States,

---

[10] Heinrich Siegler, *The Reunification and Security of Germany* (Bonn: Siegler and Company, 1957), p. 83.
[11] *Ibid.*

fearing that the Soviet definition of democratic parties and organizations would differ irreconcilably from its own, also rejected this proposal.

At the base of this diplomatic impasse lay the superpowers' utter distrust of each other's *intent*. There is a certain irony in the Soviet Union's repeated demand that the Allies return to the German policy decided upon at Potsdam, for *objectively* speaking, the Potsdam agreements had constituted a satisfactory settlement in 1945. Their viability five years later, however, depended upon one vital *subjective* factor: each superpower had to have confidence that the other would not attempt the absorption into its own orbit of the whole of a reunified Germany. By 1950, that confidence was precisely what was lacking. Hence, no diplomatic formula, however ingenious, could be devised.

Meanwhile, the fate of Germany was being decisively altered by the development of the Pleven Plan. It was hoped that by the creation of an international army and the mixing of officers and troops of different nationalities under a unified command, German armed power might be so effectively interwoven with that of the other members that its disturbing implications would be minimized. In February 1952, Bonn approved the EDC proposal, with the condition, however, that Germany would have to be accepted within the community as a sovereign and equal partner. Since the EDC idea not only satisfied the United States' sense of urgency over strengthening NATO, but also went far to allay its fear of an independent German army, the quid pro quo demanded by Bonn seemed acceptable in American eyes. Thus, the seeds of a separate West Germany were sown by America's fear of the Soviet Union.

To the USSR, EDC looked ominous, for it foreshadowed the incorporation of West Germany into the NATO alliance. In an effort to forestall this development, the Soviet Union in 1952 offered to consider several new concessions on the issue of German reunification. On March 10, it accepted the American demand for the guarantee of democratic rights to all Germans. In a dramatic reversal of its earlier stand, the Soviet Union even offered to allow Germany an independent armed force sufficient for the requirements of national defense.[12] In a subsequent note on April 9, it also accepted for the first time the principle of free all-German elections, subject to supervision by a commission made up of

---

[12] *Ibid.,* pp. 84–85.

representatives of the four powers.[13] As a vital part of this settlement, however, Germany was to pledge not to join any alliance directed against any member of the anti-Hitler coalition.[14] This, of course, meant NATO, which the Soviets maintained was directed solely against them.

American distrust, however, was by now too firmly entrenched. Given the conviction of hostile Soviet intent, the new proposal seemed fraught with dangers. Compared with the proposed EDC, the United States declared, the Soviet proposal for limited German national forces was a "step backward" in the search for peaceful cooperation.[15] Nor was the abstention of a reunified Germany from all military coalitions acceptable. In American eyes, the USSR would attempt to absorb all of Germany, and without German resources, NATO would be seriously weakened. Hence, the United States responded that any all-German government must be free to join any alliance whose objectives were compatible with the principles of the United Nations.[16]

Stalin's death in March 1953 was followed by some Soviet gestures of accommodation, but these were seen merely as a cunning new tactic. In the words of General Alfred M. Gruenther, then Supreme Allied Commander, they were no more than "a confidence game."[17]

Subsequent diplomatic efforts foundered upon this rock of mutual suspicion. The Berlin Conference of Foreign Ministers in 1954 failed to break the deadlock over Germany despite certain modifications of the Western stand included in the new Eden Plan. Shortly thereafter, the Soviet Union amazed the Western powers with a startling proposal. On March 31, 1954, the USSR announced that it intended to apply for membership in NATO. The Soviets argued that if NATO were indeed a true collective security pact, and not a closed alliance directed specifically against the Soviet Union, the Western powers could have no excuse for excluding the USSR. If, on the other hand, they did in fact deny the Soviet application, their real intentions would be unmasked. The American reaction was one of stunned disbelief, although

---

[13] Werner Feld, *Reunification and West German-Soviet Relations* (The Hague: Martinus Nijhoff, 1963), p. 106.
[14] Siegler, *op. cit.*
[15] Feld, *op. cit.*, pp. 132–133.
[16] *Ibid.*
[17] Alfred M. Gruenther, quoted in *The New York Times*, September 1, 1953.

among Western diplomats in Moscow, there were some who held that the Soviets were actually serious. A new realization among the Soviet leaders of the perils of atomic warfare, these observers maintained, had caused a genuine reassessment of the world situation, a clearer grasp of the dangers of war in a world of nuclear weapons, and a determination to avoid such a holocaust.[18]

The State Department, however, declared that it had "no evidence" that Moscow was "sincere" in seeking an end to the cold war. The Soviet Union, it said, was trying instead to recover from its failure at the Berlin Conference to "undermine Western security."[19]

The United States thus rejected the Soviet bid out of hand. When criticized by other NATO nations for acting precipitously and without consulting its allies, the United States defended its behavior by stating that it had "wanted to avoid any impression that the proposals were getting the slightest consideration."[20]

Sincere or not, the USSR came out ahead in the episode. Those Soviet policy makers who believed their own statements about the United States could now draw psychological support from the fact that NATO had "proved" its true intentions. Those who were more cynical could use the rejection as excellent propaganda. At any rate, the Soviet Union charged that the State Department "was so fearful of a possible positive reaction by Western Europe to the Soviet's NATO proposal that [it] did not wait to get a full text before issuing a negative commentary."[21] The harsh tone of this statement, of course, only hardened the United States' conviction of *Soviet* hostility.

The USSR then presented yet another proposal for a European settlement. Declaring that the EDC project was leading to a threat to European security in the form of a revival of German militarism, the Soviets proposed a new and wider conference toward an all-European security pact along the lines of Locarno. Pending a final reunification settlement, *both* Germanies were to be included in the agreement, while all parties were to renounce the use of force as a means for resolving disputes.

This new initiative was rejected by the United States as another

[18] *The New York Times,* April 2, 1954.
[19] Quoted in *The New York Times,* April 3, 1954.
[20] Quoted in *The New York Times,* April 4, 1954.
[21] *Ibid.*

Soviet effort to undermine the Western defense system.[22] The American press characterized the Soviet offer as a ruse, a transparent maneuver, or as a baited trap. Instead of dissuading the United States from its policy of German rearmament, the Soviet proposal produced the opposite effect. The United States took it as a signal to intensify the pressure for the ratification of EDC.

At this point, however, the four-year agony of the EDC proposal was drawing to a close. In August 1954, after one of the most tumultuous sessions in French parliamentary history, it went down to defeat. The State Department was dismayed, for the defeat of EDC also destroyed four years of American policy toward Germany. After four years of delicate diplomacy, the death of EDC appeared to put NATO right back in its vulnerable state of 1950. Since the USSR appeared as menacing as ever, it now seemed preferable to embark upon a possibly more dangerous course with respect to Germany than to allow the situation to drift further:

The real answer lies in the immediate admission of West Germany to the North Atlantic Treaty Organization. . . . Either the Germans are to be trusted or the Communists will rule Central Europe. . . . Germany can be trusted as long as she retains a republican form of government . . . with the E.D.C. out of the way, the decks have been cleared for action on an alternative—returning Germany to an independent position in Europe. It's a chance to take, but not nearly as dangerous a chance as leaving Europe at the mercy of Soviet Russia today.[23]

The admission of West Germany to NATO was, of course, precisely what the Soviets wanted above all to prevent. The defeat of EDC was greeted in the Soviet Union with pleasure and relief. On October 6, Molotov declared that the USSR stood ready to discuss any new proposals. Its only condition was that the EDC was not to be replaced by an alternative project for remilitarizing Germany.[24] In American eyes, however, this condition was unacceptable, for if a sovereign Germany were *not* armed and brought into the Western defense system, it was regarded as far too likely to be attracted to the East.[25]

---

[22] The New York Times, November 15, 1954.
[23] Quoted in the New York Herald Tribune, August 31, 1954.
[24] Siegler, op. cit., p. 87.
[25] The New York Times, August 31, 1954.

This made the vicious circle complete, for if the American goal *were* in fact attained, the Soviet Union could only regard this as clear-cut confirmation of its longstanding conviction that the United States would stop at nothing to implement its hostility toward the USSR.

An alternative plan for German rearmament was indeed advanced by the United States. By October 23, 1954, barely two months after the defeat of EDC, the Paris Agreements, providing for the revision and expansion of the Western European Union (WEU) to include Germany, were drawn up and signed. The Three-Power Occupation of Western Germany was formally ended, and the Bonn republic became a fully sovereign state in all matters save those pertaining to Berlin and the final peace treaty. West Germany was to proceed to equip twelve conventional divisions that were to be incorporated into the structure of the Western European Union. WEU in turn was accepted by the NATO Council as part of the North Atlantic Treaty system.

The Soviets reacted strongly: "These decisions . . . have been dictated by the aggressive circles of power striving for world dominion on the basis of pursuing the notorious policy of strength."[26] They warned that the ratification of the Paris Agreements would create an entirely new situation in Europe, perhaps postponing indefinitely the final reunification of Germany. In its effort to prevent such ratification, the Soviet Union, in October 1954, strongly intimated that the all-German free elections, so long demanded by the United States, might in fact be held in 1955 if plans to remilitarize Germany were abandoned.[27] This offer was repeated in January and again in February 1955.[28]

It was too late, however. German reunification was now relegated to second place in American priorities. Overriding all else was the imperative of NATO defense. First, the Soviets' urging that a conference to discuss their proposal be convened in the fall of 1954 was taken not as a sign of anxiety but as proof of insincerity, for as Secretary of State Dulles remarked, "the Soviets knew very well that such high-level conferences could not be prepared on such short notice."[29] Molotov accordingly proposed a delay—on

---

[26] Quoted in *The New York Times,* October 24, 1954.
[27] Siegler, *op. cit.,* pp. 87–88.
[28] *Ibid.,* p. 88.
[29] U.S. State Department, Press Release, No. 648, November 16, 1954.

the condition that the Paris Agreements not be ratified until the conference had taken place. The United States saw this condition as the real objective: to paralyze Western defense.

The USSR, for its part, saw the United States' *rejection* as its real objective—to let nothing prevent the Americans from reviving a Wehrmacht

intended to serve imperialist circles not only as an instrument in their plans of aggression but also as the gendarme of Western Europe. . . . The adherents of so-called negotiations from a position of strength base their arguments on mental acrobatics. . . . They assert that they want negotiations in order to ensure peace and security. And with this aim in view they intend to revive the Wehrmacht which undermines peace. . . . They assert that they wish to settle the German problem. And with this aim in view they intend to revive the Wehrmacht which will prevent a peaceful settlement of the German problem.[30]

Events now moved steadily to a denouement. On May 5, 1955, the Western powers ratified the Bonn Convention, granting sovereignty to the Federal Republic and recognizing Bonn as the sole legal representative of the German people. On May 9, Germany was officially admitted to NATO. The Soviet reaction was to call the Warsaw East Bloc Conference in May 1955, which concluded a multilateral alliance forging the military capacities of the Eastern bloc into the structure of a "Soviet NATO."

The United States had maintained from the beginning that NATO had been created to meet a clear-cut menace. The USSR now maintained just as stoutly that the Warsaw Pact had been dictated by the threat to its security. "The Warsaw Treaty was forced upon us," declared Nikolai Bulganin in November 1955. "It was the result of the position of the Western states, and we are ready to renounce it when a system of European security is created and the Western powers will part with the North Atlantic Treaty and Paris Agreements."[31] No other course was possible any longer.

---

[30] Statement by Polish Premier Cyrankiewicz at the first session of Moscow Conference, November 29, 1954, Polish Embassy, Press Release, No. 87, December 6, 1954.

[31] Nikolai Bulganin quoted in Kazimierz Grzybowski, *The Socialist Commonwealth of Nations—Organizations and Institutions* (New Haven and London: Yale University Press, 1964), p. 183.

"When military blocs are set up against us, when our countries are surrounded by military bases and when atomic war threats are made, we cannot remain idle."[32] A leading American newspaper retorted that "it cannot be too firmly driven home that Russian conquest of neighboring states preceded and provoked NATO; that the Russian advanced bases in Central Europe preceded and necessitated NATO's base system."[33]

The Warsaw Pact was not the innovation in the military relations of the Soviet bloc that NATO had been in those of the West. The Soviet Union had long had bilateral treaties of mutual assistance with Czechoslovakia, Poland, Rumania, Hungary, and Bulgaria; and other bilateral treaties had been in existence among the Eastern European states.[34] The 1955 pact thus only formalized what had been a reality for several years. It did, however, add one new element. The original pact excluded East Germany; but after one more inconclusive conference on Germany at Geneva in 1955, an East Bloc conference was held at Prague in January 1956, which provided for the establishment of an East German army and its subsequent inclusion in the structure of the Warsaw alliance.

Thus, the division of Germany was sealed by policies that had their roots in the superpowers' fear of one another's hostile intent. While fears and divergent perceptions are intangible, they tend to set limits to the range of policy alternatives. In the case of Germany, genuine compromise and accommodation were beyond those limits.

In retrospect, the tragic element in this development is plain. But the question remains, as Arthur Schlesinger, Jr., has put it, whether it was an example of Greek tragedy, "the tragedy of necessity," where the feeling aroused in the spectator is "what a pity it had to be this way"—or of Christian tragedy, "the tragedy of possibility," where the feeling aroused is "what a pity it was this way when it might have been otherwise."[35] It seems that in the case of the superpowers and Germany, perception helped to transform a tragedy of possibility into a tragedy of necessity.

---

[32] Speech by Bulganin at Warsaw Treaty Conference, *The New York Times,* May 12, 1955.
[33] The New York *Herald Tribune,* May 14, 1955.
[34] Grzybowski, *op. cit.,* p. 173.
[35] Schlesinger, *op. cit.,* p. 52.

eleven

PERCEPTION AND POLICY DURING THE CUBAN MISSILE CRISIS OF 1962

President John F. Kennedy, in reviewing the thirteen days of the Cuban missile crisis of 1962, estimated that the probability of disaster at the crucial point of the confrontation had been "between one out of three and even."[1] In the light of this estimate, mankind's escape from the nuclear abyss seems awesome. A slight shift of the pendulum might have doomed more human lives to sudden extinction than ever before in history. Previous calamities, whether man-made or natural, would have been dwarfed by comparison. The fact that two mortal men should have held such terrible power demands that we study the event with every tool at our command in order to prevent its recurrence. Mankind might not be so fortunate a second time.

A great deal has been written about the missile crisis, particularly in the United States. Virtually every member of the small group of men who participated in the deliberations of those crucial thirteen days has expressed his thoughts in print. Numerous writers on both sides of the Atlantic have subjected the event to careful scrutiny. No analysis exists, however, that focuses on the role that perception played in the interaction of the Soviet and American leadership and how this perception affected the decision-making process. This chapter will address itself to this task. An effort will be made to determine President Kennedy's and his advisers' perceptions of Premier Nikita Krushchev and the Soviet leadership before and during the crisis. The linkages between these perceptions and the policy decisions by President Kennedy will be exam-

---

[1] John F. Kennedy, quoted in Theodore Sorensen, *Kennedy* (New York: Harper & Row, 1965), p. 705.

ined. And the relationship between Soviet perceptions and policy will be analyzed. The circumstantial nature of the evidence may necessitate considerable speculation. A short factual review of the events precedes the presentation of the main hypothesis.

The missile crisis was the climax to rising tensions between the superpowers during 1961. The Soviet Union's action in testing nuclear weapons of unprecedented explosive force had triggered off a major debate over fallout shelters in the United States; the erection of the Berlin Wall had made the tension almost palpable; and the memory of the abortive American-sponsored invasion of Cuba was still fresh. But as yet there had been no direct confrontation.

In mid-October 1962 hard evidence that the Soviet Union was secretly building offensive missile bases in Cuba with headlong speed had been gathered by United States intelligence services. High-altitude photographs had disclosed a medium-range ballistic missile site near San Cristóbal and one near San Diego de los Baños. Tanker trucks, power and instrument installations, missile guidance stations, and erector launchers were clearly visible. And pictures of cylindrical shapes on incoming Soviet freighters confirmed the worst.

The American leadership, which had had evidence of the missile sites by October 15, now weighed its decision silently. For one week the President and his closest associates constituted themselves as an executive committee of the National Security Council and pondered the alternatives. The deliberations were intense, but no word leaked out to the public. The President continued his preparations for the forthcoming political campaign and, as late as October 18, met with Soviet Foreign Secretary Andrei Gromyko, who professed ignorance of the offensive nature of the missile sites in Cuba.

Inside the White House and Pentagon, the War Council considered the alternatives along a kind of "escalation ladder." Six possible responses developed in ascending order of severity: first, do nothing; second, submit an American appeal to the United Nations Security Council; third, make a secret approach to Castro; fourth, conduct a naval blockade of Cuba; fifth, conduct a "surgical air strike" to eliminate the bases; and sixth, launch an invasion of Cuba. The War Council eliminated the first three alternatives as ineffective and the last as unwarranted. The discussion centered around the alternatives in the middle range. The problem confronting the American planners was the classic one of deterrence strategy: how to combine both capability and credibility so that the Soviet leader would be checked by the actual and potential display of American power. Too little power could be interpreted as surrender, too much power as a bluff. Only controlled and flexible use of power at every step would make deterrence effective in the mind of the opponent.

An immediate invasion of Cuba was ruled out because it might have provoked the war which deterrence was designed to prevent. An air strike at the missile bases was also rejected, since Soviet personnel would have been killed at the sites and such an action would have been difficult to justify by the nation that had made Pearl Harbor a symbol of infamy. A quarantine seemed to hold out the best hope for a solution. It would entail the requisite show of strength by throwing a naval ring around Cuba, especially if it were coupled with a demand that the Soviet Union dismantle its bases there. Yet it offered the Soviet Union a way out: Khrushchev could avoid a direct confrontation by ordering his ships to change their course. Furthermore, a quarantine would entail no violence, at least not immediately. Thus, on the evening of October 22, President Kennedy announced the American decision to impose a quarantine and added that "any nuclear missile launched from Cuba against any nation in the Western Hemisphere" would be regarded "as an attack by the Soviet Union on the United States requiring a full retaliatory response on the Soviet Union."[2] The issue was now squarely joined between the superpowers in the most dramatic military confrontation of the cold war. It was clear to participants and onlookers alike that Castro's Cuba was only a pawn. The United States had announced a check to the king.

The announcement was accompanied by an unprecedented peacetime mobilization of military power in the United States. The Polaris fleet was moved within striking range of the Soviet Union, and for the first time Strategic Air Command (SAC) bombers were dispersed to civilian airfields. Half of the SAC force was on airborne alert. If necessary, the United States was ready to deliver an equivalent of 30 billion tons of TNT upon the Soviet Union. An atmosphere of impending showdown also pervaded the Soviet Union, where all military leaves were canceled. The next seven days took the world to the brink of war.

---

[2] *Department of State Bulletin,* 47 (November 12, 1962), 715–720.

On October 23, Secretary of State Dean Rusk obtained the unanimous support of the Organization of American States (OAS) for the quarantine. The NATO Allies came to the support of the United States, though with misgivings, and not without reminding the United States of its behavior during the Suez crisis. The United Nations Security Council met in the afternoon: the United States demanded the immediate withdrawal of the offensive weapons under international inspection; the Soviet Union condemned the blockade as piracy and asked for its immediate termination. Neither resolution was voted on and the Security Council presented a spectacle of complete helplessness. October 24, United Nations Day, took the world a step closer to the brink. Acting Secretary General U Thant advanced a plan for a two-week cooling-off period to explore the issues. Khrushchev accepted the proposal, but Kennedy rejected it on the ground that the issue of removing the missiles was not negotiable. An appeal by Khrushchev to the British pacifist leader Bertrand Russell to use his influence to effect a general lowering of temperatures was also rejected as irrelevant by the United States. On October 25, Ambassador Adlai Stevenson challenged Soviet Ambassador Valerian Zorin to admit the existence of the missiles, stating that he was prepared to wait for his answer "until hell freezes over." Toward evening, the Russian tanker *Bucharest* approached the blockade zone, and the American destroyer U.S.S. *Gearing* steamed to meet it. Since the Russian vessel carried no contraband, it was allowed to proceed. Khrushchev claimed that the ship had not stopped; the United States claimed that the captain had acknowledged inspection. Neither side backed down.

On October 26 it was learned that several Soviet ships bound for Cuba were changing their course. But, on the other hand, continued photo scrutiny of the missile bases indicated a speed-up in their construction since the announcement of the quarantine. The American offensive had to gather speed before the sites were ready and the missiles operational. President Kennedy spoke of possible "further measures" and did not rule out an air strike at the bases. He also pointed out the numerous possibilities for accidental war if the Soviet Union would not comply. That evening a letter from Premier Khrushchev arrived that looked like a conditional surrender. In it, the premier indicated his willingness to withdraw the missiles, provided Cuba was guaranteed against invasion. This seemed like a fair offer.

On the morning of the following day, however, the White House received a second letter from the Soviet leader that was much tougher in tone and more demanding in content. This time a deal was suggested: the United States was to dismantle its missile bases in Turkey, and the Soviet Union would withdraw its missiles from Cuba.

The War Council now had to make a crucial decision. Superficially, the Soviet proposal seemed reasonable. It expressed a widespread feeling among neutralists that both sides should compromise and sacrifice something. It was generally approved in the United Nations, and several distinguished Western commentators, such as Walter Lippmann, supported it. Nevertheless, the War Council turned down the proposal. First, President Kennedy felt that the first Soviet letter reflected more clearly than the second the Soviet leader's real feelings. And second, to bargain away NATO bases under pressure would be to undermine the entire alliance and engender a Munich psychology. Each time the Soviet Union would gain a strategic advantage in the cold war, it might offer to give it up in exchange for an existing NATO base, until the alliance would be totally dismantled. Thus, by turning down the barter offer, the United States in effect presented the Soviet Union with an ultimatum: remove the bases or further measures will be taken. The brink had been reached.

On Sunday morning, October 28, the confrontation came to an end. Kennedy's gamble on the first Soviet letter had paid off. The Soviet leader reiterated his offer of withdrawing the missiles in return for an American "no-invasion" pledge. The American President accepted immediately and welcomed Khrushchev's "constructive contribution to peace." Other differences were settled in short order. Castro refused to admit on-site inspection by the United Nations to survey the dismantling of the bases, but the United States decided to forgo such inspection and continued to rely upon its own aerial surveillance. The missile sites were completely stripped within a few weeks and outgoing Soviet ships laden with shrouded shapes that everyone took to be missiles brought the crisis to an end. The world had gone to the brink of nuclear hell and come back.

THE HYPOTHESIS

The basic thesis of this chapter is threefold: first, the proposition that, before the crisis entered its acute phase on October 15, the leadership of each superpower had lost hold of the reality of the other. Thus, President Kennedy was convinced that the Soviet Union would never attempt to place offensive missiles into Cuba; and Premier Khrushchev was convinced that he could do so and the United States would take no forceful action. In other words, both leaders permitted their desires to control their perceptions: Kennedy perceived the Soviet leader as prudent, rational, and respectful of the status quo, and Khrushchev perceived the American President as weak, irresolute, and lacking in determination.

Second, and equally important, both leaders managed to gain a much clearer and more realistic perception of each other during the heat of the thirteen days. Thus, Kennedy learned that Khrushchev, though far from irrational, was still capable of taking dangerous risks and of holding invalid assumptions of America's vital interests; Khrushchev learned that Kennedy, though apparently lacking resolve in the Berlin Wall and Bay of Pigs episodes a year earlier, was nevertheless capable of taking a forceful and determined stand in Cuba in October 1962.

Most important, both leaders corrected their perceptions to conform more closely to reality and based their policy decisions on this more realistic appraisal. This ability on both sides may well have saved humanity from nuclear destruction.

PERCEPTION AND POLICY BEFORE THE CRISIS: KENNEDY AND KHRUSHCHEV

The evidence indicates that neither President Kennedy nor his top aides were prepared for the possibility of Soviet offensive missiles in Cuba. Robert Kennedy described the reaction of the group of men assembled by the President on October 15, shortly after the missiles were discovered: "The dominant feeling at the meeting was stunned surprise. No one had expected or anticipated that the Russians would deploy surface-to-surface ballistic missiles in Cuba."[3] The President, in Theodore Sorensen's words, "had not expected the Soviets to attempt so reckless and risky an action in a place like Cuba."[4]

Prior to October, the President and his advisers were thus predisposed to disregard clues that otherwise might have been examined much more closely. During September, for example,

---

[3] Robert F. Kennedy, *Thirteen Days* (New York: Norton, 1969), p. 24.
[4] Sorensen, *op. cit.*, p. 673.

numerous Soviet ships on their way to Cuba were noticed to be riding "high in the water." These ships were later identified as those that had carried the offensive missiles, but at the time, intelligence sources largely dismissed them as innocuous lumber ships. A large increase in Soviet personnel in Cuba was detected as early as August, and a U-2 flight over Cuba on August 29 revealed evidence of the construction of surface-to-air missile (SAM) sites. At the same time, however, Soviet Ambassador Anatoly Dobrynin assured both Robert Kennedy and Sorensen that Soviet intentions in Cuba were peaceful. He apparently succeeded in dispelling any doubts that might have lingered in the minds of the two men or in the President's.

President Kennedy's perception of Premier Khrushchev before the crisis as a rational statesman too prudent to risk anything so dangerous as a direct threat to the security of the Western Hemisphere thus led directly to a policy of nonaction with regard to Cuba. If the President or his advisers had perceived the Soviet leader differently, surveillance of the Soviet vessels and of the island would probably have been much more thorough. The clues that were ignored would have led to far more careful analysis, and, in all probability, the missile bases would have been detected earlier. Thus, the "selective inattention" that characterized the American leadership led to the discovery of the missiles only when it was almost too late. "Psycho-logic," the tendency to ignore or explain away evidence that conflicts with needs and wishes, was also at work. Not only did Kennedy perceive Khrushchev as prudent and rational, but he also desired a détente with the Soviet Union. To admit the possibility of Khrushchev's plan to place offensive missiles in Cuba would have jarred the American President's mental picture most severely. Kennedy did not want an offensive Soviet missile base in Cuba in the same way in which Zermatt, the famous Swiss ski resort, did not want typhoid fever and refused to acknowledge its existence until epidemic proportions had actually been reached.[5]

On the Soviet side, some speculative reconstruction is necessary. The critical determinants of Khrushchev's perception of Kennedy as weak probably were three events that had taken place during

---

[5] Roberta Wohlstetter, "Cuba and Pearl Harbor: Hindsight and Foresight," *Foreign Affairs* (July 1965), p. 699.

the first year of the Kennedy administration: the Bay of Pigs invasion, the Vienna conference, and the Berlin Wall. In all these cases, Kennedy did not perform according to Khrushchev's criteria of firmness and strength. In April 1961, Kennedy initiated an invasion of Cuba, but then failed to complete it and allowed more than 1,000 Cuban refugees to be taken prisoner by Castro. Khrushchev no doubt studied the events of the Bay of Pigs. He would have understood it if Kennedy had left Castro alone or if he had completely destroyed him. But when Kennedy was rash enough to strike at Cuba but not bold enough to finish the job, Khrushchev probably decided that he was dealing with an inexperienced young man who could be intimidated and blackmailed. Khrushchev's decision to place offensive missiles into Cuba was the final gamble of this assumption. In Vienna, in June 1961, while Kennedy talked of the dangers of miscalculation that lead to war, Khrushchev threatened him with a separate Soviet peace treaty with East Germany. And when, in August 1961, Khrushchev built his wall between East and West Berlin, Kennedy did nothing to remove it.

Khrushchev did not announce publicly that he saw Kennedy as weak, but there are strong indications that this was so. In September 1962, the Soviet premier had a meeting with Robert Frost who was visiting the Soviet Union. The aged American poet reported Khrushchev as saying that democracies were "too liberal to fight."[6] In the course of a conversation with the American businessman William Knox on October 24, 1962, Khrushchev reportedly said about Kennedy: "How can I deal with a man who is younger than my own son?"[7] An immature man, almost a boy in the Soviet premier's eyes, might not stand up under the pressure of a powerful and determined adversary. Henry Pachter, in his analysis of the missile crisis, stated that "Kennedy seemed open to blackmail. Ever since the confrontation at Vienna, Khrushchev professed to doubt that Americans would stand up in a test of will power."[8] And Edward Crankshaw, in his biography of Khrushchev, wrote that "Kennedy's fumbling at the Bay of Pigs affair and his accep-

---

[6] Cited in Arthur M. Schlesinger, Jr., *A Thousand Days* (Boston: Houghton Mifflin, 1965), p. 821.
[7] Cited in Elie Abel, *The Missile Crisis* (New York: Bantam Books, 1966), p. 133.
[8] Henry M. Pachter, *Collision Course* (New York: Praeger, 1963), p. 25.

tance of the Berlin Wall suggested that he might be the President most amenable to such a lesson."[9]

In addition to perceiving Kennedy as weak, Khrushchev also perceived Cuba to be of less than vital importance to the United States. Roger Hilsman has suggested that "American attitudes toward Latin America, particularly Cuba, derive from an intimate history, which the Soviets seem not to have fully understood."[10] Another observer described the Soviet premier's perception of the American interest in Cuba in the following terms:

He [Khrushchev] ridiculed the Monroe Doctrine, perhaps the most revered political text in American diplomatic history. Historically, the Monroe Doctrine has encompassed vital national interest. Yet Khrushchev claimed it to be totally outmoded and irrelevant to the current era of international politics.[11]

In 1961, Khrushchev had seen Kennedy act with greater firmness with regard to Berlin than with regard to Cuba. Kennedy might go to war over Berlin, but not over Cuba. With the missiles installed in Cuba, greater pressure could later be placed on Berlin. The place to strike first, then, was Cuba.

On balance, it is most doubtful whether Khrushchev would have placed offensive missiles into Cuba had he not perceived Kennedy as weak and Cuba as relatively unimportant to the United States.

It should be pointed out here that Khrushchev, like his American counterplayer, seemed also to have been the victim of psychologic. He saw what he wanted to see and minimized discordant evidence, thus arriving at the clear picture that allowed him to act. Kennedy may have talked about miscalculation and the need for conciliation at Vienna, but he did nothing to accede to Khrushchev's demands. He may have let the wall go up in Berlin, but he gave no indication of giving up Western interests in the city itself. And even though the Bay of Pigs may have been a fiasco, the American President made numerous policy pronouncements underlining the continuing special concern of the United States for Cuba and the nation's determination to oppose any further Soviet initiatives in the Western Hemisphere.

---

[9] Edward Crankshaw, *Khrushchev* (New York: Viking, 1966), p. 281.
[10] Roger Hilsman, *To Move a Nation* (Garden City, N.Y.: Doubleday, 1967), p. 182.
[11] Joseph G. Whelan, "Khrushchev and the Balance of World Powers," *The Review of Politics* (April 1961), p. 149.

In sum, then, before the crisis entered its acute phase, both leaders saw what they wanted to see. In Kennedy's case, this led to inaction, in Khrushchev's to swift and determined action.

PERCEPTION AND POLICY DURING THE CRISIS:
THE AMERICAN SIDE

The thirteen days of the missile crisis can be divided into two distinct phases: the first, or secret, phase, which began with the discovery of the missiles on October 14 and ended with President Kennedy's speech on October 22; and the second, or public phase, which came to an end on October 28.

On the American side, President Kennedy made three crucial decisions during the first phase and three more during the second. Each of these decisions flowed directly from his image of himself or of his opponent. Kennedy's perception of Khrushchev had changed significantly since the discovery of the missiles. While Kennedy still perceived the Soviet leader as a rational man who would not risk a nuclear war once convinced of the American determination to get the missiles out of Cuba, he now saw another dimension in the Soviet leader's personality: volatility and the capacity for dangerous, even reckless, action. This dual perception was responsible for the fine sense of balance that dominated Kennedy's subsequent decisions; his sensitively calibrated crisis management; and his adroit use of power, without erring in applying too much or too little. Let us examine the three decisions President Kennedy made during the secret phase of the crisis.

First, the President decided to seek advice from a group of men with different political outlooks. The most prominent members of this executive committee were the President, Robert Kennedy, Lyndon Johnson, Dean Rusk, Robert McNamara, Maxwell Taylor, John McCone, Adlai Stevenson, McGeorge Bundy, and Theodore Sorensen. Others participated in some of the deliberations, notably Dean Acheson, George Ball, Douglas Dillon, and Arthur Schlesinger, Jr.

Kennedy had learned from the Bay of Pigs disaster about the danger of one-sided, uncontested viewpoints guiding the decision-making process in foreign policy. On that occasion, most of the new President's advisers had perceived a Cuba ripe for an anti-Castro uprising that could be sparked by a handful of Cuban refugees. Almost everyone close to the President had seen what he wanted to see, not what the reality actually was. Kennedy had also learned from Barbara Tuchman's *The Guns of August* how miscalculations can lead to war. In order to minimize this possibility, he wanted to avail himself of the widest possible range of opinion to assist him in reaching a decision. As he put it to his brother, "I am not going to follow a course which would allow anyone to write a comparable book about this time, *The Missiles of October*."[12] And in order "not to be dragged along in the wake of events, but to control them," Kennedy was determined to keep the committee deliberations secret. "If our deliberations had been publicized, if we had had to make a decision in twenty-four hours," Robert Kennedy wrote after the conclusion of the crisis, "I believe the course that we ultimately would have taken would have been quite different and filled with far greater risks."[13] In essence, the President's decision to be seriously responsive to a group of advisers with a wide variety of viewpoints and to encourage frank and uninhibited discussion in that small group, removed from all publicity, was a decision to reject psycho-logic, to make sure that opinions with which the President might be out of phase emotionally would nevertheless be weighed on their objective merits. Most important, perhaps, the decision to assemble the executive committee was the alternative to an immediate military strike; Kennedy rejected the latter because he perceived Khrushchev as not only a dangerous but also a "rational, intelligent man, who, if given sufficient time and shown our determination, would alter his position."[14] In short, the President's perception of the Soviet leader provided guidance not only for what to do but, perhaps more important, for what not to do.

The naval blockade of Cuba was by far the most important decision the President took during the secret phase of the crisis. An analysis of the discussion of the six alternatives reveals significant linkages between the perceptions held by the participants and the decisions that were actually made. Kennedy ruled out nonaction from the very beginning, even though he realized that the emplacement of Soviet missiles in Cuba would not have substantially altered the strategic balance *in fact*. But he was convinced that the balance would have been substantially altered in *appear-*

---

[12] John F. Kennedy, quoted by Robert Kennedy, *op. cit.*, p. 127.
[13] *Ibid.*, p. 111.
[14] *Ibid.*, p. 126.

ance; and in matters of national will and world leadership, as the President was to say later, "such appearances contribute to reality."[15] "If we did nothing, we would be dead,"[16] Schlesinger quotes him as saying, and "the worst course would be to do nothing," he said to Sorensen.[17] Douglas Dillon, commenting on the first meeting of the committee, observed that "the first reaction of the President, with the others in full agreement, was that we simply could not accept the fact of Soviet missiles in Cuba, trained on the United States."[18] Defense Secretary McNamara who argued at first that "a missile was a missile," regardless from where it was fired, soon changed his mind, apparently persuaded by the President's distinction between reality and appearances.

To bring the crisis to the United Nations was dismissed as a dilatory tactic and to make a secret *démarche* to Castro was seen as futile. The first three levels of response were thus considered to be too weak, even though no one on the executive committee seriously argued that the missiles posed an objective military threat. The President, in the last analysis, "was concerned less about the missiles' military implications than with their effect on the global balance of power."[19] Given this definition of the situation, there was little alternative but to initiate a forceful remedy.

Perception of self and of the adversary also played a crucial role in the discussion of the higher levels of escalation. An invasion of Cuba was rejected almost immediately since Kennedy did not wish to make it appear that his primary aim was the overthrow of Castro. The possibility of an air strike against the missile bases, however, was considered most seriously and for several days was deemed to be the only real alternative to the naval blockade. Several committee members argued that an air strike was the quickest and safest way to eliminate the missiles. A blockade, they argued, might well be irrelevant since the missiles were already on the island. Robert Kennedy, however, found such a course to be incompatible with his perception of the American heritage. "Sunday morning surprise attacks on small nations are simply not in the American tradition," he said; and he added, "My brother is

[15] John F. Kennedy, quoted in Sorensen, *op. cit.*, p. 678.
[16] John F. Kennedy, quoted by Schlesinger, *op. cit.*, p. 811.
[17] John F. Kennedy, quoted by Sorensen, *op. cit.*, p. 694.
[18] Douglas Dillon, quoted in Abel, *op. cit.*, p. 35.
[19] Sorensen, *op. cit.*, p. 683.

not going to be the Tojo of the 1960's."[20] Schlesinger suggests that most of the members of the committee turned away from the air strike route as a result of Robert Kennedy's statement.[21] The President displayed a keen sense of empathy with his Soviet counterplayer. "They cannot permit us to kill a lot of Russians and then do nothing,"[22] he said, adding: "It isn't the first step that concerns me but both sides escalating to the fourth and fifth steps."[23] Reflecting on the crisis in a speech at American University, in the summer of 1963, he put it most succinctly: "Nuclear powers must avert those confrontations which bring an adversary to a choice of either a humiliating retreat or a nuclear war."[24] An air strike would have done that, a blockade did not. In his book on the missile crisis, Robert Kennedy stressed his brother's empathy with Khrushchev's position:

Always he asked himself: Can we be sure that Khrushchev understands what we feel to be our vital national interests? Has the Soviet Union had sufficient time to react soberly to a particular step we have taken? All actions were judged against that standard.[25]

The evidence suggests that, in the last analysis, Robert Kennedy's argument against a "Pearl Harbor in reverse" and John Kennedy's empathy with and multifaceted perception of Khrushchev led away from the physical violence of an air strike to the more limited and nonviolent course of the quarantine. Specifically, the placement of Soviet missiles in Cuba was perceived as a challenge to the American will. A low-level response would have made America *appear* weak, even though little would have actually changed. An air strike, on the other hand, would have made America appear immoral. Thus, the course that was the most compatible with the executive committee's perceptions of the United States was the quarantine.

The third decision during the secret phase of the crisis involved Kennedy's perception of his adversary's intention. Khrushchev, in Kennedy's view, was intent on presenting the United States with a

---

[20] Robert Kennedy, quoted in Abel, *op. cit.*, p. 51, and in Schlesinger, *op. cit.*, p. 807.
[21] Schlesinger, *op. cit.*, p. 807.
[22] John F. Kennedy, quoted in Robert Kennedy, *op. cit.*, p. 36.
[23] *Ibid.*, p. 98.
[24] John F. Kennedy, quoted in Abel, *op. cit.*, p. 193.
[25] Kennedy, *op. cit.*, p. 125.

fait accompli when the missiles were in place. In the President's words: "They thought they had us either way. If we did nothing, we would be dead. If we reacted, they hoped to put us in an exposed position with regard to Berlin, Turkey, or the UN."[26] Hence, Kennedy decided to keep the committee deliberations secret and to announce the quarantine decision to friend and foe alike in a surprise speech, thus presenting Khrushchev with his own *fait accompli*.

The quarantine speech of October 22 ushered in the public, or direct, phase of the crisis. During the next six days, President Kennedy made three more crucial decisions, each based on his perception of himself or of Premier Khrushchev. After obtaining the unanimous support of the Organization of American States for the quarantine on October 23, he drew the blockade line on the morning of October 24. The first two decisions pertained to the enforcement of this line.

On October 24, Acting Secretary General of the United Nations U Thant sent identical letters to Kennedy and Khrushchev urging suspension of both the blockade and of further arms shipments to Cuba for two weeks. While Khrushchev accepted U Thant's suggestions almost immediately, Kennedy decided to put off a reply until the following day. To accept the suggestions, would, in Kennedy's view, have relieved the diplomatic and military pressure on Khrushchev that the quarantine had set in motion, and that was precisely what the President did not want to do. Kennedy wanted to impress on Khrushchev his determination to stand fast. Thus, he decided to refuse negotiations until Khrushchev showed some willingness to dismantle the missile bases. Once again, Kennedy acted on his perception of Khrushchev as a rational man who, if shown determination without violence and given sufficient time, would alter his position. Accordingly, on October 25, the President rejected U Thant's proposal in the following words: "The existing threat was created by the secret introduction of offensive weapons into Cuba, and the answer lies in the removal of such weapons."[27]

The second decision concerned the first actual encounter between Soviet and American ships on the high seas. "The greatest

---

[26] John F. Kennedy, quoted in Schlesinger, *op. cit.,* p. 811.
[27] John F. Kennedy, quoted by Abel, *op. cit.,* p. 148.

danger of war as we saw it then," Assistant Defense Secretary Paul Nitze recalls, "was that we would sink a Russian ship trying to run the blockade. If that happened, it seemed highly doubtful that Khrushchev would hold still without further action."[28] In the afternoon of October 25, several Soviet ships approached the quarantine line, with the tanker *Bucharest* in the lead. Even though the ship was thought to carry only oil, which was not on the contraband list, "there were those on the ExCom," Robert Kennedy recalls in his memoir, "who felt strongly that the *Bucharest* should be stopped and boarded so that Khrushchev would make no mistake of our intent and will."[29] The President, however, permitted the ship to pass through the blockade line with only a signal from an American destroyer. This move clearly was based on Kennedy's perception of Khrushchev as a man who, if pushed too hard, might initiate violence. In the President's words, "We don't want to push him to a precipitous action—give him time to consider. I don't want to push him into a corner from which he cannot escape."[30]

The most crucial decision that Kennedy made, however, involved the two fateful letters sent to him by Khrushchev on October 26 and October 27, respectively. When, on October 26, Kennedy received Khrushchev's first letter hinting at his willingness to remove the missiles in exchange for a pledge from the American President not to invade Cuba, the President and his advisers were inclined to respond favorably. Only Dean Acheson who felt that Khrushchev, when writing the letter, must have been "either tight or scared," thought that "so long as the President had the thumbscrew on Khrushchev, he should give it another turn every day."[31] On October 27, however, just as the President was about to draft an affirmative reply, the second letter arrived in which the Soviet leader raised the price for the removal of the missiles. In this letter, which had been released simultaneously to all the news media, Khrushchev asserted that if Kennedy wanted him to remove the Soviet missiles from Cuba, he would have to remove the American missile base in Turkey. On the same morning, there occurred the only casualty of the missile crisis: Major Rudolf Anderson, Jr., a U-2 pilot, was shot down by Soviet surface-to-air

---

[28] Paul Nitze, quoted in *ibid.*, p. 134.
[29] Kennedy, *op. cit.*, p. 73.
[30] John F. Kennedy, quoted by Robert Kennedy, *op. cit.*, p. 76.
[31] Dean Acheson, quoted in Abel, *op. cit.*, p. 162.

missiles over Cuba. Under this pressure, the consensus against an air strike in the executive committee almost broke down. In Sorensen's words, "Our little group seated around the Cabinet table . . . felt nuclear war to be closer on that day than at any time in the nuclear age."[32] Schlesinger reports that

We had no choice, it was argued, but a military response, and our tactical analysis had already shown that strikes at the bases would be of little use without strikes at the airfields, and strikes at the airfields of little use without further supporting action, so once the process began, it could hardly stop short of invasion.[33]

Nevertheless, Kennedy refused to bomb the bases. He still believed that a determined, but nonviolent, posture by the United States would persuade Khrushchev to retreat, and that an air strike might well push the Soviet leader over the thermonuclear brink.

Most difficult of all, of course, was the specific problem of responding to Khrushchev's two contradictory messages. "No one knew which letter superseded the other; no one knew whether Khrushchev was still in power."[34] Robert Kennedy made the suggestion that the President should respond to the first letter. After all, it had arrived first and probably indicated more accurately than the second the Soviet leader's real perception of the crisis. The President, apparently reluctant to bargain away the Turkish bases under Soviet pressure and fearful of threatening the unity of NATO, agreed to gamble on the first letter, thus rejecting the Cuba-Turkey exchange proposal. This decision was so crucial that it deserves careful analysis.

Robert Kennedy wrote the following account of his brother's rejection of the Cuba-Turkey deal:

He obviously did not wish to order the withdrawal of the missiles from Turkey under threat of the Soviet Union. On the other hand, he did not want to involve the United States and mankind in a catastrophic war over missile sites in Turkey that were antiquated and useless.[35]

The fact remains, nevertheless, that President Kennedy risked precisely such a catastrophic war. The rejection of the Cuba-Turkey

---

[32] Sorensen, *op. cit.*, p. 714.
[33] Schlesinger, *op. cit.*, p. 827.
[34] *Ibid.*, p. 829.
[35] Kennedy, *op. cit.*, p. 95.

swap was in effect an ultimatum to Khrushchev. Kennedy let Khrushchev know that, unless he dismantled the bases within the next day or two, military action would follow. "The expectation was a military confrontation by Tuesday and possibly tomorrow,"[36] the President's brother said of that Saturday. And the President said on Saturday night, "Now it can go either way."[37]

To argue, as Sorensen does, that "the President had no intention of destroying the Alliance by backing down"[38] seems superficial. The evidence suggests that the answer must be sought at a deeper level and that Kennedy's perception of himself and of the United States played a crucial role in the decision. "We cannot tell anyone to keep out of our hemisphere," young Jack Kennedy had written twenty-two years earlier in *Why England Slept*, "unless our armaments and the people behind these armaments are prepared to back up the command, even to the ultimate point of going to war." In his speech of October 22, 1962, he had said, "One path we shall never choose, and that is the path of surrender and submission," adding, with specific reference to the missiles, "It is difficult to settle or even discuss the problem in an atmosphere of intimidation."

It seems that President Kennedy, in his eagerness to impress his determination upon Khrushchev, may have confused weakness with compromise. In his desire not to appear weak, he apparently never fully distinguished between the danger of the missiles remaining in Cuba and the danger resulting from a removal of the missiles through compromise. Certainly the latter danger was much smaller, but the President seems to have perceived both as equally unacceptable challenges to the American will. A deeply ingrained reaction against the "Munich syndrome" and the determination not to appear weak—stemming perhaps from his encounter with Khrushchev in Vienna—made him risk nuclear war over missile bases in Turkey, which, by his own admission, were obsolete and useless and which, by his own order, should have been dismantled two months earlier. Thus, after twelve days of almost incredible balance and restraint, he risked nuclear Armaggedon on the thirteenth day over what appeared to be a side

---

[36] *Ibid.*, p. 109.
[37] John F. Kennedy, quoted by Abel, *op. cit.*, p. 179.
[38] Sorensen, *op. cit.*, p. 714.

issue. Fortunately for mankind, his luck held and he won his gamble. But by turning down the barter deal, Kennedy placed the decision over peace and war squarely into the hands of Nikita Khrushchev.

PERCEPTION AND POLICY DURING THE CRISIS:
THE SOVIET SIDE

We have seen that Khrushchev probably perceived Kennedy as lacking determination and that this perception was probably responsible for his conviction that Soviet missiles could be placed in Cuba without eliciting a forceful American response. We shall now attempt to demonstrate that, in the course of the public phase of the crisis, Khrushchev gradually learned to perceive the American President differently and that this changed perception led directly to the decision to withdraw the missiles. Naturally, since there is hardly any access to the Soviet decision-making process, this analysis must be based largely on circumstantial evidence, but even the bits and pieces that can be assembled add up to an impressive case.

Khrushchev's perception of Kennedy as weak seems to have been so firmly embedded that the Soviet leader pursued his course without hesitation and despite some telltale signs in September and early October that Kennedy might not be soft to further Soviet initiatives in Cuba. When, on September 4, Kennedy publicly warned the Soviet Union that if Cuba were ever to become an offensive missile base, the United States would take action to protect itself, Khrushchev responded with a tough public statement: "Today one cannot attack Cuba and expect the aggressor to go unpunished for the attack. If such an attack is made, it will be the start of the unleashing of war."[39] Khrushchev probably regarded Kennedy's warning as political oratory and felt that a threat of war would be sufficient to deter the United States from responding forcefully. Because of this perception, the Soviet leader was unable to see that Kennedy was "drawing a line, and making it extremely unlikely that he would back down if that line was crossed."[40] Even when Kennedy activated the reserves,

---

[39] Nikita Khrushchev, cited in *Digest of the Soviet Press* (October 10, 1962), p. 14.
[40] Wohlstetter, *op. cit.*, p. 701.

Khrushchev seemed to remain unaffected. Arnold Horelick suggests some other reasons that might have prompted Khrushchev to continue the missile program. These reasons included the expectation that the United States would respond with diplomatic action, namely, that Kennedy would consult with his NATO Allies and be persuaded to adopt a nonviolent approach and that the OAS would probably oppose any military action by the United States.[41] These expectations were all based on the assumption of a fictitious Kennedy, one that Khrushchev needed in order to implement his missile program.

The first decision that confronted the Soviet leader during the public phase of the crisis was how to respond to Kennedy's quarantine speech of October 22. It seems that the Soviet leadership was as stunned by the American response as the executive committee had been when it first learned of the Soviet move on October 15. There was no immediate reaction from the Kremlin. Dean Rusk said to George Ball on the morning after the speech, "We have won a considerable victory. You and I are still alive."[42] Neither in Berlin nor anywhere else did a Soviet move materialize. A front-page editorial in *Pravda* on October 24 condemned the United States for a "crude form of blackmail that is bringing down catastrophe upon all mankind" but concluded by declaring that "in the situation that has arisen, a special responsibility falls on the United Nations."[43] This reaction suggested that the Soviet leadership had been thrown off guard by the blockade and now adopted a policy of "wait and see." Though Khrushchev was probably confused by the American move, his precrisis perception of Kennedy had yet to be shaken. After all, Kennedy had thus far only called for a blockade. He had not yet proved his determination to enforce it.

The blockade line was drawn on October 24. Khrushchev now had to make the crucial decision of what to do about it. In the morning of that day, the Soviet leader issued a stern warning: "If the United States Government carries out the program of piratical actions outlined by it, we shall have to resort to means of defense against the aggressors to defend our rights."[44] In the afternoon, he

---

[41] Arnold L. Horelick, "The Cuban Missile Crisis: An Analysis of Soviet Calculations and Behavior," *World Politics* (April 1964), p. 381.

[42] Dean Rusk, quoted in Abel, *op. cit.*, p. 110.

[43] Cited in *Digest of the Soviet Press* (November 12, 1962), p. 4.

[44] Nikita Khrushchev, quoted in Abel, *op. cit.*, p. 126.

summoned to the Kremlin the American businessman William Knox who happened to be in Moscow on behalf of Westinghouse International. Elie Abel renders a vivid account of this meeting, which deserves to be quoted in full:

> Knox arrived fifteen minutes late to find Khrushchev in a state of near-exhaustion. He looked like a man who had not slept all night. For three hours he treated Knox to a succession of threats, complaints and peasant jokes. It was true, he said, the Soviet Union had missiles and attack planes in Cuba; moreover he would use them if need be.
>
> He wanted the President and the American people to know, Khrushchev added, that if the United States Navy tried to stop Soviet ships at sea, his submarines would start sinking American ships. And that would mean a third world war. Khrushchev complained that he could not understand Kennedy. Eisenhower had been troublesome enough, but Eisenhower was a man of his own generation. "How can I deal with a man who is younger than my son?" he asked the astonished Westinghouse man. Then, extending a stubby index finger across the table in Knox's direction, he talked of weapons, offensive and defensive. "If I point a pistol at you like this in order to attack you," Khrushchev said, "the pistol is an offensive weapon. But if I aim to keep you from shooting me, it is defensive, no?"[45]

This exchange suggests that Khrushchev's perception of Kennedy was shaken by October 24 but not yet undermined. This ambivalence was reflected in Soviet policy decisions on that day. Khrushchev issued orders to some of his ships to change course. The ship that was ordered to test the blockade was a freighter that carried no contraband. On the other hand, Khrushchev ordered to speed up the construction of the missile sites. His ready acceptance of U Thant's proposal for a cooling-off period suggests that such a period would have given him the necessary time to render the missiles fully operational.

Khrushchev probably changed his perception of Kennedy sometime during Thursday, October 25. Kennedy's rejection of U Thant's proposal, his insistence that the missiles be removed, his warning that "further action will be justified should these offensive military preparations continue," and the continuing massive arms build-up in the United States probably persuaded Khrushchev that Kennedy was not bluffing. What Khrushchev now began to perceive was that Kennedy was determined to get the missiles out

---

[45] *Ibid.*, pp. 132–133.

of Cuba, that he was planning to bomb Cuba if necessary to attain this objective, and that such an attack could precipitate a nuclear war. The note of desperation that permeated his personal letter to Kennedy suggests this sudden recognition. He wrote:

Mr. President, we and you ought not now to pull on the ends of the rope in which you have tied the knot of war, because the more we pull, the tighter the knot will be tied. . . . Only lunatics or suicides who themselves want to perish and destroy the whole world before they did, could do this.[46]

The perception of acute danger was reinforced by the strategic realities of the situation. Khrushchev had known that the American military machine was exceedingly powerful. But so long as he felt that Kennedy was unwilling to use this power, he had felt relatively safe. As soon as this assumption became questionable, however, the terrible consequences became obvious. If war came, Khrushchev had the choice of either being overwhelmed in a limited air or naval engagement in the Caribbean or of having his country devastated by a nuclear attack. Neither alternative was acceptable. Hence, Khrushchev's new perception of Kennedy as having "tied the knot of war" and willing to commit "suicide," if necessary, to get the missiles out of Cuba probably led him to write his personal letter to the American President.

There has been considerable speculation about the sequence of the two Khrushchev letters. The actual timing of the notes and the reasons for their contradictory content may never be fully known. Michel Tatu suggests that the Cuba-Turkey letter was prompted by the reaction of other Presidium members that Khrushchev had backed down too quickly. He advances the hypothesis that the Cuba-Turkey swap proposal constituted a middle approach between the offer contained in Khrushchev's personal letter and the demands of Soviet hard-liners who insisted on an American withdrawal from all foreign bases.[47] Henry Pachter, in his *Collision Course*, suggests that the second letter, proposing the Cuba-Turkey exchange, had actually been drafted and sent first, but through the regular diplomatic channels of the foreign ministry. The personal letter, Pachter contends, was actu-

---

[46] Nikita Khrushchev, quoted in *ibid.*, p. 152.
[47] Michel Tatu, *Power in the Kremlin* (New York: Viking, 1969), p. 263.

ally written and sent later, but directly by Khrushchev without clearance with the foreign ministry. Hence, it overtook the other, more formal and demanding, communication.[48] The evidence seems to support Pachter's thesis. The Cuba-Turkey letter mentions Kennedy's rejection of U Thant's proposal but does not make reference to Kennedy's warnings about a possible air strike, nor does it make reference to the military arms build-up. This seems to suggest that the slow letter, proceeding through channels, had been overtaken by events. Khrushchev's new perception of Kennedy, now reinforced by the ominous events of October 26, probably prompted him to write the personal letter indicating his desire to avoid a showdown and his willingness to remove the missiles in exchange for a pledge from President Kennedy not to invade Cuba. When Kennedy did indeed respond to the personal letter rather than to the barter proposal, Khrushchev did not press the matter; he had become convinced that Kennedy would bomb Cuba if he did. In a revealing speech before the Supreme Soviet on December 12, 1962, Khrushchev related how the crisis appeared to him on that day. "Immediate action was necessary," he said "to prevent the attack on Cuba and to preserve peace."[49] He added that "In these circumstances, if one or the other side had failed to show restraint, failed to do all that was necessary to prevent the outbreak of war, an explosion would have followed with irreparable consequences."[50] He also gave the Supreme Soviet a detailed and vivid account of the military preparations that President Kennedy had made:

Several paratrooper, infantry, and armored divisions, numbering some 100,000 men were allocated for the attack on Cuba. In addition, 183 warships with 85,000 sailors on board were moved toward the shores of Cuba. Several thousand war planes were to cover the landing in Cuba. About 20 percent of the U.S. Strategic Air Command planes, carrying atomic and hydrogen bombs, were kept aloft around the clock.[51]

Hence, when Kennedy pledged not to invade Cuba, Khrushchev was ready to withdraw the missiles and thus to terminate the

---

[48] Pachter, *op. cit.*, p. 68.
[49] Nikita Khrushchev, cited in *Digest of the Soviet Press* (January 16, 1963), p. 5.
[50] *Ibid.*
[51] *Ibid.*

crisis. "We are interested that there should be no war in the world," he wrote Kennedy on October 28.[52] He now firmly believed that Kennedy had been ready to risk war over the missiles in Cuba and perhaps even over obsolete missiles in Turkey.

A word should be said about Khrushchev's self-image during the crisis. First, it was possible for Khrushchev to withdraw the missiles without severe damage to his self-esteem. In December, he told the Supreme Soviet: "Our purpose was only the defense of Cuba."[53] With a pledge from Kennedy not to invade Cuba, Khrushchev could claim that he terminated the crisis with the main Soviet objective accomplished. Second, Marxism-Leninism does not equate retreat with the stigma of defeat. Lenin's concept of "one step backward, two steps forward" could be made to apply to the Cuban encounter. Indeed, anything other than withdrawal might have seemed like reckless adventurism under the circumstances, a shortcoming that Lenin had once condemned as an "infantile disorder."

With all this said, however, the fact remains that retreat for Khrushchev probably was not easy. It takes an honest man to admit that his perception of an adversary might have been wrong all along. It takes a flexible and resourceful man to change his policy upon such recognition. And it takes a strong and courageous man not to place the preservation of his ego before the preservation of the human race.

President Kennedy's and Premier Khrushchev's perceptions of themselves and of each other deeply influenced the course of the Cuban missile crisis. Both saw what they wanted to see before the crisis. As a result, Kennedy lowered his guard in Cuba, and Khrushchev shipped his missiles.

Kennedy viewed the missiles basically as a challenge to the American will. They had to be removed, not because they made America weak, but because they made her *appear* weak. And in order to get them out, Kennedy went to the brink of war. Khrushchev was able to withdraw the missiles with his ego and self-esteem substantially intact. Had he not been able to do so, had he been forced to *appear* weak, nuclear disaster might well have been the consequence.

---

[52] Nikita Khrushchev, quoted in Kennedy, *op. cit.*, p. 210.
[53] Nikita Krushchev, cited in *Digest of the Soviet Press* (January 16, 1963), p. 5.

Each leader showed empathy with the other's perception of the crisis. Robert Kennedy wrote that

The final lesson of the Cuban missile crisis is the importance of placing ourselves in the other country's shoes. During the crisis, President Kennedy spent more time trying to determine the effect of a particular course of action on Khrushchev or the Russians than on any other phase of what he was doing.[54]

Khrushchev's ultimate recognition of Kennedy's determination and his flexibility at the brink showed similar empathy and self-restraint.

There is one final sense in which perception was perhaps decisive. Neither leader could say to the other, "Do as I say or I shall kill you;" but each was reduced to saying, "Do as I say or I shall kill us both." Force, in the crude physical sense, was no longer a predictable instrument of national policy. Each superpower could have annihilated the other, but by so doing, would have destroyed itself. To put it crassly, since everybody was somebody, nobody was anybody. Since physical force on each side was equally devastating and thus virtually canceled out, subjective perceptions and appearances of power loomed particularly large. Psychology thus superseded hardware, and a state of mind became decisive. The missile crisis was in essence a nuclear war, but one that was fought in the minds of two men and their perceptions of themselves and of each other. Fortunately for all of us, these were good men with political wisdom, moral courage, and a gift for empathy. They grasped not only with their minds but also felt deeply in their hearts both the burden and the terror of the human condition in the nuclear age.

---

[54] Kennedy, *op. cit.*, p. 124.

twelve

"THROUGH A GLASS, DARKLY; BUT THEN FACE TO FACE"

As we conclude this study, it is difficult to avoid a feeling of sadness. Why do men behave like this? Why such blindness? Why such stubbornness? Can we learn anything from the tragic past so that it might serve as prologue for a better future?

These are difficult questions. History is mankind's great laboratory. But it does not yield its secrets easily. As the knowledge of a person's past gives us some clues about his future, history provides us with some clues about a nation's future. It never repeats itself exactly. If it can teach us anything at all, it teaches through analogy, not identity. But by what mental processes do we select the right analogy? What lessons do we choose to select from the myriad of events of the past? The answer is that we choose those that we *perceive* as meaningful. *Perception,* thus, is crucial.

Let us now, toward the end of the book, make an attempt at definition. Perception in world politics may be defined as the total cognitive view a nation holds of itself and of others in the world. As such, it includes, of course, both reality *and* distortion. There is little doubt that many nations much of the time see themselves and others the way they really are; but, as the examples in this book have shown, it is equally clear that some nations some of the time see themselves and others in partially distorted or even totally distorted ways. Hence, I have tried to isolate from the composite picture of reality and illusion the elements of illusion, and then I have attempted to determine what effects these have had on decisions of national policy.

In this endeavor, it has been useful to consider four different dimensions of perception in world politics. First, there is a nation's *self-image;* how does a national leader perceive himself? The question, "Who does he think he is?" may be posed in a spirit of genuine inquiry. Second, one must consider a nation's perception of the nature and *character of its counterplayer.* How does a national leader view the character of his ally or adversary? Third, how does a nation view another nation's *intentions toward itself?* What, in other words, does it expect to happen? And finally, how well do nations perceive each other's objective *power and capabilities?*

Four dangers must be guarded against in any perceptual approach to world politics. First, nations are clearly more than groups of people living on pieces of territory. Large political entities cannot be dealt with in the same manner as individuals. Hence, wherever possible, I have tried to focus on the perceptions of individual leaders or of small groups whose actions were accessible to empirical analysis. Second, nations probably exist more in time than in space. Thus, I have adopted a historical approach and dealt with three nations only: China, Russia, and America. It is hoped that by thus limiting the breadth of the analysis, we have gained in depth. Third, there often exists a fine distinction between perception and judgment. Policy decisions often include both elements, and the task of separating them frequently is difficult, if not impossible. Finally, it is worth pointing out again that, in the mosaic of world politics, perception is only one part of the pattern. I believe that we have found a key to *one* riddle, but I know that there are many keys yet to be found for the other unsolved riddles.

What, now, are the major insights that are revealed by our five examples in Chinese-American relations? In all of recorded history, the most rigid and enduring self-image was probably that held by Imperial China. She saw herself at the center of the universe and as the hub of virtue, learning, and civilization for over two millenia. This image of herself excluded the possibility of learning anything from anybody else, since one could learn nothing from barbarians. The empire was self-contained and self-sufficient, and foreign barbarians were thought to inhabit small islands separated from civilization by "intervening wastes of sea."

It is probably not enough to say that the Chinese had false perceptions of the early Americans with whom they came in contact. It may be more accurate to say that they had *no* concept at all to account for the strange new phenomena they were encountering. The first meeting with the West must have been an experience comparable to an invasion from a hostile foreign planet. The early attempts to fit the Western powers into the long familiar pattern of tributary relationships doomed Imperial China from the start. Her decision to give the barbarians the right to try their own citizens on Chinese soil in order not to sully her hands was the beginning of extraterritoriality in China. And to meet foreign firepower with pronouncements of superior virtue was to invite the dismemberment of the empire through military force. Thus, China's self-image prevented her from learning anything at all for half a century; and when at last the image cracked, it was already too late.

Before the first encounters between China and the United States, American perceptions of China were marked by respect and veneration. With physical contact, however, this respect quickly gave way to a kind of benevolent contempt. The Americans came to regard the Chinese as wards in their own country. By 1900, the barbarians perceived the Chinese as heathens to be civilized, and Imperial China now perceived the barbarians correctly—as the agents of her destruction.

As the Nationalist revolution engulfed China, first under Sun Yat-sen and then under Chiang Kai-shek, the perceptual relationship between China and America underwent significant changes. While Americans continued to regard themselves as benevolent guardians of China, they now perceived Chiang Kai-shek not only as the hero and future hope of China, but also as a steadfast friend of the United States and an enemy of communism—in short, as an ally in a global moral battle. It could never be admitted that the anti-Western passions of the new revolutionary China also extended to the United States; nor could it be admitted that the wartime alliance wih Chiang Kai-shek was more an outgrowth of the power balance of the time than a common crusade against the forces of evil. Alliance had to be made synonymous with friendship. And finally, Americans tenaciously refused to see that nationalism and communism in China had been born in the same anti-Western mold. Chiang Kai-shek, the Christian general, was endowed by America with all those qualities that were considered virtuous and moral. In return, the United States fully expected to be regarded with similar enthusiasm and respect.

When Mao Tse-tung's communism emerged victorious from the

Chinese civil war, Americans, burdened with the Chiang Kai-shek image of the past, were unable to deal pragmatically with the new situation. They could not suddenly abandon a heroic Christian leader who for so long had been perceived as America's trusted friend. Nor, however, could they save him from disaster. Hence, many Americans found refuge, if not comfort, in the myth of China's loss through the machinations of subversives in the American government itself. The denouement of China had been so unthinkable that only treason could explain it. Thus, the extravagant American image of Chiang Kai-shek contributed substantially to America's failure in China. Ironically enough, the object of this image also felt abandoned and betrayed by his former ally. And on the Chinese mainland, America was suddenly confronted with a new and fiercely hostile presence.

The Korean War became the great watershed in Sino-American relations. On the American side, it marked the death of the image of China as the heroic underdog and the birth of a new image— that of a hostile and menacing power to be reckoned with. The Chinese Communists, in turn, learned to perceive the United States as their archenemy, bent on their destruction.

The most crucial perception on both sides during the Korean War no doubt was that of the enemy's intent. General MacArthur firmly believed that the Chinese Communists neither would nor could intervene in Korea. He perceived the soldier of the People's Liberation Army of 1950 in the same way that he had perceived the defeated Chinese Nationalist soldier of 1949—with considerable disdain. The Chinese, on the other hand, were convinced that MacArthur, in his drive toward the Yalu River, would not stop at the border but would invade China herself. Hence, military intervention was seen as the only possible recourse.

Once the Chinese intervention had occurred, MacArthur's image of China's power began to play a decisive role. When the Chinese infiltrated 200,000 men into North Korea and dealt MacArthur's army a devastating blow, the American general was unable to accept this fact. And when the Chinese broke contact temporarily before striking again, MacArthur ascribed this move to their need for rest. The old images died hard, and MacArthur blundered into the trap of his own misperceptions. The tenacity with which Americans held on to their old images was exemplified in official State Department declarations to the effect that the war was not being waged against the Chinese people, but only against their Communist leaders. Since no one knew how this distinction could be put into effect on the battlefield, it was soon abandoned. But it demonstrated the utter incapacity of many Americans to admit that the Chinese Communists had secured a genuine power base and a measure of popular support.

The old images, in short, helped prevent a more pragmatic policy, helped prevent Americans from seeing a massive Chinese intervention coming, and ultimately almost led to disaster on the fields of battle in Korea.

Perception has also had a tragic impact on the war in Indochina during both the French and American phases. After the Chinese intervention in the Korean War, American leaders expected a similar intervention on the side of Ho Chi Minh. Even though the Chinese never intervened in armed combat, this expectation led to policy decisions of the gravest consequence. France, whose presence in Indochina before the Communist victory in China had been perceived by the United States with considerable misgivings, now became the defender of the West in Asia. The perceptions that America entertained of communism in Europe were automatically transferred to the Asian scene. The United States began to fight a war by proxy in Indochina. Military aid to France increased by leaps and bounds until by 1954 the United States was paying over half of the cost of the Indochinese war.

American perceptions of Ho Chi Minh also underwent dramatic changes. In 1946, most Americans had seen him as a nationalist resisting the incursions of French colonialism. By the time of the Korean War, he had become, in the view of most American leaders, a puppet of Chinese Communism. A man had to be either a nationalist or a Communist but could not really be both. The towering shadow of Mao Tse-tung was seen to hover over the figure of Ho Chi Minh.

Thus, the Indochinese war, which had begun as a local nationalist uprising with Communist leadership cadres, was now perceived by the United States as a mortal test of wills between a Communist monolith and the forces of the free world. When the showdown came between France and Ho Chi Minh at Dienbienphu in 1954, a massive military intervention by the United States was averted only by the narrowest of margins.

China's perception of hostile intent by the Americans was as one-dimensional as that of the United States. The Chinese saw themselves in deadly peril. American aid to France had to be balanced with Chinese aid to Ho Chi Minh. A vicious circle was created in which the border line between real and imaginary threats tended to blur and finally disappear altogether. A spiral of Hobbesian fear was set in motion. Each side vividly felt the terrible fear it had of the other but could not enter the other's counter-fear or even understand why it should be particularly nervous. The stage was thus set for an even more tragic encounter.

As the American presence in Indochina displaced that of France in the late 1950s and as this presence gradually changed to a massive military intervention of half a million men during the 1960s, American perceptions again were crucial. American leaders remained the prisoners of their cold war images at the very time when communism had in fact ceased to be monolithic and was breaking up into political and ideological fragments. They continued to see the shadow of China looming over North Vietnam. Mutual perceptions of both character and intent now became true devil mirror images. Each side compared the other's declarations to those of Hitler. Both evoked analogies to Munich in their own need to stand up against each other. Both saw themselves as the torchbearers of truth and justice in the world.

Fortunately, however, both China and America by now had developed a healthy respect for each other's military power. American leaders reiterated that they had no wish to encounter China on the field of battle. And Chinese leaders, despite countless references to Americans as paper tigers, exercised a policy of extreme restraint. Of course, the split with the Soviet Union and the shock waves of the cultural revolution probably made China less willing to risk war with the United States. And equally, the deep divisions within America over the Vietnamese war made her leaders most reluctant to risk an even wider war with China. But it is altogether possible that both China and America had learned to perceive each other's power quite correctly in Korea and that this more realistic appreciation served as a restraining memory.

The most significant misperception in the relations between the young American republic and Czarist Russia occurred on the American side. When Catherine the Great and Czar Alexander II embarked on policies that happened to be helpful to the United States, the Americans assumed, without any evidence whatsoever, that Russia's policy was fashioned in response to American desires. The truth was that the fate of the United States was a matter of complete indifference to Czarist Russia.

When Catherine the Great refused to lend troops to King George III to crush his rebellious subjects, the American revolutionaries assumed that the czarina's refusal stemmed from her affection for the American fighters for independence. When Czar Alexander sent his fleet to New York and San Francisco during the American Civil War, the North assumed that the ships had come for the purpose of helping the Union cause. And when the czar sold Alaska to the United States, the Americans purchased it as a debt of gratitude for past Russian favors.

Actually, in all these cases, the czars followed the dictates of their national interest. The fact that these interests happened to converge with those of the Americans was purely coincidental. The czars never considered the Americans as very important. In fact, in comparison with the European powers, the United States was perceived as virtually irrelevant.

When, under Czar Nicholas II, American and Russian interests began to diverge and ultimately to collide, the Americans went to the other extreme. Even though Nicholas' policies had as little to do with the United States as those of his predecessors, the Americans—once again relating these policies to themselves alone —overreacted in the opposite direction. Affection now turned to suspicion, and romanticism gave way to hatred. Thus, the consequence of basing policy on legends rather than on facts was naïveté and lack of balance.

The tragedy of the Russo-American encounter in 1917 was that both Wilson and Lenin perceived each other and their nations with a total lack of empathy. Wilson attempted to fit the events in Russia in 1917 into the framework of the American experience, and Lenin perceived the United States through the prism of Marxism alone.

On the American side, there probably was *no* experience that could have equipped the American people to perceive the Bolshevik Revolution for what it really was: a political and social upheaval of earth-shattering proportions that remade an entire society. The American Revolution had not been marked by excessive violence, and the Civil War had been fought and won to preserve a union, not to destroy it and supplant it with a new political order. Thus, the absence of any comparable historical experience probably doomed the United States to misperceive completely the revolutionary process in Russia. There was simply nothing in the American experience to relate to. The reports about the events in Russia that were written in the summer of 1917 by David R. Francis, the former grain merchant, and by Elihu Root, the elderly statesman who "did not like filth," demonstrate this total lack of empathy in its starkest form. The expectation that democracy, American style, would flourish in Russia and that such self-government would lead to renewed Russian enthusiasm for the war demonstrated how little the American leaders understood the revolutionary forces that were reshaping the Russian nation.

Lenin and Trotsky, on the other hand, perceived the United States so much through Marxist lenses that the reality of America was completely lost to them. Their absolute commitment to Marxism made for distortion a priori. America had to be adjusted to fit the Marxist categories. Perception thus took place within a closed and predetermined system. Moreover, to the Bolsheviks, nothing mattered but their revolution. They could not conceive that it could have appeared otherwise to anybody else. Even the fact that a world war was in progress was of little consequence to them.

Thus, with equal egocentricity, Americans and Bolsheviks perceived themselves as secular crusaders for the good life on earth and saw each other as anathema. Each made a distinction between the other's "good people" and "evil government" and saw the latter as a transitional phenomenon to be removed from the face of the earth with all possible speed. Hence, even though in 1920 there were few objective causes for conflict between America and Russia, these perceptions had made the two nations into mortal enemies.

The years preceding the establishment of diplomatic relations between the United States and the Soviet Union illustrate the tenacity with which negative images and stereotypes can live on, despite the growing impact of objective forces that point in the direction of flexibility and change.

Throughout the decade of the twenties, Americans took great delight in using Russia as a mirror of their own accomplishments. By the thirties, the tables had turned and Russia now used America as a mirror of its own successes. When Lenin adopted the NEP, Americans saw this decision as the triumph of capitalism in Russia. When the Great Depression overtook America, however, Stalin perceived it as "the first swallow of the impending spring" of communism. Both nations saw only what they wished to see, and new facts were conveniently adapted to fit the old perceptions.

It took the catastrophe of the depression to make Americans somewhat more receptive to new facts. Suddenly the United States discovered that it needed the Russian market for its goods. The Russians in turn discovered that they needed the American goods. And both Russia and America began to realize that they shared a common interest in defending themselves against the rising menace of Germany and Japan.

What is striking is that it took the two nations so long to establish diplomatic relations in the absence of any major objective power rivalries between them. The negative images that each maintained about the other no doubt retarded the process toward rapprochement. Had this rapprochement come earlier and had it been more solid, perhaps the rise of the Axis powers might have been stemmed and the disasters that followed might have been averted. When the war made allies of America and Russia, the old images prevented real trust and genuine collaboration. And no doubt these images—latent and beneath the surface though they were—came to the fore again at war's end and hastened the coming of the cold war.

The fate of Germany after World War II is a fearful example of the evolution of a vicious perceptual spiral. Both Russians and Americans distorted incoming information to fit their images of the other's hostile intent. With every step up the spiral, the prophecy came nearer to fulfillment, until the image became fact. The result was a divided Germany, half of it rearmed and integrated into the North Atlantic Treaty and the other half equally rearmed but committed to the Warsaw Pact.

It is amazing how many formulas came to grief on these mutual perceptions of hostile intent. Both the Pleven Plan and EDC on the Western side and proposals for free all-German elections and an all-European security pact on the Soviet side failed to be accepted. Americans perceived Soviet offers as ruses, transparent maneuvers, or baited traps. Russians saw American initiatives as aggressive designs, capitalist tricks, or imperialist expansion. Each side, of course, saw its own moves as purely defensive.

The greater danger in this cold war struggle lay in the possibility that the extreme images of hostile intent that each side held of the other might have driven the spiral of suspicion and counter-suspicion to the desperate step of a preventive war. If each side had continued to believe that the other was its mortal enemy, this view might have influenced behavior to such a point of rigidity and compulsiveness that the inevitable conflict could have become a self-fulfilling prophecy. It took a near catastrophe to introduce a larger measure of reality into the relations of the superpowers—the Cuban missile crisis of 1962.

In essence, the story of the Cuban crisis is the story of the two most powerful men in the world, who first saw what they wished to see but were able to correct their misperceptions and thus pull back from the edge of nuclear destruction.

President Kennedy at first perceived Premier Khrushchev as a prudent statesman who would never take the gamble of placing offensive missiles in Cuba. Ambiguous evidence was adjusted to this desire to see Khrushchev as a man of peaceful intent. Thus, Soviet ships with large hatches, riding high in the water on their way to Cuba, were dismissed as lumber ships. When the truth was revealed, the American leadership was taken by complete surprise.

Premier Khrushchev, on the other hand, first perceived the American President as irresolute and weak. After all, Kennedy had seemed to lack resolve in the crises of the Berlin Wall and the Bay of Pigs. Hence, Khrushchev was convinced that he could place offensive missiles into Cuba and Kennedy would take no forceful action. Thus, before the crisis erupted into the open, both leaders saw what they wanted to see. As a result, Kennedy lowered his guard in Cuba and Khrushchev shipped his missiles.

During the acute stage of the crisis, self-images played a crucial role. It is striking how much emphasis Kennedy placed on appearances. He admitted, in fact, that the missiles had to be removed, not because they made America weak, but because they made her *appear* weak. They symbolized an unacceptable challenge to the American will. Thus, if America did nothing, the President said, she would "be dead."

Fortunately, Kennedy was equally concerned with the Soviet leader's self-image. He knew that Khrushchev would not withdraw the missiles if this forced *him* to appear weak. The pledge not to invade Cuba was Kennedy's recognition of this truth and bears testimony to the American leader's gift for empathy. "The final lesson of the Cuban missile crisis," in Robert Kennedy's words, was "the importance of placing ourselves in the other country's shoes."

Both men changed their perceptions only in response to mortal danger. While this is a sad reflection, it is also true that lesser men, when confronted with such peril, tend to hold on to their misperceptions with redoubled tenacity. Even men of great intelligence, when confronted with disaster, often use this intelligence not to question their false images, but instead to shore them up. Intelligence alone, as the Cuban missile crisis shows, is no guarantee for survival in the nuclear age. Great moral courage, a respect for facts, and above all, a gift for empathy are also needed.

Our ten case studies have demonstrated that false images affect policy, often disastrously. But perhaps an even more significant conclusion emerges from the case studies: men do not easily abandon misperceptions through rational analysis but primarily through trauma and catastrophe. Most national leaders will not examine their prejudices and stereotypes until they are shaken and shattered into doing so. Man, in short, learns and grows largely through suffering.

As a comment on the human condition, this observation is both accurate and tragic. As a comment on man's political condition in the modern world, it is many times more tragic since it involves mankind, not just man. If one examines the lead-time before wars, the amount of available time for growth and change becomes shorter and shorter. In Napoleonic times, national leaders had months; in 1914, they had weeks; Kennedy in 1962 had just thirteen days. Under such conditions, rationality and self-analysis become absolutely essential.

It is, of course, a truism that a statesman's perception of the truth is all he has to go on. He cannot postpone a decision until all the facts are in, until maturity of judgment has developed and historical perspective has illuminated the situation. He must decide and act *now* even though he may be aware that his vision may be blurred. He cannot *but* act on incomplete knowledge and so can never prove that his vision is correct. Once all the facts are in, foreign policy has become history. In this sense, the statesman's task is a trying and cruel one and the scholar, who does not have to face this existential imperative, owes him a measure of empathy and tolerance.

Nevertheless, the nuclear age demands that the statesman must constantly strive to improve the accuracy of his perceptions. In this light, the crucial question that now confronts us is this: What can be done to make sure that the reality principle governs

Chinese-American and Soviet-American relations? Reality is complicated enough, and everything must be done so as not to render it even more complex by adding to it our unsubstantiated misperceptions. How can we eliminate or at least minimize the pernicious influence of stereotypes and misperceptions that have dominated relations among these three great nations for so long? Toward this end, we shall now advance a number of concrete suggestions.

First, national leaders should guard against the dangers of psycho-logic: the tendency to see what they want to see and to respond to situations, not on the basis of empirical evidence, but on the basis of their subjective wishes. The wish must never be father to policy; only facts can be.

In Indochina, for example, many Americans who felt that it was important for the United States to win the war also felt that a meaningful victory was *in fact possible.* Conversely, many Americans who felt that a defeat would not seriously endanger American security also felt that victory was *in fact impossible.* In both cases, the chances are considerable that at least part of the basis of these views was related to psychology and *not* to the substance of the evidence. This is psycho-logic. It may influence the thinking of hawks as well as doves in foreign policy.

One cannot, of course, simply tell statesmen not to misperceive. But one can guard against psycho-logic by including in the leadership group people with different temperaments and outlooks. This is what President Kennedy did when he pondered the alternatives during the Cuban missile crisis. It takes a man with a strong ego, however, to encourage other men to tell him not what he wants to hear, but what he ought to know. Thus, wise leaders will tend to have "devil's advocates" around them. ·

Second, and related to psycho-logic, is the all too human tendency to ignore conflicting evidence and to give more weight to supporting evidence once a decision has been made. Psychologists describe this phenomenon as "reduction of cognitive dissonance." It is simply the temptation to rationalize a decision by listening to those who support it and ignoring those who oppose it. Usually, the more difficulty the policy maker has in reaching a decision, the greater will be his tendency to justify it afterward. President Johnson's justification of his Vietnam policy following the decision to Americanize the war, and his tendency to surround himself with advisers who supported that policy, were classic examples of "dissonance reduction," or more simply put, of reassuring himself that he had made the right decision.

The wise leader does not reduce such dissonance but remains receptive to it and encourages it. He tends to resist internal pressures toward a consistent mental picture. He always remains open to new evidence that might become a new objective basis for a change in policy.

Third, policy makers often transfer an image automatically from one place to another or from one time to another without careful empirical comparison. Thus, Americans transferred their image of monolithic communism from Europe to Indochina, where the actual situation was entirely different. When images are transferred from past to present, they usually become analogies. Facile analogies to Munich or to Hitler that were used at different times by American, Soviet, and Chinese leaders often served as seductive symbols for their peoples but did not necessarily have a realistic basis. The mature policy maker knows that each challenge to his nation has its own distinct reality. While there may be similarities to past events, there are also differences. A statesman must remain conscious of both.

Fourth, the mature statesman will take care not to fall into the traps that his ego might ensnare him in. He will not view his nation as the center of another nation's policy—witness the errors of the young American republic in its relations with Czarist Russia. He will not mistake alliances for friendship when there is little or no friendship—witness American errors vis-à-vis Chiang Kai-shek. He will not try to explain every phenomenon abroad in terms of his own historical experience—witness Wilson's explanation of the Russian upheavals in 1917 or Lenin's explanation of America. The wise statesman will admit the possibility that new concepts must be learned in order to assimilate new experiences. Imperial China's failure to do so led straight to her destruction. Moreover, he will make an effort at all times to keep perspective on *himself*.

Fifth, the statesman must be able to change his perceptions of himself and others without the dreadful catalyst of war. It is a tragic commentary on the human race that it took a Great Depression, a major war in Asia, and a close brush with atomic holocaust to bring such changes about. The wise leader will decontaminate his policy of shopworn slogans and base it on realities, not on anachronistic ideologies or on fictions. He will encourage his people to use their minds to learn new facts, not offer up their bodies in defense of shadows.

Of all the virtues that a statesman in the post-atomic era must possess, perhaps the greatest is a gift for empathy. It is no longer enough to understand another nation with one's mind; one must learn to feel its essence with one's soul. This is how Kennedy and Khrushchev successfully averted a holocaust over Cuba. That men can learn to act like this, gives one hope for our survival.

All of us must leave the garden of our misperceptions and venture forth into the larger world. As Sigmund Freud discerned so brilliantly, ancient myths are not fairy tales but glimpses of deep psychological truths. Why were Adam and Eve expelled from the Garden of Eden? Because they had tasted the fruit of the Tree of Knowledge of Good and Evil. They had not become *less* by doing so but *more*. "And the Lord God said, Behold, the man is become one of us, to know good and evil." The Fall was not *merely* an act of rebellion, it was *also* an act of maturity.

The myth of Eden records the painful fact that each person must leave his garden in order to become fully human. The overtones of woe with which this myth has echoed down the ages testify to the reluctance and the pain with which wisdom—and hence full humanity—is born. We yet have to accept our Fall.

ABOUT THE AUTHOR

JOHN G. STOESSINGER at the age of eleven fled from Nazi-occupied Austria to Czechoslovakia. Three years later, he again fled via Siberia to China where he lived for seven years.

DR. STOESSINGER came to the United States in 1947, and received his B.A. from Grinnell College in 1950 and his Ph.D. from Harvard University in 1954. Having previously taught at Harvard, Wellesley, M.I.T., and Columbia, he is now Professor of Political Science at The City University of New York at Hunter College. In 1969, Dr. Stoessinger led the International Seminar on International Relations at Harvard.

DR. STOESSINGER's The Might of Nations: World Politics in Our Time (1962) was awarded the Bancroft Prize in International Relations in 1963. He is also the author of The Refugee and the World Community (1956), Financing the United Nations System (1964), Power and Order (1964), and The United Nations and the Superpowers (1970). He is currently Book Review Editor of Foreign Affairs and is a member of the Council on Foreign Relations.

8/23 **DATE DUE**

DEC 17 1976			
FE 7 '78			
GAYLORD			PRINTED IN U.S.A.